OLD TOM GIN

THE ESSENTIAL LIQUOR REQUIRED IN THE BAR ROOM

First published
in 2015 by
Jacqui Small Llp
74–77 White Lion Street
London N1 9PF

Text copyright
© Aaron Knoll 2015
Design and layout copyright
© Jacqui Small 2015

Publisher **Jacqui Small**
Senior Commissioning Editor **Fritha Saunders**
Managing Editor **Emma Heyworth-Dunn**
Commissioning Editor & Project Editor **Joanna Copestick**
Editorial Assistant **Alexandra Labbe Thompson**
Picture Researchers **Amberley Lowis & Vicky Warrell**
Designer **Robin Rout**
Production **Maeve Healy**

Special photography by **Sasha Gitin** and **Simon Murrell**

British Library Cataloguing-in-Publication Data
A catalogue record for this book is available from the British Library.

ISBN 978 1 910 25409 7

Printed and bound in China.

jacqui
small

GIN

The Art and Craft *of the* Artisan Revival

in

3OO

Distillations

Aaron Knoll

This book is dedicated to friends, family and gin drinkers everywhere.

Contents

The History
of Gin

The

Pliny the Elder
knew a thing or two
about smells, and
believed the aroma of
juniper could ward off snakes.

How a plant such as juniper catches the eye of a human, and how they are both then inspired to engage in a long, mutually beneficial relationship, is a complicated thing. There has to be an initial attraction that makes a person look closer at a plant in the first place. That attraction can sometimes be one of appearance, sometimes one of accessibility, or even necessity. But no matter what that first attractor might be, it is most often its usefulness to the other species that determines whether or not it gets a second look. To take from the world of marketing – and, much later, of gin: 'You sell a first sip with the appearance and the ad campaign, but you sell a second sip with the actual product itself.'

We can use this lens to look at how juniper first captured the eye of our distant ancestors, and trace it through history to understand how it came to be the primary flavouring in gin. Though we begin with a look at the prehistory of juniper, this particular strain underlies the narrative in each of the other histories contained in this chapter. Essentially the whole story of gin is how mankind fell in love with juniper. And it begins at the very beginning.

Juniper has a knack for finding a niche, and thriving in it, having been grown successfully in all of its many different forms of species in numerous eco-regions for hundreds of thousands of years. Despite this, its range expanded further after the last ice age, which was 10,000 years ago. Junipers can be found in

Aroma of Gin

tropical Africa, the forests of eastern Europe, Tibet, the Pinyon-Juniper woodlands in the deserts of the western United States, and nearly anywhere else in the northern hemisphere. As juniper was so common it should come as no surprise that many people around the world used the plant as part of their daily lives.

As far back as the Palaeolithic era the coniferous juniper shrub was in common use. Archaeologists have discovered that the Lascaux Cave in France, famous for its thousands of engravings and paintings, was lit by the juniper branch. And indeed researchers found

that the branches doubled as wicks for the inhabitants of the cave. There's a certain romanticism around the notion that the very painters who left us some of the best examples of Stone Age art, more than 15,000 years ago, created their vivid depictions of aurochs and deer to the light of an illuminated juniper branch.

The Lascaux Cave is by no means the only Palaeolithic site where evidence of juniper use has been found. Charcoals from burnt juniper have been found in sites in Western Macedonia and in Neolithic sites in what is now modern-day Jordan, as well as along the Dalmatian coast and in Adriatic settlements elsewhere in Europe. Though we can't be sure if the berries themselves were the objects of desire, or whether it was the branch on which they had grown, their presence is a sign that people were indeed aware of the aromatic properties of juniper. The sweet, piney, fresh air and charred pine aromas of burnt juniper are, after all, hugely memorable.

It's worth pointing out that thus far, the sites I've mentioned are all places where juniper was known to have been growing indigenously at the time people were recorded as using it. This is certainly a situation where accessibility and necessity drove the use of the conifer. After all, the juniper plant is short and readily available, with branches that are easy to grab. To track the transition of juniper from a plant of convenience to one of desire, we have to look for evidence that juniper was being found and used in places outside of its native range. This is a tall order for a conifer that has found a niche nearly everywhere in the northern hemisphere.

However, by at least 1500 BC (and possibly much earlier), we find evidence of exactly that. Research shows that whatever utilitarian or aromatic properties our distant ancestors discovered, they warranted special treatment and the transport of the plant to new areas. Kyphi is a well chronicled and much researched ancient Egyptian incense or perfume that took the form of a scented paste. Among its ingredients are many plants that will seem familiar to anyone who has ever looked up a list of botanicals for a gin: orris root, mint, cinnamon, cassia, cardamom and juniper to name but a few. Perhaps this is one of the earliest historical examples of the aroma accord that underlies many gins being put to good use.

JUNIPER HAS BEEN USED FOR ITS CURATIVE POWER by cultures going back as far as the ancient Egyptians. A papyrus that dates to 1550 BC suggests juniper as a cure for headaches, or a mixture of oil and the berry to cure tapeworm affliction. Aristotle was writing about the curative powers of juniper in Europe during the fourth century BC.

Among the most detailed records of juniper's medical prowess is Pliny the Elder's work during the first century AD. Juniper, it was said, could cure stomach pains, and even repel snakes. Additionally, a whole slew of ailments including 'affections of the uterus', 'griping pains in bowels' or even convulsions 'can be treated by drinking a mixture of white wine with juniper berries'.

Galen wrote in the second century AD that juniper berries 'clear out material in the liver and kidneys… it thins thick viscid humours' and 'produce[s] urine flow to a moderate extent'.

Arabic scholars in the 9th and 10th centuries AD wrote of juniper's abortive properties. Some even suggested proactive use of juniper might prevent an unwanted pregnancy.

By the 11th century, knowledge of distillation had arrived in Europe. At this time monks in Italy were distilling 'aqua vitae' or 'water of life' from wine. It's important to note that these early spirits held symbolic power for these men of faith. But as they experimented with these waters, they sought to imbue them with additional healing properties using the pharmacopoeia of the day. Though there aren't precise records available, it's most likely that juniper was among the early ingredients they experimented with. Firstly, because it grew rampantly all over Italy and secondly, because of its acknowledged curative powers.

A PLAGUE OF JUNIPER

It was during the mid 14th century that some pathogens hitched a ride on some fleas, which hitched a ride on some rats, and helped spawned one of the deadliest pandemics in the history of the world. By the 1350s Europe was gripped with feelings of 'helplessness, agony and horror'.

Bearded John, better known as John of Burgundy, wrote the bestseller of his day, *Treatise on the Epidemic*. First published in 1365, his text was translated into at least four other languages and over one hundred different versions. John's treatise held that the origin of disease was bad air. Juniper was among those ingredients that, when burned, would help protect its burner from the plague. Demand for juniper was high and growing among the masses of Europe, desperate for anything to help them escape the horrors of the plague.

In this time of death, 'life waters' were also becoming more widely available to the masses. But in addition to their healing properties, people soon discovered you could get drunk from them. By the early 1500s municipalities in Germany were struggling with this. Though laws were on the books against such a practice, people drank these medicines for pleasure. But environmental pressures would challenge this growing demand. The 'Little Ice Age' brought cooler

Gin as

ABOVE *The Ebers Papyrus contains several juniper-based cures.*

RIGHT Medieval distillation equipment was crude and was unable to produce quality spirits.

Medicine

temperatures and crop failures to Europe at this time. Wine prices rose, which created pressure to find an alternative drink.

Salesmen were peddling 'false' juniper water, distilled from grain, during the early 16th century. Largely unregulated by authorities, the strong juniper flavour masked the harsh off-notes of the grain spirit, and the common man, being the dolt that he was, was thus fooled into consuming an inferior product!

During the 17th century, we start to see medical juniper paired with ingredients we'd recognise as being staples in gin. In *The London Distiller*, written by John French, the author suggests a Water to Procure Sweat with a mixture of dried angelica, marigold flowers, aniseed and juniper. For his lesser Plague Water he recommends a botanical bill, which adds aniseed, angelica, lavender, elderflower, gentian and mace.

little bit of Pink Gin did indeed help the bitter medicine go down.

Another gin drink which evolved out of a medical necessity was the Gin and Tonic, but the full history of that classic drink is explained further in the Drinking of Gin chapter on page 184.

JUNIPER AT PORT AND SEA

Scottish physician James Lind discovered through experiments in the 1750s that citrus fruit was effective in preventing scurvy among sailors. Citrus was originally preserved mixed with rum aboard ships, but by the mid 19th century, Lauchlan Rose discovered how to preserve lime juice with sugar. His patented Rose's Lime Juice became standard issue aboard ships in the Royal Navy. Officers were picking up gin while at port (while the ensigns still had their grog, a 4:1 ratio of water to rum), and mixing their daily lime rations with it.

In the 1820s, German doctor Johann Gottlieb Benjamin Stewart saw an opportunity while living in Angostura, Venezuela. With all of the foreign navies using the city as a port, he created a bitters recipe and subsequently advertised it as a cure for seasickness. A

THE BITTER TRUTH

Modern medical and scientific capabilities have verified that juniper does indeed have some medicinal properties. In 2005, scientists at the University of Zagreb found that *Juniperus communis* essential oil has some antibacterial and anti-fungal properties. Meanwhile, scientists in Macedonia found that the berries of a local juniper, *Juniperus oxycedrus*, was equally effective, and in 2013 scientists in Egypt and Saudi Arabia found that oils in *Juniperus phoenicea* were capable of protecting the liver.

Gin might not stop the plague, repel a snake, nor save the world, but it does taste good. So at least it's got that going for it.

RIGHT Apothecary bottles were originally made of earthenware but later on glass was used.

I

IN LOOKING TO HISTORY for the absolute first objective origins of a gin, we end up going down a lot of side roads. For in a world before gin was conceived, what did a 'proto-gin' look like? Certainly the idea that juniper berries could be drunk outside of a medicinal context is one consideration. But for the purposes of this section we define a proto-gin as a combination of juniper berries and alcohol. Following this trajectory, we can see that throughout history juniper was used in conjunction with several other alcoholic substances including wine, mead and beers. It not only illustrates the wide range of experimentation that existed globally, but also suggests that it was perhaps inevitable that juniper berries would one day be combined with a neutral grain spirit.

PLINY THE ELDER'S PROTO-GIN

If we set our criteria as a 'substance that could in theory get you drunk flavoured with juniper', one of the first proto-gin recipes we encounter was written in the first century AD. Born in AD 23, Pliny published his magnum opus *Naturalis Historia* in AD 77–79. Among the volumes are works on botany, astronomy and medicine. It's here in Book 24 that we see something which bares only the faintest resemblance to gin:

[Juniper] is prescribed for convulsions, ruptures, griping pains in the bowels, affections of the uterus, and sciatica, either in a dose of four berries in white wine, or in the form of a decoction of twenty berries in wine.

A decoction is created by boiling something until its essence is extracted. Boiling juniper berries in wine concentrates the flavours by extracting the volatile aromatic compounds, resulting in an intensely bright pine/coniferous flavour resembling gin. The husks of the berries are often filtered out after the decoction.

PROTO-GIN FOR THE COMMON MAN

By the Middle Ages, juniper was continuing to be used as a substitute for pepper by the lower classes: one use of the berry that endured for centuries, due to the latter's rarity. There's a faint hint here of juniper becoming

Proto-Gins

subversive, giving the common folk a small taste of the aromatics and spices often reserved for those with the means to afford it.

To see another example of this, we look north to the Nordic countries of northern Europe. What Hannele Klemettilä described as the 'common man's wine' was in fact just mead flavoured with juniper berries. The tradition of flavouring drinks with juniper continued to evolve. Perhaps this drink is a medieval percursor to Sahti, which evolved into Finland's folk beverage and is one of the oldest styles of beer still being made and drunk today. Authoritatively, Sathi's production can be dated back to the 14th century.

Sahti is often made with juniper berries in addition to hops, which are used as a flavouring agent. In a traditional preparation, the spirit would also be filtered through juniper twigs and served in a vessel made of juniper wood. What is interesting is that although Sahti is more of a beer than a gin, it's perhaps one of the first pieces of evidence we have that juniper was used to flavour drinks that were designed to be consumed recreationally. In southern Europe, juniper continued as a medicine and an apothecary ingredient, but we're not that far from a point where others would soon join the Finns in enjoying drinks that included the flavour of juniper in them.

MONASTIC PROTO-GINS

An oft-repeated historical anecdote says that the next proto-gin was being distilled in Italy in the 11th and 12th century AD. The monasteries were a place of research and exploration, and these monks were experimenting with medicine rather than recreational spirits. The techniques required for distillation were likely understood by way of others having learned the art somewhere in the Middle East, by way of Abu Musa Jābir ibn Hayyān, a Persian scientist alive during the Islamic Golden Age of the eighth century AD, who is credited with the invention of the alembic still.

The monks were busy experimenting with distilling wines rather than distilling their own grains from scratch. These spirits distilled for medical purposes were then made either more palatable or more medically effective by the addition of herbs grown in the region. Drinks historian Geraldine Coates notes that it is very likely that juniper was among those ingredients with which they experimented since it 'grows rampantly all over Italy'. As of now, our most recent proto-gin was a pot-distilled wine flavoured by the herbs and botanicals of the Italian countryside. It is highly likely that it included other native plants such as heather, sage and rosemary, although the ingredients available in monks' medicinal utilitarian gardens were much wider than this.

It's within this pharmacological tradition that we get the origin of the term 'aqua vitae' – which means 'water of life' – and later gave birth to the names of several spirits, including whisky and aquavit. Although they didn't have the word for it, it's highly likely that monks were distilling something that, by the legal definition, could be called 'gin'.

This same proto-gin would continue to be made throughout the following centuries and would make an appearance in the mid 16th century as *Geneverbessenwater* (translated as juniper-berry water). This pharmaceutical spirit first appeared in Dutch print in 1552 and was essentially crushed berries, sprinkled with wine, and then distilled in an alembic still.

YET ANOTHER PROTO-GIN FOR THE COMMON MAN (SORT OF)

Antoine de Bourbon, better known by history as the Count de Moret, may seem an unlikely source of drink for the common, everyday, working person. His father, Henry IV, was the king of France from 1589–1610. Before his assassination, Henry consorted with at least four mistresses, in addition to his two wives. His affair with Jacqueline de Bueil, the Countess of Moret, resulted in young Antoine. The king legitimised his son, who would go on to become an abbot at Saint-Etienne.

His contribution to the history of gin lay in creating a fashion for a juniper berry wine that he is credited with inventing. It's likely that he was making this wine in the late 1610s through to the 1620s. Though history hasn't left us any detailed notes containing a recipe or ingredients, writers later indicated that it was the consumption of

this drink to which he owed his long life and sterling health.

Additionally, due to the cheapness of creating this drink, it was said that Count de Moret called it 'the wine of the poor'. Here we have another example of juniper's widespread availability being invoked to subvert power and grant some sort of luxury to the working classes.

Young Antoine's contributions to gin in helping fuel a fashion for drinking juniper for enjoyment is an important milestone in proto-gins. Not bad for someone who died of battle wounds at the age of 26. We'll give him points for taste and pleasure, but I'm not sure we can give him points for a long life.

RIGHT *Pliny the Elder authored many books that formed the* Naturalis Historia, *published in* AD 77–79.

THE EVOLUTION OF THE DRY SPIRIT that we know as gin today, and how it evolved from the genevers and burnt wines of the 15th century, can be traced back to trade. So too can the story of why certain botanicals are common in gin.

The proto-gins we looked at are all tightly tied to the base spirit. In these cases, it was wine. For parts of Europe that were fortunate enough to be located between 30 and 50 degrees latitude, grapes grew freely and easily. For many of the places in Europe where gin was evolving, such as Germany, the Low Countries including the Netherlands, and the United Kingdom, they were not so fortunate. Here, they were largely reliant on other nations for their wine imports, so as long as their medicinal waters or recreational spirits relied on wine for distillation, they were subject to the whims of war – and the climate. During the period in which the seeds of gin first sprouted, we saw a little bit of both.

In the late Renaissance, Europe was undergoing some pretty significant climate change. The onset of what modern-day scientists call the 'Little Ice Age', a prolonged period of decreased temperatures that affected the world for a few hundred years, began to intensify suddenly in the late 15th and early 16th centuries. One such cold snap resulted in widespread viticultural failures in 1511, and would hit again in subsequent years. Distillers of all sorts were forced to innovate. The move towards grain was not driven by taste, but by necessity.

They first turned to the next most common source of alcohol that was widely available: beer. Soon distillers were able to coax grains into releasing their sugars through malting. Grain distilling was thus born. And soon brandy sellers would have something to worry about, because grain distillates, although harsh, nasty, brutish and somewhat unpleasant, were cheaper. This was partly because they were unregulated, and partly because suitable grains were grown locally (and distillers could use lower-quality grain that had been rejected for breadmaking).

So, with their awful-tasting spirits, grain distillers sought to compete with the brandy sellers of the world.

Fortunately for distillers in these regions, they lived in an era of rich cultural exchange, with access to cheaper exotic overseas ingredients. In the early 17th century, the Dutch East India Company was establishing a monopoly over exotic spices like nutmeg, cloves and black pepper. It's not by coincidence that these once rare luxuries previously only afforded by the wealthy, such as those that had been used in the 1495 proto-gin, were coveted by all, and one day would all be relatively common ingredients in gin.

Juniper grew locally in all of the regions mentioned above, and therefore was the most widely available botanical. It was also incredibly effective, and so genever was born. Crude grain spirits flavoured with juniper caught on and became popular in the Low Countries. However, these halcyon days were not to last. Two

Gin and Trade

groups became concerned about this new use of grain.

First, the breadmakers and the nation's rulers had their say. In 1601, in the region that now spans Luxembourg, Belgium and parts of modern-day Germany and France, the ruler Albert VII, Archduke of Austria, and his wife, Isabella, banned distilling spirits from either fruits or grains for concerns of food security. This only served to diffuse the craft, forcing it out of the Low Countries into nearby regions with less regulation. Albert and Isabella's mandate pushed genever distillation to places outside their control. Some of those cities, such as Hasselt and Scheidam, are still renowned for their genevers today, while cities that were under their control are left to wonder what might have been.

The other group saw the grain distillers as a more pressing threat. The brandy sellers of Germany had some luck with their petitions to parliament, and they succeeded in pushing the craft to the countryside, where it could prosper unchecked. Grain distilling was the cat that was out of the bag, and it wasn't going anywhere. Places that sought to tax rather than prohibit grain distilling were to benefit.

LEFT *Bols genever, a forerunner to gin as we know it, is still produced in the Netherlands and parts of Belgium.*

OPPOSITE *William III, Prince of Orange from 1672, fuelled a fashion for genever after he took the British throne in 1689.*

Trade and economic concerns drove the switch to grain, and futhermore helped define the places where the fledgling industry could thrive. In the Low Countries, places that didn't ban genever were able to turn it into a source of income for the Crown, with records of taxation existing as early as 1606. German authorities struggled a bit more, with distillers from the countryside coming into Augsburg to peddle their juniper-berry water door-to-door. Even as the government looked more into regulating grain distillation as a legitimate craft by taxing it as it did other spirits, it found that wine, and therefore brandy in the recreational sense, were too far out of reach for the common man. Economic concerns led to the regulation of the craft, which in turn led to the legitimisation of a craft that was once left only to the poor.

The Thirty Years War was the bloodiest and most violent war Europe had seen up until that point. Lasting from 1618–1648, the English and the Dutch fought together as allies for part of the war. The Dutch soldiers were given rations of genever, which their newly found brothers-at-arms were glad to partake of. It's been suggested that this is the origin of the term 'Dutch Courage', though the term didn't appear in print until the 1820s. Whatever they called it, the English soldiers returned home with a taste for genever. This fondness for imported spirits filled the king's coffers and by 1643, spirits were taxed as luxury goods, especially imported ones. This was all well and good for genever until the first of the Anglo-Dutch Wars broke out in the 1650s over control of the seas and the aforementioned rich trade routes. In 1674, right at the end of the third war between the two nations, there were suddenly 'strong water shops' appearing everywhere. At first a partnership, then later a war, the taste for Dutch spirits was not going anywhere. And despite a serious tax break, imported spirits reigned supreme.

Imported spirits were expensive, especially so during the 17th and 18th centuries, subject as they were to the whims and love affairs of those in power. If you liked a spirit, you were doubly motivated to try and produce it yourself. For those who fell in with brandy, there was little they could do. The grapes weren't going to grow in the British countryside. Apples did, but the complex cider economy and the resulting spirits' awful taste

kept them from ever rising above a niche spirit. Grain was available too, but the good stuff was spoken for. So distillers were distilling the worst of the wort, the dregs and the leftovers. Needless to say, despite a business climate that seemed to be oriented towards creating local products, this didn't happen for quite some time. But when it did, these products would take over.

There was a steady trend upwards from the 1680s onwards where locally produced British spirits were produced in ever increasing numbers, though the biggest jump coincided with the Dutch King William of Orange ascending to the throne in 1689. It was hip to be Dutch. So genever was in fashion. But being French was out, even more so, and imports of all foreign spirits were banned outright. William also took other steps that would allow anyone to make or sell spirits, mostly for the increased revenue that came from excise taxes. Even at this early point, before the gin craze had begun, it was all about taxes and revenue.

The 'gin craze', when it did start in the 1700s, could be seen through one lens as reflecting wealthy and merchant class anxieties and through another as showing the story of how a government came to regulate an industry as a means of increasing revenue for the Crown.

When licences for vending gin were prohibitively expensive, people and the distillers' companies campaigned against them. Distillers and hawkers didn't follow the laws. When the 1729 Gin Act called for a £20 annual licence for retailers as well as a tax per gallon, the distillers organised against it.

Throughout the 1730s, the royal Crown passed act after act attempting outright prohibition. The 1736 Gin Act prescribed a £50 licence for selling gin, and giving £5 to anyone who informed on someone who was dispensing in violation of the Act. In the 1740s when the war of Austrian secession broke out, the strategy changed. The fee for a licence to sell gin was reduced to one pound. Over 20,000 licences were taken out by 1744. The Crown was doing well. Even though the tax was doubled under the Gin Act of 1751, it didn't elicit outrage or force vendors out of business. It in fact turned the profession into a respectable one.

However, *1751* (the year of Hogarth's famous print,) *Gin Lane*, see page 19) is often cited as the end of the gin craze. What happened? The industry was regulated into a profitable commodity for the Crown. It did in fact reduce sales; however, other facts were at play in the public's fickle drinking tastes. High-quality beer such as porter was becoming more widely available, and at cheaper prices than throughout most of the gin craze. Secondly, the climate was to strike again. Bad harvests in 1757 and onwards were so meagre that distilling was banned outright. Gin hadn't gone away, but it seems that even without regulation *per se*, gin might have been on its way down.

Thus far, gin had turned from being grape-based to grain-based, due to trade. And the gin craze took care of itself, although not before the Crown found a way to make a pretty penny from it. Though some would be quick to give reformers credit for quelling the gin craze, the truth is likely to be somewhere in the middle, with external factors likely to have been equally complicit in the change in preferences.

While the early evolution of gin was influenced by a complex array of factors mostly centred around trade, there were further developments in the 19th century, when gin would be adulterated with sugars and sweetening agents and called Old Tom to create a better flavour. Thereafter a taste for dry gin would emerge, also driven less by trade, until emerging trends for cocktails would force gin to evolve once again.

BELOW *The spice trade in the Dutch East Indies was centred around Indonesia.*

'*The fear of the house of correction, imprisonment, or danger of the gallows, make little impression upon them, if any at all.*'

W HEN SIR JOSEPH JEKYLL, the octogenarian Parliament member, wrote the above words, he was appealing to his upper-class peers and the merchant class's fear of crime and violence. The cause was deemed to be Mother Gin, so nothing short of prohibition would do.

What Jekyll was really afraid of, was the rise of the lower classes. Wages were rising and the lower classes had time and money for leisure. This represented a threat to the social order. The fact that they opted to spend their new-found wealth on gin was purely incidental. It wasn't the gin itself, as much as the highly visible people that Jekyll and his reformer peers targeted.

Perhaps there was a festering, deeper implication to the poor people's beverage of choice. Gin was originally an upper-class beverage. What was once a luxury, or an expensive imported spirit, was now being made cheaply by all manner of people across London. This wouldn't have escaped the notice of the upper classes. As gin moved downwards, it seemed that the hierarchy of luxury and power was not as static as it seemed. If gin could move down, why couldn't the poor move up?

Those who were drinking the gin understood the symbolic importance of it as well. Just as when William of Orange took to the British throne in 1689, and people emulated the style of his court by drinking Dutch gin, the lower classes sought to emulate those of higher social status, and that included drinking gin.

There is some truth to the notion of a gin craze in London during these times. People were indeed drinking more gin than they had before; however, it's within this larger climate that we can begin to understand why reformers were exaggerating the truth just a bit. In 1723 the death rate in London exceeded the birth rate, and would do so for 10 years. In 1725, just 17 people died from drunkenness. At its very worst, the death rate from drinking peaked in 1735 at 69 people. It continued to increase after 1735; however, deaths from drunkeness continued to decline. A simpler explanation for the high rate of deaths in this period is that plague was still present in 1720s London, hygiene was poor and infant mortality was high, yet gin became an important target.

Gin and Power

An oft-cited example of just how out of hand things were during the gin craze, was this sign hung outside a well-frequented Whitechapel dram shop.

> **Drunk for One Pence**
> **Dead Drunk for Twopence**
> **Clean Straw for Nothing.**

It makes a great story, but evidence suggests it was constructed, and recognised, as apocryphal even around the time it first appeared. However, the slogan has endured to this day. Hogarth included it in *Gin Lane, 1751*; other writers repeated it when they provoked anxieties that were created by gin. It even persists in a number of modern-day books as an example of how crazed the time was. Give one point to the reformers on this one. The number of gins shops in the city is also often cited as evidence of how wild the times were. In parts of the East End or Whitechapel, it's certain that there was one gin shop for every 7.5 residences. In London proper, it was closer to 1 in 38, often on a par with the number of ale shops. What was really at stake here was the story of how those with the power distorted the gin story to their own ends and how their power has endured to this day in how we tell the story of gin.

ABOVE RIGHT *Crocker's Folly in London's St John's Wood, a gin palace-style pub built in 1898 and recently restored to grandeur.*

OPPOSITE *Hogarth plays up the perceived societal costs of drinking gin in his* Gin Lane, 1751 *a companion piece to his* Beer Street.

A

2014 INTERNET SURVEY REVEALED that at least one in five respondents felt like gin was a 'feminine' drink, nearly three times the number that felt it was a masculine drink. How did our preferential quaffs get so tied up with male and female? In modern times we've seen gins segregated by this invisible line. One marketeer speaking in 2003 tried to explain new contemporary gins such as Citadelle (page 119) and Bombay Sapphire (page 92) as being the feminine counterpoint to masculine gins such as Beefeater (page 91) or Tanqueray (page 111). Bloom Gin (page 92) was positioned, early on, as a feminine gin, while Langley's No. 8 targets the 'discerning gentleman'. Are gins really masculine or feminine? What is the relationship between gender and gin? It lies in an interesting history that suggests there might be some reason why a feminine association with gin has endured.

In the 15th century, distilling was primarily a woman's role. Contemporary books of the era included engravings showing women working the stills. At this time, distilling was largely a domestic and medicinal homemaking duty. As distilling moved from the home space to the public space, and from the medicinal to the recreational, increasing numbers of men became involved in distilling (but not in the gathering of herbs for the process). The end products were regulated closely by the government. It's this period of increased regulation that might have led to increasing prosecution of women under new rules. In the 17th century, when German laws were passed to reduce the amount of spirits distilled from grain on the market, women may have been disproportionately targeted and affected then, too. The same pattern would again be seen under the Gin Acts of 18th-century London.

Gin presented a bevy of opportunities for women in London during the early 18th century, and anyone who described gin as 'Ladies Delight' would have been right in more ways than one.

Young women, driven by increased employment opportunity, flocked to London. These opportunities equated to more money, and in turn enabled women access to spheres normally off-limits. The early 1700s in London was one of the few times in history when men and women would be found drinking together in the same social space. There were other opportunities to have

Women

drink as well. Ale houses selling beer were also common; however, women only rarely visited them on their own. Ale costs were higher than those of gin. Dram shops dispensing gin had lower prices due to an incredible amount of competition, in some places as many as one per every five homes, and seemed more interested in moving quantity than increasing profit. It was also the case that the number of women involved in the gin economy from start to finish created a more welcoming atmosphere, or established early on that gin was a drink for women.

It's the gin economy that presented the second opportunity for women in this era. For young women in search of opportunities and wages, the gin trade required no skills for entry and was lacking in strong trade organisations. There were relatively few barriers to entry. Between 1725 and 1750, upwards of a quarter of the gin sellers in parts of the city were women. These same sellers were much less likely to be licensed and operating within the good graces of the law as well.

With great opportunity came great risk, especially for unmarried women who occupied a lower rung of the social ladder in 18th-century London. When the 1736 Gin Act offered rewards for informers who went after sellers operating without licences under the 1736 Gin Act, it was this same group who made up nearly 70% of those who were charged with violations of the Gin Act. Of those prosecuted, nearly all were single women and many were unable to pay the fine, so a large number of them were incarcerated as a result of these new laws. Others in London noticed the skewed rate of prosecution, as it seems to have temporarily forced women out of the trade, or underground, to weather the storm.

It seems that the image of 'Mother Gin' might have been strongly linked to a drinking community that, at the time, had a stronger female representation than other businesses. Madame Geneva was indeed a woman. Is it any wonder that a woman was made the centrepiece of William Hogarth's *Gin Lane* and *Beer Lane*? Her grotesque, distorted appearance stokes the flames of what gin might have meant for his audience.

and Gin

During the late 1700s, with inexpensive, persuasive prints like *Gin Lane* making their rounds, the culture of drinking would change, and again women would find themselves painted as victims of drinking culture rather than participants. But not all trends are forever, and again we saw a brief reappearance of the co-ed drinking spaces of the early 18th century one hundred years on.

Gin palaces were vast, elaborately decorated factories for quickly dispensing as much gin as possible. Unlike pubs, the gin palaces removed any accoutrement that may have encouraged one to linger. With an emphasis on volume, gin palaces were well situated to take advantage of the 1825 reduction of duties on spirits. Cheap gin was back, and during a brief golden era, women and men were drinking in the same social sphere. Informal observations of the palaces found more women than men in gin palaces near factories. But still, the social restrictions, led by temperance advocates at this time, made it clear that respectable women didn't drink, and they didn't drink gin.

Or maybe they did, but just came to calling it something else. It was clear at this point, as gin became more professionalised, with brands such as Booth's and Tanqueray already becoming well established, the reputation of gin itself was increasing. However, for those like Hogarth who chose to use gin as a symbol to advance their agendas, such as the Temperance movement, gin would still remain a powerful icon whose history would precede it.

Nowadays, distilling, and spirit production in general, remains an overwhelmingly male-dominated profession; however, with the explosion of new distillers around the world, the profession is opening up. Joanne Moore became the master distiller at G & J Greenall Distillery in Cheshire in 2006, while women have prominent roles in many new American and British distilleries as well.

It is easy to look at the history and see how anxieties and opportunities created a strong feminine association with the spirit. However, it's harder to see how that differentiation has endured outside of its historical underpinnings. Fortunately, the drinks industry has moved far away from the original creation of gin categories based on stereotypical gender attributions. Perhaps we should take solace in the findings of that original survey. Nearly 70% of people find gin to be gender agnostic. Marketeers might still find benefit in selling a gin to women as supposed to men, or vice versa. Campaigns might target one audience over another. Let's toast our Martinis, whether made with Tanqueray or Bloom, based on taste alone, and not expectations. To Madame Geneva! And to maybe putting that Hogarth print back in the closet.

ABOVE RIGHT *During the early European Renaissance Era it was women who were responsible for distilling spirits in a domestic setting.*

GIN IS CONSIDERED TO BE THE PERFECT SPIRIT FOR A COCKTAIL. Although the spirit existed in many forms throughout the 17th and 18th centuries, it is through the cocktail and the fashions associated with it that gin really evolved.

The term 'cocktail' is of disputed origin. Perhaps it comes from the French word *Coquetel,* which referred to a mixed drink consumed by French officers during the American Revolutionary War? But it was in America that the art of the cocktail was perfected.

Drinks' historians have noted that cocktails were the 'first uniquely American cultural product to capture the world's imagination'. Once a morning pick-me-up cocktails were common by the 1850s, and by 1862 Jerry Thomas's seminal guide *How to Mix Drinks: or The Bon-Vivant's Companion* was published. While Thomas included a few recipes for gin drinks in his book, including Gin Punch (raspberry syrup, sugar, lemon, orange, pineapple and water, shaken with ice) and Gin Julep, he also included recipes for several types of gin. Domestic gin at the time was created by flavouring the white spirit with juniper oil and simple syrup. English gin comprised juniper and turpentine dissolved in alcohol, but Thomas also offered a suggestion for a London Cordial gin, which took out the turpentine and added angelica, coriander and simple syrup. Clearly, much gin at this time was sweetened.

The invention of the Martini helped create a growing fashion for unsweetened gins. By the time cocktail culture emerged, gin would have a central place in it. But it wouldn't be the gins of Jerry Thomas's era. It would be a drier style altogether and one we are familiar with today.

Overlapping with the rise of the Martini and 1887 reprint of Jerry Thomas's seminal work, the first golden age of the cocktail saw an explosion of new recipes, several of which have survived roughly intact today. The Tom Collins was in print by 1876, followed by the Martinez in 1884 and the Martini by 1896. This wave of creativity continued until the early years of the 20th century, when the Negroni was invented in 1919, a beautiful day for gin drinkers everywhere.

On 17 January 1920, the US nation went dry. Well, sort of. It became illegal to sell, buy or traffic alcohol. But not to drink it. So those who could afford to stockpile were in the good graces of the law.

There are many theories as to why cocktails were the drink of choice during the Prohibition era. One says that so many people were drinking rotgut 'bathtub gin' made from the worst of toxic spirits that cocktails were necessary to make poorly made alcohol palatable. While there is likely to be some truth to this story, it's important to note that many English gin distilleries did a brisk

Prohibition

business with a lot of small Caribbean islands and Canada during these lean times. Another story suggests that although the fashion at the time was more for beer during pre-Prohibition times, American drinkers were forced to spirits because it was harder to hide beer and beer-making equipment. It's as if spirits were custom–made for Prohibition.

Gin was well suited to this challenging drinking climate. As we saw during the gin craze, gin was a playground wherein distillers could manipulate a spirit to make it more palatable. Whisky took years to age and was off the table. Vodka was many years away from being in fashion, and to add insult to injury, it would have been incredibly difficult to make a clean-tasting spirit, with no flavourings, under challenging circumstances. Rum was more challenging again. But gin could be flavoured, and therefore if you were to opt for bathtub gin rather than rum-running gin (naturally) you were likely to go to gin. After all, juniper had been effective in this role once before, so why not an Act Two?

Another legacy attributed to American Prohibition is the so-called cocktail hour. That time between afternoon and dinner time was filled with a period during which one could have a drink or two before going out to a dry dinner. Though the term itself was in use long before Prohibition, it had sprung into popularity by the mid 1920s. The *New York Times* was covering its expansion

to France and dresses were being advertised with bare sleeves! Perfect for cocktail parties. Prohibition was still several years from ending, but cocktail hours were at least enough of an open secret to be freely advertised.

Dorothy Parker, a member of the Algonquin Round Table – a group of sharp-witted writers who gathered at the Algonquin hotel in NYC during Prohibition – is perhaps unfairly credited with a certain quote about Martinis that ends with 'Four and I'm under the host'. History has long linked the legendary table with Gin Martinis, though Parker's biographer says she was a Scotch woman. In terms of understanding the links between drinks and culture, it's enough to note that the idea of these smart people playing practical jokes and making racy quips under the special kind of heightened awareness that could only be fostered by a fine gin Martini suggests that the place of gin was clear, even in this time of official prohibition.

When Prohibition ended, the *New York Times* jumped in, mid-cocktail-hour-trend, to do lifestyle pieces on their occurrence all around the city and beyond. In 1933, the cocktail closet jumped out from the ad pages onto the front pages. Gin leapt out of the bathtub into our glasses, back on top of the world for a short while.

By 1934, people in Paris were trying to turn cocktail hour into French wine hour. But don't cry for the British gin makers. The colonies were back.

and Cocktails

Gin hit a rough patch in the 1940s. World War Two was hitting its stride as the rocket engines of the era used 180-proof grain alcohol as a propellant. With distillers around the world turning their grain into rocket fuel (the other kind), the domestic market turned to other, less vital sources for inebriation.

Domestic gins were being made out of cane, molasses and potatoes and sales were crashing, either because of a shortage or because of the taste. Though juniper and other botanicals could play their part in covering up the taste of a base spirit, people had already become accustomed to the clean tastes of Tanqueray or Gordon's.

Around the same time, another spirit was slowly beginning its ascent. Vodka had gone from being a marginal spirit on the periphery of the cocktail world to one that was rapidly gaining mainstream acceptance.

more likely that it was the memorable scenes in the film that did the trick.

Gin bottomed out in the late 1960s, but Stateside it began growing again through the 1970s and 1980s. It wasn't growing like vodka but remained in vogue through the short-lived neo-temperance movement of the 1980s. Just as the *New York Times* was extolling the drink's steady perseverence, *Time* magazine was writing it off, along with its signature cocktail, as an 'antique'. The symbol of the Martini was a battleground throughout the decade. The three-Martini-lunch, re-popularised by modern-day revivalists such as TV's *Mad Men*, was a symbolic (and largely mythical) field for discussing the role of drink in society.

Gin was also at a creative low. While the big names in gin such as Gordon's, Beefeater, Tanqueray and

Gin Renaissance

Mentions of vodka in the *New York Times* tripled between 1953 and 1954, and would more than double again before the decade was complete.

A 1954 article mentioned the 'vogue for vodka', suggesting that you always serve snacks with it, and to add lemon and orange peel to the bottle. Odd that even then, its neutrality was being thwarted at the very source: the bottle itself. Great Britain, home of gin, got in on the vodka trend. In 1954 the real deal was imported into London for the first time since 1917.

James Bond seems to get his share of credit and blame for gin's fall and vodka's rise. In Ian Fleming's 1953 book *Casino Royale*, Bond orders a drink familiar to many modern-day cocktail aficionados: the Vesper. Though this drink is linked to James and his love of vodka, it also contained a good quantity of gin, an ingredient so important to the drink he called it out by name. 'Gordon's' he said, 'in a three to one ratio with vodka. Any old vodka'. Naturally the drink was shaken rather than stirred. Perhaps James Bond's preference for any old vodka to cut his gin was so striking that many converted; however, it's

Seagram's were advertising and dominating their respective markets, little was being done to open up the world of gin to new taste buds. You either liked your father's gin or you didn't like gin. That is until 1987 when Bombay Sapphire launched. Here was a gin that rocked the shelves of the liquor store. The bottle stood out with its bright blue, unusual square shape. Its botanicals were clearly enumerated on the back of the bottle, where the illustrations tied tradition to the exotic feel of India. However, it was the taste that truly changed the path of gin. Bombay Sapphire has a bright, almost exotic note of coriander that it is now familiar, but at the time it pushed much further than any of the other major gin offerings. It also had a strong, citrus-forward profile that was particularly noticeable in cocktails. Although it seems tame today, it was perhaps the most different gin on the shelf at the time. Bombay stands on its own as a good gin today; however, it's hard to remember just how radical it was when it launched. Though not gin as gin-drinkers of the time knew it, by the year 2000, the Bombay Sapphire Martini became a cocktail you asked for by name.

Top Gins that are Leading the Renaissance and Why

1987 Bombay Sapphire
Set the stage for the renaissance, pushed the envelope of what gin can taste like, emphasising less-traditional notes and disclosing the botanical bill.

1996 Crater Lake Gin
A daring mid 90s US launch pushed the envelope by adding juniper via post-distillation infusion.

1997 Tanqueray Malacca
Perhaps a bit ahead of its time, vanilla, citrus and a touch of sweetness. Brought back in 2013.

1999 Hendrick's/Martin Miller's
Launched the same year in the UK, both prominently feature cucumber. They inspired a generation of gin drinkers to look beyond just the juniper.

2004 Jensen's Bermondsey London Dry Gin
A revival of sorts influenced by out-of-production gins, its roots are in the style of gins produced in the early 1900s.

2005 Aviation American Gin
House Spirits helped pioneer the notion that there is another genre of gin with its floral and gently spiced take on gin.

2006 Bluecoat American Dry Gin
Playing the blue to the England's redcoat, Philadelphia Distilling put a stake in the ground for American gin with its citrus-forward take.

2006 G'vine Floraison
Grape spirit base with a floral, spicy, complex and decidedly non-traditional take, G'vine made it clear that experimentation with gin was global.

2007 Death's Door Gin
Raised the bar for 'local' in gin. Local Washington Island wheat, local coriander, local fennel. It represents its place.

2008 Citadelle Réserve
Early to the game with its original gin, Citadelle Réserve broke new ground by ageing its gin in French oak casks.

2011 Few American Gin
Features a rich grain-forward base spirit, that's neither genever nor traditional gin, and every step is done on site at the distillery.

2012 Filliers Dry Gin 28
The famous Belgian genever distillery launched a bright floral gin based on a nearly century-old recipe.

2012 City of London Dry Gin
The first distillery in the city of London in over 200 years, the renaissance returns to gin's roots.

In the middle decades of the 20th century, gin advertisements were primarily made only by the big names. When people called their gins, they usually called something that had been around for centuries. In only one short decade, a pronounced sea change in gin culture manifested itself.

RIGHT *These greenhouses built to showcase the botanicals used at Bombay Sapphire's distillery in Hampshire, in the UK, were designed by the renowned Thomas Heatherwick Studio.*

GIN HAS EXPERIENCED A HUGE CRAFT REVOLUTION MUCH IN THE SAME WAY THAT BEER HAS.

Having experienced a big decline in popularity during the 1960s, as beer did, gin's revivial got underway in the 1970s and 80s. The re-emergence of cocktails during the 1990s, together with the introduction of new and radical brands such as Bombay Sapphire and Hendrick's really kicked off the revolution in Europe.

By the year 2000, revellers in New York City welcoming in the new millenium went on Bombay Sapphire Martini benders to celebrate. And in a newspaper piece at the time, a couple described their perfect Martini as 'Bombay Sapphire with a drop of Martini and Rossi Vermouth.' In 2005, they were still calling the Bombay Sapphire Martini by name, only this time straight up with an olive. The gin had become a status symbol, and in a short time rose to a level of prominence that put it on par with the centuries-old brands. Many are quick to give credit to the advertising and marketing team, and plenty of that is fair. But you only serve a first sip through marketing. You serve the second, and every taste after that, with a good product. Bombay Sapphire found an opening, and it ran with it.

MORE YOUNG BLOOD

Some of what is now regarded as the old guard of American craft distilling hit the market in the mid 1990s. Anchor Brewing Company launched Junipero in 1996, Bendistillery's Crater Lake Gin hit the market the same year, while Citadelle, from a Cognac distillery in France, and Plymouth Gin, the renowned brand famous for its relationship with the British Royal Navy, had both made it onto shelves Stateside by the late 1990s as well.

Many of the big names joined the bandwagon. Tanqueray Gin, which had been a staple for years, launched Tanqueray Malacca, and drinkers who had no taste for gin found themselves singing its praises. Its sweeter, floral-forward profile didn't catch on the way Bombay Sapphire did, though, and it was discontinued in 2001. Drinkers had to wait another 12 years before getting to try it again.

The brand that perhaps has done the most to change taste buds this century, in large part due to its unique and distinctive advertising campaign, was Hendrick's, launched at the beginning of the millenium. A dry gin, tweaked to be more floral forward by the addition of rose and cucumber, then macerated post-distillation, helped popularise the idea that gin could de-emphasise the juniper and still be considered a gin. Suddenly you'd hear of people who said they disliked gin making an exception for Hendrick's.

Other gins that emphasised this floral-forward style continued to proliferate. Throughout the next decade gins that deviated from the trend proliferated. G'vine's Floraison, Magellan's signature blue gin, Martin Miller's Westbourne and standard gins, as well as a much more successful offshoot of the Tanqueray brand – Tanqueray 10 – were all widely available by 2005 and 2006, which would be the year that American craft distilling really began to embrace gin wholeheartedly.

Brands such as Junipero, and other launches like Leopold's were out there. However, I'd say the watershed moment was when Rogue, North Shore, Philadelphia Distilling and House Spirits all released their gins in 2006. House Spirits' Aviation American Gin might have done the most to push the word forward that this was the beginning of something. A well-circulated essay by House Spirits' distiller Ryan Magarian declared his gin among several others as a new category in itself. 'New Western Dry Gin' was the name, and within it he lumped a great deal of the new gins coming onto the market, including the already well-known Hendrick's and Tanqueray 10, among many other smaller distilleries' efforts.

By 2005–2006, American craft distilling began to embrace gin wholeheartedly. The terms 'New Western Gin', 'New American Gin' and 'Contemporary Gin' exploded onto the scene as gin traditionalists attempted to define what was becoming of the once narrow category. These gins defied tradition by emphasising or complementing juniper with other notes. Although the rapid proliferation of this style of gin can be attributed to the 'craft spirits' revolution in the United States, it's

OPPOSITE *Australia is in the vanguard of the new boutique distilleries, complementing, in the case of Melbourne, the long-established culinary scene.*

The Rise of Craft Gin

hardly specific to a single region or nation. Many suggest that it was gin's lean years that led to an appreciation of citrus-forward vodkas and therefore the citrus and floral-forward gins of the current times; however, it's more than likely that it was attributed to a relaxation of rules in the United States and a changing culture that led many men and women to take up distillation as Prohibition era regulations were loosened. People who had differing ideas of what gin could be were now putting out their own spirits, just as craft brewers had decades ago, when craft beers carved out their space on shelves around the country. Certainly, craft distilling owes a lot to the trailblazers of the brewing movement (notice many of the early distillers in the States who put out gins were also brewers first).

The fact that this new style of gin went worldwide, even before Aviation and other West Coast gins of that ilk hit the market, is why we prefer the more location-agnostic term of 'contemporary gin'. Many distillers in the US and elsewhere are making juniper-forward styles of gin as well.

BECOMING A WORLDWIDE PHENOMENON

There have been a few reasons cited for the fascination with gin. The first is one of production. Many new distilleries were opening, with the hopes of bringing a whiskey or other aged spirit to market. As those take time to age and mature before they can be sold to keep the doors open, distillers turned to other unaged spirits. The vodka market was saturated with well-recognised brands and the spirit offered little wiggle room for creatively putting their own spin on things. Gin was the perfect temporary fix.

It could be made, bottled and sold nearly immediately. It was something that could be truly unique. And especially in the early days, there wasn't a lot of noise in the sector. It was a perfect place to carve out a niche. Distillers appealed to people to help keep the doors open, and in doing so, helped cultivate a taste for gin that varied widely from the classics.

Many distillers did put out a gin purely to make ends meet, but equally as many produced gins because they 'loved gin'. They probably didn't change tastes as much as they filled a gap in the market for a new, particular taste in gin.

Another oft-cited reason is popular culture. *Mad Men* and its sexy, stylised interpretation of Madison Avenue and the New York City of the 1960s is given credit for repopularising old cocktails (there is even a specific *Mad Men* cocktail app). The site promotes classic gin drinks like the French 75, the Gibson and even the Sloe Gin Fizz. It was through popular culture that cocktails were re-romanticised and gin was brought back into style.

It probably didn't hurt, but there were many articles already proclaiming the noughties the decade of the cocktail. Bartenders were already experimenting with novel concepts by the early 2000s, with the revival of old standbys happening in the second half. Cocktail-culture revival definitely helped gin (because it was an ingredient in so many drinks), but it was not the sole cause.

Whatever the cause, in the United States there were only 70 craft distilleries in 2003 and by 2014 there were over 600. There are at least 150 craft gins on the market today in the States alone, with new ones coming along almost every day it seems. The craft spirits revolution is not just limited to the United States, though. The City of London Distillery founded in London was the first distiller in over two centuries to distil within the city limits when it opened its doors in 2012. Sipsmith Independent Distillers, Sacred Spirits Company, Cotswolds Distillery and many others have opened as well. Londoners have never been better serviced with a diverse range of domestically produced gins since perhaps the days of the gin craze. Craft spirits have taken off in Canada, too, with at least 30 gins on the market as of 2014, with more on their way.

Australian distillers are struggling with high taxes, but that hasn't stopped creative distillers from Kangaroo Island Spirits, Four Pillars or the Melbourne Gin Company from putting out excellent gins. Spain, France, Germany, and even places you might not expect to look for an excellent gin, like Colombia or New Zealand, are awash with locally crafted spirits.

Some traditionalists still bemoan the gin renaissance and the proliferation of non-juniper-forward gins. I like to think that it's perhaps the most exciting time to be a gin drinker, ever. There are more options and more creativity in this small section of the drinks market than there has ever been before. Though many see the seeds of the explosion beginning with a couple of UK renegades marketing to vodka drinkers, the US quickly embraced gin and made it a place to create something local. The explosion has spread from there, so much so that not even 10 years after the first hints of something about to break, the craft gin revolution is truly worldwide, and distillers everywhere are finding some way to make gin truly their own.

Gins launched in the last 10 years are as diverse in taste as they are in bottle shape.

The
Appreciation
of Gin

How Gin is Made

THERE ARE TWO IMPORTANT COMPONENTS to how a gin is made. First, there is distillation, which is the trade or required skill, and it is this process that affects the end product. Secondly, there's the choice of aromatic material and botanicals. Without the plant world, we wouldn't have gin as we know it today, so the Botany of Gin section (see pages 42–59) explores the great variety of botanicals, ancient and modern, that are available to the modern gin distiller.

Nearly all of today's gins are designed and distilled with a two-stage process in mind. In the first stage of creating a gin, a producer ferments some sort of grain or fruit, then distils it to create a base spirit. In the second stage, the base spirit is re-distilled with aromatic botanicals, including juniper, to create the final product. This is the short of it. The complete story of how a gin is crafted from start to finish is a lot more complicated. We'll start at the very beginning.

Creating the Base Spirit

The clear, generally neutral spirit that results from the first step of the gin-creation process is what might be more commonly known as vodka. Unlike vodka, though, the goals here can differ. Whereas vodkas often aspire to be as neutral as possible, for gin – especially contemporary gin – a completely neutral character is not always the most desired outcome. When distilled, some fruits or grains can impart an earthy depth, or brightness, that an expert gin distiller can use to great effect when botanicals are added. Whether distilled multiple times until the final base spirit is truly neutral, or whether the goal is a quirky spirit with character, a distiller begins with something that they wish to ferment.

Much produce can be made into a base spirit. Some of the more common base ingredients include corn, wheat, potatoes or grapes. More exotic items that can be fermented at this step include bananas, apples or even carrots.

When working with grain, the first step is to malt it. This involves getting it wet and allowing it to sprout. Germination begins and the small seeds start converting starch into sugars that, ideally, would be helping nourish the young plant. Of course, distillers have other plans for that sugar. Malting isn't equally easy across all grains and that's why you'll see barley

included in many recipes. Barley has very high levels of the enzyme that does the converting, and it can help kick other grains into gear, assisting the malting process.

Once the grains have converted their stored starch into usable sugars, the distiller needs to halt the germination to ensure the fruits of the sprouting are available for distillation. The sprouted seeds are heated, thereby killing them, and then the sugars are ready to use.

As explained earlier, a distiller can use almost anything as a base spirit for gin. If working with potatoes, or another starch-heavy grain, the distiller adds either malted grain or an enzyme to help break it down directly. If starting with a fruit juice or other sugar-heavy fruit, a distiller doesn't need to worry about this step, as they already have the sugar that's necessary to begin the next phase.

The distiller adds yeast and moves the mash to a fermentation vessel where the small bacteria will digest the sugar, creating carbon dioxide and alcohol. Given time, a fermented, alcohol-laden liquid will be created in the vessel. The liquid is siphoned out, leaving behind the solids, and is then poured into a still where the good stuff can be separated from the not-so-good (i.e. toxic) stuff.

OPPOSITE *Stills are are often given pet names. This one is 'Christina'.*

USING A STILL

The choice of still is one that many distillers love to talk about in their promo material, as many are quite proud of these impressive pieces of equipment. Many also feel that their choice of still says a lot about the type of distiller they are. Take the pot still, for example. It looks like its name might indicate. Heat is applied to the bottom of the still and the alcohols are converted to vapours, then re-condensed by passing through a tube that is submerged in cold water.

The pot still separates a spirit in stages. The first alcohols to be condensed are the foreshots, or the toxic stuff you wouldn't want to drink, such as nail polish remover. The next stuff up is the heads, which are high in congeners (flavour) and ethanol. These are mostly used to add character, because the hearts are the right, bright, smooth literal centre of most spirits we drink. The tails are often murky tasting, and are often left discarded.

The innovation of the column still is that it separates these various parts of the spirit in physical space, by having various plates where the alcohol can condense, before being evaporated again. Since there is no more concept of 'time', the still can be run non-stop. The column still is also called a continuous still.

Smaller distillers who use columns do not run their stills 24/7, but many large-scale column stills are in constant use. These columns are actually appendages that are added onto a pot still. Also, unlike their large-scale cousins, these stills produce a neutral spirit that isn't completely neutral in flavour. They tend to maintain some of the base ingredient's

flavour. This is why you get some modern-day small-scale distillers producing apple-based vodkas and gins that manage to retain some of the apple's original flavour notes.

Pot stills tend to produce a base spirit that has flavour and character. Such stills are often associated with artistry, 'small-batch' and craftsmanship, whereas column stills are often associated with pure, clean and large-scale operations. But neither is inherently superior to the other. The real artistry lies in the art of a distiller knowing how to use their equipment to make a good product. It's okay to fall in love with the romance of a certain distilling process, but products should always be judged on their own merit.

It is also possible to make a gin in a single step. For example, a distiller could add juniper and other botanicals to the mash and distil a gin in a single pass; however, in practice very few distillers do this. The heads and tails of an initial distillation contain toxic, or otherwise unpleasant, compounds; however, those same heads and tails contain aromatic notes from the botanicals that the distiller might want to include.

So right now what we have is a neutral grain spirit. If this were a book about vodka, we could quit here and dive into the tasting notes. But not so fast. This is gin, remember, and we have the all-important second step: in which juniper and the other botanicals are added to the neutral spirit.

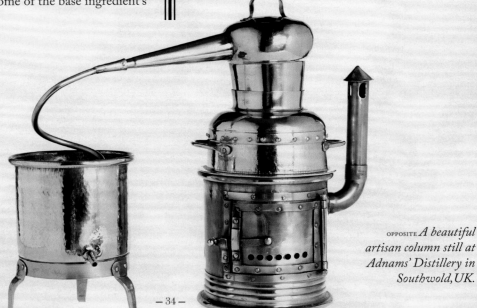

RIGHT *A pot still is used to separate a spirit in stages known as foreshots, heads and tails. The result is a characterful base spirit.*

OPPOSITE *A beautiful artisan column still at Adnams' Distillery in Southwold, UK.*

The Types of Gin Making

JUST AS VODKA DISTILLERS can stop at the end of step one, some gin distillers begin at the start of step two. Many distilleries have reputations for creating a good, high-quality neutral grain spirit, so specific gin distillers often purchase that neutral spirit and use it as the starting-off point for their gin. These sorts of relationships range from partnerships between small-scale distilleries (such as between a gin distiller and a vodka distiller, or a gin distiller and a whisky distiller, depending on the desired character) to industrial partnerships where neutral grain spirit is purchased from a massive, somewhat anonymous factory. While many distillers take pride in designing a spirit from start to finish, the use of neutral grain spirit need not necessarily indicate an inferior gin. If a distiller is looking for a truly neutral character, the use of a neutral spirit can be a convenient launching-off point to keep costs down. With the base spirit in place, the gin making can now begin. There are several different methods available.

COMPOUND GIN

IN ORDER TO BE CALLED GIN, a spirit must derive its flavour from a juniper infusion. It is possible for a spirit to technically labelled a gin without ever being re-distilled. While this is true of many supermarket brands of gin, where flavouring agents are added to a neutral grain spirit to create a drink that is superficially gin, we're talking here about the addition of real juniper.

This is the principle behind a famous recipe by mixologist Jeffrey Morganthaler and the many homemade gin kits (see page 195) that are widely available in which juniper is infused in vodka. Compound gins aren't limited to the home and the bottom shelf, however. There are some high-quality compounds out there. For example, Crater Lake Spirits in Bend, Oregon makes its Crater Lake Estate Gin by infusing local juniper berries after distillation. These gins are sometimes referred to as 'bathtub gins' as well. Though not necessarily a style designation on its own, it has been seen by some as a preferable name for gins produced by this technique, because it distinguishes a creative choice from the negative associations of a compounded gin.

Bathtub gin is produced by adding aromatics or extracts to the neutral spirit, without a further process of distillation. If the flavours from the botanicals are imparted without distillation, then it is by definition a compound gin. However entwined the word 'compounded' is with an assertion of quality, its important to keep in mind that the word encompasses an entire spectrum of gins.

LEFT *Crater Lake Estate Gin, made by infusing local juniper berries in a base spirit, is known as a bathtub gin.*

OPPOSITE *Copper House Distillery uses juniper, cardamom and coriander as well as other botanicals such as orris root.*

DISTILLED GIN

THIS IS, BY FAR AND AWAY, the most common type of gin out there. These sort of gins begin with an initial run of a spirit, and then that spirit is run through the still again, only this time with botanicals. This 'second' distillation generally assumes a high-quality starting product, which means that there's a lot more artistry in this second half of the process. If the first half is about ensuring that the bad stuff is gone, this second process is focused on taste and aroma. To that effect, there are several different techniques that distillers can use to give their gin the character they desire. Each will extract different aromatic molecules from the plants they are working with, and therefore each will have its pros and cons. Truly all methods are equal at this stage, separated only by the skills of the men and women working at the still.

The first two methods involve maceration. In the first one, the distiller will put the botanicals directly into the liquid. That liquid will then be directly heated and re-distilled. There's a variation on this method that might be more aptly described as the 'tea' method wherein a bag of botanicals is dropped in the still, then heated similarly, creating a swirling broth, that once boiled and re-condensed will have its gin-like character. A second type of maceration results in a lighter style of gin. The botanicals are steeped in the liquid for a period of time, often no more than a day, and are then filtered out. The resulting liquid (which could rightfully be called a bathtub or compounded gin at this point) is then re-distilled, without ever heating a single botanical.

Of the first method, critics might allege that 'cooking the botanicals' spoils the flavours or releases undesirable aromas. Steeping extracts, phenols and tannins may add a bitter character to the gin. Though the critiques are true, several of the biggest names in the history of gin, such as Beefeater and Tanqueray, distil their gins in this fashion. Clearly, method alone does not guarantee an inferior product.

The truth lies closer to the fact that this method simply releases 'different' aromas and a skilled distiller needs only to be aware of what they are doing to ensure a quality gin.

ABOVE *At Sipsmith, the still room is used to store the distillery's experimental gin blends.*

LEFT *Tanqueray places botanicals directly into the spirit before directly heating and re-distilling the gin.*

OPPOSITE *Servicing the stills at Hendrick's distillery in Girvan, Scotland.*

STEAM DISTILLATION

THE NEXT SET OF METHODS has been moved forward by the next generation of distillers. These methods often result in a much lighter, more botanically rich, but less intense style of gin.

The first method is based on the principle of steam distillation. It's also alternately called vapour infusion or the 'gin basket' method. What they all have in common is that the actual aromatics and botanicals do not touch the liquid in the still. They can be either suspended above the liquid or located in the neck of the still, so that the aromatic infusion occurs as it's about to re-condense. A distiller who locates botanicals just above the liquid, does so with the expectation that the aromatics will drip down and mix with the liquid below, creating a more full-bodied flavour profile. Locating them in the neck better preserves delicate flavours. In both cases, steam distillation is a better way to extract the essential oils, which are what gives a gin its character.

However, even this method has its detractors. Some distillers allege that the simple act of heating a botanical destroys the most delicate of volatiles. The only solution to this conundrum is to reduce the temperature. Fortunately, many distillers are well versed in physics. By using a vacuum, the boiling point of a substance can be significantly lowered, to the point where very little heat needs to be applied. This means that heat-sensitive volatiles can now be distilled and re-condensed. A couple of notable distilleries that do this are the Sacred Spirits

Company in London, and Greenhook Ginsmiths in Brooklyn, New York.

Thus far, all of these distillation techniques have described situations where the botanicals are all placed into an apparatus together at one time. There's a certain artistry and challenge in these tasks, because a slight change in botanical essential oil content can result in a change in the flavour of the end product. Many smaller distilleries label their bottles with 'batch' and 'bottle' numbers to differentiate between distillations and manage the expectation that the product might differ a little bit from run to run. One might wonder then, how larger distilleries are often able to maintain a consistently reliable product that seems unfailingly similar from batch to batch.

There are a couple of different ways that distilleries can help mitigate this. The first happens after distillation. A distillery may blend the results of several batches together for consistency. Smaller differences across a wide number of distillations may be evened out by averaging the botanical profiles of each distillation by mixing them together. The other method is actually part of the distillation process. Though uncommon, some gin distillers are known to distill each botanical individually. That way they can ensure that the expression of coriander is where they want it; the notes of their juniper are true to their vision, and so on. They then precisely blend the various distillates together to create the final product.

LEFT *Greenhook Ginsmiths uses vacuum distillation in order to keep temperatures down during re-distillation.*

NEAR RIGHT *The distillery floor at Iceberg Gin in Newfoundland, Canada. Water from melted icebergs is used to dilute the company's gins.*

FAR RIGHT *Martin Miller's, Long Table and Iceberg all take the origin of their water very seriously.*

Gin Dilution

The final step for many distillers is to reduce the strength of the spirit that comes off the still to one suitable for consumption. Pure ethanol, for example, comes out of the still at 190 proof, or about 95% alcohol by volume. This is in fact the upper limit, 'as pure as you can get' by distillation alone. Some legal designations, such as London gin in the European Union, require the gin with botanicals to come out of the still at a minimum of 140 proof, or 70% alcohol by volume. Obviously, very few gins are bottled at this proof. Many are diluted prior to sales. In the United States, gin cannot be less than 40% alcohol by volume; in the European Union gin cannot be bottled to less than 37.5% ABV and still be sold as gin.

Many distillers take this dilution step very seriously and pay very close attention to the water they use. Martin Miller's Gin's identity is tightly tied to the Icelandic sourced water that it uses to dilute its gin. Iceland is prominently featured on the bottle and the 'purity' of its water is often referred to in its marketing materials. Another example is Iceberg Gin from Newfoundland, Canada. Ed Kean, a sea captain from the Canadian Maritimes, scouts and harvests hunks of icebergs, which are melted to make the water for its vodka and gin. Long Table Distillery in Vancouver proudly sources its waters from the Coast Mountain Range. Spring 44 Distilling cites its source as artesian mineral spring water from the Buckhorn Canyon in Colorado. The list goes on. As you can see, this final step is far from an afterthought for many distillers who believe that the quality of the water they use is just as important as the botanicals and grains that go into the product.

Non-chill Filtering

Though we'll be diving into aromatics a little bit later on, there's another step that some distillers take at this point. Many aromatics are soluble in alcohol but are not soluble in water. This basically means that when you add water or ice, the gin becomes cloudy. Fans of absinthe, pastis or ouzo might recognize this effect, often referred to as either a louche, or the ouzo effect. For absinthe, a louche is a highly desired characteristic; for gins not so much, as distillers will go to lengths such as chill filtering to improve the clarity of the spirit. It's a simple process, which involves chilling the gin to around or below freezing and then passing the spirit through a filter to remove the particles that contribute to the cloudiness. Many distillers have chosen to differentiate themselves recently by electing to not use this process and calling their gins 'non-chill filtered'. A few examples include Vor Gin from Iceland, Dodd's Gin from England and Letherbee Gin from Illinois in the United States.

There are many different ways to make a gin. What's important to note is that although each process has its advocates, each method has produced a well-received gin. If no process alone can guarantee a perfect end product, our journey will take us on a closer look to the other important part of the process that creates this botanical spirit. Whether put in a bag, suspended in a basket or thrown in a tub with the mash, the journeys of these plants is what distinguishes one gin from another.

The Botany of Gin

Common Botanicals

LEFT *The juniper in flower.*

Juniper

THE JUNIPER BERRY that gin drinkers are most familiar with comes from the *Juniperus communis* plant, but it's worth taking a look at the larger botanical picture and the family tree that this specific juniper plant comes from. Junipers are conifers, closely related to the cypress family that contains such giants as the Sequoias and American coastal Redwoods. There are over 50 different species of juniper within the genus *Juniperus*, and they have a nearly worldwide distribution, found on five different continents and occupying a vast range of niches, from deserts to alpine boreal forests.

What distinguishes junipers is the distinctive berry, but they're not really berries, they're cones, like pine cones. As the plant grows, the scales (which are fleshy, as opposed to the woody ones associated with pine cones) coalesce and form a solid berry-like appearance. This fleshy outer covering protects the seed inside. When the cone matures (often taking as long as 18–36 months to do so), we have what we call the juniper berry. Though its colour varies across species, generally it's close to the bluish-purple hue exhibited by some of the more common junipers, including *Juniperis communis*. When dried, it appears darker in complexion, approaching a purplish-black.

Junipers can also be distinguished by their pine-like needles or scaled leaves. These leaves vary greatly in texture, but all of them are evergreen. The size of the plants ranges widely from low, creeping junipers that rarely exceed 30cm (1ft) in height to some that are most definitely trees and tall ones at that.

This incredible diversity within the family of juniper might look like a boon to the gin distiller; however, much of this botanical range is of no use to the enterprising gin maker. Some juniper varieties are mildly toxic to humans. For example, the Eastern Red Cedar (*Juniperus virginiana*), widely grown throughout the United States as a decorative tree, or seen growing in disturbed roadsides or pastures as a weed, has poisonous berries so it should not be consumed, let alone distilled in gin. *Juniperis sabina*, a variety native to Eurasian mountains also has been shown to have negatively affected pregnant mice. Not really the kind of thing you want to eat or drink, although they might make beautiful ornamental plants. The Plants for a Future charity only ranks six species of juniper as having a moderate edibility rating. Though many junipers have traditionally been used by peoples around the world, very few have made it into modern-day kitchens.

Among the species that do make good additions to spirits, distillers have taken the plunge. Among the first was the United States' Bendistillery, that makes a compound gin (meaning the juniper is added after the spirit is distilled) using *Juniperus occidentalis*, also known as western juniper or sierra juniper. Western juniper is native to the Cascade and Sierra Nevada mountain ranges of the Western US. It generally grows at altitude, and although usually the size of a small bush, exceptional examples are found near Lake, Oregon, towering 23m (75ft)+ high into the sky. Quite a tall juniper.

Usually though, when we speak of gin, we speak of *Juniperus communis*, a.k.a the common juniper whose name is fitting because it is represented in native plant populations in boreal forests from Siberia to Canada, Norway to Iceland and Greenland, and literally anywhere in between that I've left out. Remarkably, the plant is dioecious, which in other words means it has a lot in common with people. There are lady plants and there are guy plants. In order for the female plants to bear cones, the pollen from a male juniper must make it all the way over to the branches of a female juniper. Without wind, the common juniper wouldn't be all that common whatsoever. Among junipers, the common variety also has a particularly long maturation time for its seeds, testing the patience of gin distillers around the world. A berry might take three years to become ripe and be ready for harvesting.

Harvesting is a challenge in and of itself. More commercial operations might strike a juniper branch with another branch, dislodging only the ripe berries. Other smaller-scale juniper harvesting is done with a foraging mindset. Ladders, gloves, buckets and hands are all that's required to do it the old-fashioned way. Most juniper plants that are foraged are also rather small, save for an example in Letchworth State Park in Upstate New York that clocks in at a tall (for its species) 6m (20ft). They rarely top out at half that, generally opting for a creeping or more shrub-like appearance. Juniper is as common as a weed, as it is a decorative plant. It is simultaneously desired for its fruit and appearance, while also being reviled as a pest and an invasive species.

Although around the world juniper is common (still), in the land often referred to as the home of gin, the United Kingdom, is where it is now threatened with extinction. In recent times, a combination of fungus, grazing herbivores and an already small population has led to a series of interventions led by local organisations created to preserve existing juniper stock and create an environment conducive to the plant re-establishing itself across the island. On behalf of gin drinkers and juniper aficionados everywhere, we wish them the best of luck in this difficult, ongoing task.

For a plant as common as juniper, it may not seem like much is at stake when we speak about a specific region's population. Surely, the species is among the world's most successful. It's not going anywhere. The importance of its survival, especially for a place that is so connected with the origin of gin, is that the climate and local variations, or terroir, produce a discernible difference in the juniper berries' essential oil content. That is to say that juniper from two parts of the world can taste significantly different, and there's plenty of science to back this up.

Researchers in the 1990s looking at *Juniperus communis* found that Greek juniper had much less alpha-pinene (the molecule largely responsible for the signature pine character of juniper) than samples from other parts of Europe. Differences between populations in Montenegro and Iran showed that Iranian juniper samples contained almost double the content of this vital molecule. Others have shown significant variances between regions based on separate micro-climate, and the variation includes different essential oils that might add notes to juniper not often associated with juniper. Limonene, the aromatic molecule with a bright orange scent, is also found in juniper berries. In short, where juniper is grown does affect its overall flavour. So if the major gin distillers of London, founded in the 18th and 19th centuries, were using local juniper, we could lose that insight into some of the earliest gins if action isn't taken in the UK to preserve the juniper stocks. However, this implication extends beyond just the UK. It means that around the world, distillers who want to add something of a local touch to their gin need look no further than their backyards.

Juniper terroir is very real. Though many distillers still source their juniper from Italy, there seems to be a trend away from that. In addition to the aforementioned Bendistillery, other producers such as Legend Distilling, Okanagan Spirits and Long Table Distillery, all in British Columbia, forage for the juniper they use in their gin. Perhaps we're entering a new era where the provenance of your juniper is as important as the other botanicals in your mix.

Don't believe me? Master of Malt did the gin world a fantastic service in 2012 when it developed a series of gins called Origin. Each has only a single ingredient: juniper, from a very specific place (sourced by its customers). In tasting the range of gins one can appreciate just how wide the range of expressions this small berry can embody. Without further ado, here are some descriptions.

Terroir Tasting Notes

Skopje, Macedonia

Begins with green, slightly resinous juniper on the nose. Notes of black peppercorn and a touch of bright spice.

PALATE

Spiced, warm juniper with a green note at first, a resinous note on mid palate, with a hint of sea salt and almond on the finish.

Meppel, the Netherlands

Earthy with a woody juniper note set a little back on the nose.

PALATE

Slightly minty and herbal, with hints of rosemary.
Herbal finish with hints of almond.

Arezzo, Italy

Resinous and woody, the juniper is highly concentrated in the top notes. It fades quickly, leaving woody notes and a bright aroma of orange zest.

PALATE

Boldly juniper forward. Begins with a touch of citrus, vanilla cake and bright green juniper. Finishes with notes of vanillin and orange peel, with a burst of heat.

Istog, Kosovo

Piny green juniper with violets and coriander on the nose.

PALATE

Surprisingly sweet and floral. Cherries precede a slow-building pine-forward juniper, crisp and precise. The finish has a hint of almond, and a sharpness/astringency that remains on the palate, brightly juniper.

Veliki Prestav, Bulgaria

Notes on the nose that immediately call to mind coriander, juniper a bit lower in the mix, but also some floral notes as well.

PALATE

Fruity at first, but intensely herbaceous juniper on the mid palate. Floral complexity on the edges, with hints of coriander and hibiscus. Long, bright juniper-led finish.

Klanac, Croatia

On the nose, this is slightly resinous and piny juniper with hints of coriander as well.

PALATE

On the palate, it sits quiet, but it is juniper that hits the palate first. Bright and herbaceous, the finish has a peculiar hint of sloe gin. Rich, deep red stone fruit, with a long resinous finish.

Valbonë, Albania

On the nose, quiet with juniper and stone fruit.

PALATE

On the palate, it builds sharply, with hints of dark, sweetened cherries and stone fruits. Juniper shines on the back end, slightly astringent with a long, resinous juniper finish.

Coriander

Ask people 'what do you think of CORIANDER (CILANTRO)?' and you're likely to get a mixed reaction. Some absolutely love the sharp, citrussy, green flavour of the leaves. Others abhor them, perhaps lending credibility to theory that the word coriander itself comes from a Greek word for an insect.

When we're talking about gin, though, we can ignore this discussion entirely. Something magical happens to the fruits of the coriander plant when they are harvested and dried. They lose all the sharpness that's associated with the leaf and take on a warm, spicy and somewhat citrussy taste that is so prized in gin. Coriander is nearly as common as juniper itself, appearing in nearly 9 out of every 10 gins you might encounter. The primary aromatic is linalool, which on its own has a surprisingly floral aroma that some liken to the aromatic top notes in Froot Loops cereal. It's bright, and incredibly pleasant, explaining coriander's millennia-long history as both an important food and a perfumer's ingredient.

Coriander (*Coriandrum sativum*) is an annual plant closely related to carrots, fennel and parsnips. While native to southern Europe and northern Africa, it is now grown around the world and has taken up important roles in the food cultures of places as far away as Mexico and China. It rarely grows to more than 60cm (2ft) tall, and other than its notable flat green leaves, which you'd probably recognize from the supermarket, it has white flowers arranged in the shape of an upside-down umbrella, similar to Queen Anne's Lace.

Coriander might owe its modern-day popularity to its presence in the botanical bills for some of the world's longest-lived and bestselling gins. Tanqueray (1830) and Gordon's (1769) are among those that include coriander. Bombay Sapphire, although a more recent gin, also has a bright coriander top note.

By volume, coriander seed is often the second ingredient in many gins. A lot of distillers swear by the quality of Moroccan coriander, which is the most common source on the market today. Others, however, suggest that cooler, wetter summers result in a higher essential oil content, suggesting that northern Europe or Siberia might be the best source for coriander. The predictability of climate is one primary reason why many distillers and gins source their botanicals from Morocco, though this is a classic example of the trade-offs made in the interest of consistency, as well as the acute effect climate and growing region can have on a botanical.

Coriandrum

54

Character Genericus

Œnanthe Pimpinelloides
Pimpinell Dropwort

Coriandrum Sativum
Common Coriander

Angelica

ANGELICA is perhaps the most unfamiliar of the major gin ingredients, and many are surprised to learn that is nearly as common as coriander as a gin botanical. At any given point, it's likely that nearly three-quarters of the gins behind any bar you can think of (or for you collectors out there, take a look at your shelf at home) contain this single botanical. Like coriander, angelica is closely related to the carrot family (and therefore to coriander also), and the herbs which make up the Angelicus genus grow nearly everywhere in the northern hemisphere. The angelica that is used for gin belongs to a single species known as *Angelica archangelica*, native to northern Europe and first cultivated by the peoples of Scandinavia in the medieval era. As a vegetable in its own right and as an important medicine, angelica is primarily cultivated today for its stems and its roots. The stems are often candied, while the roots are what is commonly used in gin.

Angelica archangelica, better known as garden angelica, can tower upwards of 2m (7ft) tall, has broad leaves which in and of themselves stretch outwards of 1m (3ft). The bush-like plant has towering single stalks that culminate in a 'firework' shape of yellow, green or white flowers. It grows in many places around the world, but thrives in cooler climates.

The roots are harvested and dried before use in gin, and can be touchy in terms of their flavour profile. Whole roots maintain more of their aromatics than crushed roots, and crushed roots in turn are more aromatic than angelica powder. The aromatics also dissipate the longer a root is stored, so it can be important to use them as quickly as possible. Chemically speaking, Angelica root adds alpha-Pinene, beta-Pinene, and Limonene, which may be familiar, as these same aromatics are common in juniper citrus. These commonalities explain why some describe the taste as being a bitter and pungent combination of juniper and celery.

Angelica Root is also a likely ingredient in herbal spirits such as Chartreuse and Benedictine, and has historically been part of the botanical bouquets of aquavits and absinthes. It features in gins as disparate as Broker's (page 93), Hendrick's (page 110), Vaiōne (page 177) and Green Hat (page 153).

Cassia

CASSIA is the most recognisable botanical in gin yet is also often easily confused with cinnamon. Cassia comes from the bark of a tall tree native to China and Southeast Asia, growing to a height of 3–4.5m (10–15ft). *Cinnamomum cassia* refers only to this one specific tree. Though closely related to cinnamon, it's merely a cousin or close relation. Shoppers in North America might not be familiar with the difference, as cassia is often sold as cinnamon.

If sold in stick form, one can tell cassia from cinnamon by the thickness and character of the sticks themselves. Cassia is thick, and rolled as a single piece; cinnamon will be thinner and not as solid. If sold in powdered form, cinnamon and cassia are nearly indistinguishable from one another, short of chemical analysis. Both have a bright, spicy, distinctive cinnamon note owing to the presence of cinnamaldehyde. Cinnamon has a much higher quantity of eugenol, the primary aromatic component of cloves. Cassia's telltale signature is the presence of coumarin, which has a more vanilla-like scent. While in terms of volume, neither eugenol nor coumarin are the primary aromatic component, chemists can use it to differentiate between the two when the eye is unable to do so.

Truthfully, the biggest difference between the two is cost. Cinnamon is much more expensive than cassia, which has led to some referring to cassia as 'the poor man's cinnamon'. Its wider availability, lower price and equally as distinctive aromatic character have made it a common ingredient in both classic and contemporary gins.

Cassia appears in gins as classic as Bombay Dry Gin (page 92) and as contemporary as G'vine Floraison (page 120). It is among the most common gin botanicals, found in nearly half of the gins on the market today, and although more common than cinnamon, there does seem to be an overall trend towards cinnamon among newer gins. Whether that's cassia being sold as cinnamon, or true cinnamon, is a question best left to the chemists.

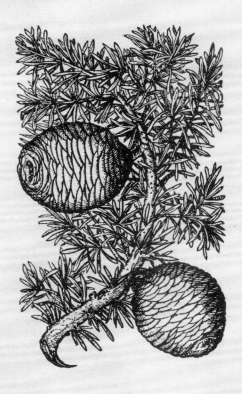

Orris Root

The ORRIS ROOT might seem more familiar if referred to by the plant's more commonly used English name, the iris. More specifically, orris root comes from any plant of the species *Iris germanica*, including Florentine Iris, best known for its inclusion in Martin Miller's Gin (page 99). Iris is a perennial, growing to about 1m (3ft) tall and generally has bright, aromatic flowers which, depending on the plant, can take on any number of colours; the most common one is a bright, vivid purple with which the name itself is often associated.

The root of the plant has been a prized fixative in perfumery for many centuries, which means that it helps hold the other fragrances in place. It does so by contributing an extra atom that helps make other aromatics less volatile. This chemical fact was, however, unknown by those who first started drying the roots for use in perfume. Widely used by the 15th century, orris root has a bright woody raspberry/violet aroma due to the molecule irone, which is distinctive on its own and important as a fixative.

For the root to be effective as an aromatic fixative, a labour-intensive process of harvesting the roots and drying them must occur. The drying process can take up to five years. The roots are often ground before use, and the essential oil only makes up a small portion of the root overall by volume. Orris root is therefore one of the more expensive ingredients in a gin distiller's arsenal, though a small quantity goes a long way. Most orris root on the market today comes from Italy, though other sources exist throughout southern and eastern Europe, Morocco and even Asia.

When it comes to evaluating orris root in gin, it will most often be present in the background, or low in the base notes. You'll be more likely to detect it by the effect it has on the other ingredients. Gins that don't contain orris root, such as single botanical blends, often tend to lose their aromas very quickly. While this is not always due to a lack of orris root, it is often one of the main reasons.

Citrus Fruit

ALL CITRUS FRUIT taken together as a gin botanical would make it nearly as ubiquitious as coriander in gins, and there is an overall trend among distillers towards emphasising citrus in their gins (Bluecoat Gin and Black Button Citrus Forward Gin to name only a couple), and expanding the range of citrus fruits used. Once gin was the domain of lemon and orange, but now grapefruit (Glorious Gin and Tanqueray 10), lime (Vaiōne and Tanqueray Rangpur), yuzu (Citadelle Réserve and Japanese Gin), bergamot (Botanivore Gin) and pomelo (Bloom Gin) are stealing the show. The diversity and range of this vast family of highly aromatic fruits are well represented by gin distillers around the world.

The primary botanicals are lemon and orange, so we'll focus on their similarities and flavour profiles here.

LEMON TREES can grow to heights of nearly 6m (20 ft) when grown outdoors in their natural habitats, though minature and dwarf versions are common as well, growing indoors but rarely exceeding 3m (10ft). Lemon peels have long been prized for their aromatic character. Native to China, most lemons today are grown in China, Mexico and South America, with smaller numbers grown in Italy and Spain.

Lemon peels, like other citrus fruit, contain a large amount of limonene, the aromatic largely responsible for the bright aroma associated with citrus. Lemons, though, have terpinene-4-ol and beta-pinene, which help give them a greener flavour profile than other citrus fruits.

ORANGES cannot be assumed to be a simple, single fruit as pictured on the side of juice cartons. You can roughly divide the world of oranges into two sub-categories. Sweet, which is the kind we drink as juice, and bitter, which is often used by perfumists as an essential oil, made into marmalades or used in the world of distilling in gins and other herbal spirits. You'll find both types in gins. Distillers who use bitter oranges might only disclose the botanical as 'orange', or might refer to it by a more specific name. Seville orange is one of the most popular types of bitter orange in the gin world, appearing in gins as classic as Beefeater (page 91) and as contemporary as Ginself (page 133). As there are over 50 different types of citrus fruit available around the world, the choice of citrus in your gin is one important way distillers are adding a local touch to their gins while playing within the traditional gin botanical bill. One of the emerging trends of the last few years is that there's been increased experimentation with citrus fruits. In 2008 you would have been hard-pressed to find yuzu or Buddha's hand in a gin. Soon we might be seeing *cam sành* or finger lime as well.

Blood Orange.

Sustain.

Tangierine.

Novel Botanicals

SOME SURPRISING INGREDIENTS

As GIN CONTINUES TO EXPAND AROUND THE WORLD, and new gin distilleries open in new places, so new botanicals, never before distilled with juniper, are starting to crop up. These surprising botanicals have one major thing in common: they're a way to link the place where a gin is distilled with the end product. The new botanicals are providing a way to 'taste' the food culture of the region or country where the gin is made, providing terroir if you will.

Local berries have been a goldmine for distillers looking to create a local spin on gin. Unagava Gin, which hails from Quebec, Canada, has selected its botanicals to create a feeling of the boreal forest. It has included **cloudberry**, a small peach-coloured berry, similar to a raspberry, which has been used for making both spirits and jams for centuries. Further west in Canada, Lucky Bastard Distillers in Saskatchewan has added the locally named **saskatoon berry** or juneberry. These wild-tasting berries have long been a fixture of the Canadian prairie underbrush and been used in jams and beers. Scottish gin Caorunn includes **rowan berries**, which are the flourishes on a weedy, fast-growing tree that is a common sight in the Scottish Highlands.

Other fruits get in on the action, too. Bulldog Gin sets itself apart by including the **longan** or dragon's eye, a small fruit which, when peeled, is milky white, with a tart sweetness similar to that of a lychee. When in season, longan fruits are a common sight in Asian fruit or vegetable markets. While Bulldog is looking to conjure up notions of the 'far away' and 'exotic', the West Winds Gin distillers in Australia looked a little closer to home and included the **bush tomato**.

A small relative of the aubergine (eggplant), its sweet, pungent and fruity, almost caramel-tasting fruits, look a bit more like raisins than tomatoes.

Australia is rife with local experimentation. The incredible biodiversity coupled with the large number of plants that are only found locally, gives distillers an untapped menagerie with which to create new and innovative gins. Kangaroo Island Spirits distil the **coastal daisybush**. For an idea of what it tastes like, perhaps its alternative name, wild rosemary, will help. Botanic Australis Gin has *Mentha australis* or **river mint**, which imparts a spearmint, but sharper, flavour to its gin.

Vegetables might not be a likely source for gin botanicals but Blanc Ocean Gin from Spain makes it work. **Seabeans**, also known as *Salicornia* or marsh samphire, add a seaweed-like note. Lichens aren't a likely source either, but Eimverk Distillery adds **Icelandic moss** to its Vor Gin. Or maybe you're more a fan of what's below the ground as opposed to above it. Elephant Gin includes **devil's claw**, a cousin of the sesame native to South Africa that was used historically to treat arthritis and aid digestion.

There's no way I could exhaustively represent the incredible diversity of plants that are being distilled in gin. But hopefully, this brief look at some of the most exotic plants that are being used nowadays helps give you an idea of just how wide open gin can be if you want it to be. There's no end to the number of ways that distillers could add a local touch to gin, and there's likely no end to the ways we'll see distillers do exactly that in the coming years.

CLOCKWISE FROM TOP LEFT *Longan fruit, rowan berry, bush tomato, saskatoon berry, devil's claw and coastal daisybush.*

Other Important Botanicals

LESSER ARCANA

Lavender

SOMEONE ONCE REMARKED THAT LAVENDER is quickly becoming the hallmark of contemporary-style gins. While it's far from being as common as any of the big names, it is starting to appear in gins on both sides of the Atlantic with surprising regularity. This woody, alpine shrub, native to the foothills of central Europe, has whitish green, narrow and pointed leaves. The flowers are a pastel purple for which the colour is named.

The leaves and flowers have an herbaceous, slightly camphorous and floral character, somewhere between rose and violet with a hint of fresh mint.

GINS WITH LAVENDER
Berkeley Square Gin (page 92)
Waterloo Antique Barrel Reserve Gin (page 162)

Cardamom

CARDAMOM is another emerging botanical that's becoming more and more common in gins. It adds a distinctive flavour and an air of exclusivity. It's the third most expensive spice in the world and a vital part of food cultures in countries as disparate as India and Scandinavia. Native to central Asia, most of the world's cardamom grows in Guatemala thanks to an enterprising coffee planter who introduced cardamom there in the 1910s.

Prized for its exotic aroma, it adds an expressive, spicy note (some recognise it as 'chai' as it is one of the key ingredients), which in large quantities can be perceived as bitter. Of the major colours, green/white and black/red, the green is often prized for the minty eucalyptus note it adds to the flavour. Despite its captivating and unique aroma, cardamom can be a challenge as its essential oils and aromatics are very volatile and degrade quickly.

GINS WITH CARDAMOM
Four Pillars (page 176)
and Sacred Gin (page 102)

Liquorice

LIQUORICE is interesting among botanical ingredients in that it contains a natural sweetener known as glycyrrhizinic acid. Although it only makes up 2–10% of the root's essential oil content by volume, it's a powerful sweetener that's over 20 times sweeter than regular sugar. Because of this, it's been speculated that liquorice was an important ingredient in Old Tom gins. Whereas some believe they were sweetened with sugar or other sweet additives, others claim that the gins themselves were distilled with liquorice to give them a sweeter profile, hence the term 'Botanically Sweetened Old Tom'. One notable example in this style is Jensen's Old Tom (page 98).

Liquorice is not botanically related to the similar-tasting fennel and anise, though it does share with them the molecule responsible for part of the flavour. Anethole, which has the characteristic 'anise' flavour, is also, curiously, the molecule responsible for the louche of absinthe also known as the 'ouzo effect' (page 41). Anethole is not as soluble in water as it is in ethanol. When you lower the strength of the spirit by adding water into it, the anethole comes out of the solution and gives the spirit a cloudy appearance. Many gin distillers chill filter their gins to prevent this; however, those that have a large quantity of liquorice notes and are not chill filtered, such as Letherbee Gin, will exhibit a cloudy louche comparable to an ouzo or arak.

GIN WITH LIQUORICE
Jensen's Old Tom (page 98)

2.

1 b

1 a, b, c.

1a

1c

Fennel

AT THE MARKET, FRESH FENNEL might be confused with celery; in gins the taste might be mistaken for liquorice or anise. Gin distillers use fennel seeds to impart a liquorice-like warmth and spice, but offset with an herbal undernote that is subtle in gins, but striking when the seeds are eaten on their own.

Fennel is an herbaceous plant, native to the Mediterranean region that is now grown all around the world. The stalks and green parts are important foods for many; however, the seeds are where the essential oil is located, and it is these that form such a valuable ingredient for gin distillers.

GINS WITH FENNEL
Spirit Hound Gin (page 161)
and Death's Door Gin (page 149).

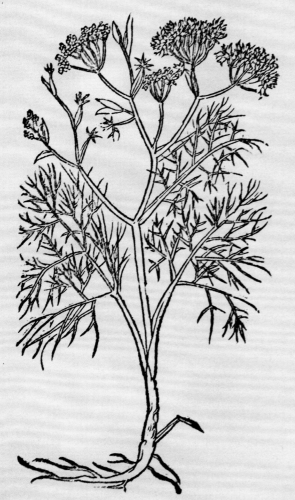

Nutmeg

NUTMEG is native to the Moluccas in Indonesia and once played an important part in the Dutch East India Company's overseas monopoly of the spice trade. Although two important spices come from the same tree, only the nutmeg seed, and not the outer covering called mace, is an important gin botanical.

Nutmeg is frequently used in perfumes, and the seeds, although toxic in large doses (not in the quantities used in gin), have a woody, citrussy, spicy, peppery and warm aroma redolent of baking spices. The essential oil of nutmeg is mostly camphene, which imparts the minty, spicy notes; however, it has similar aromatic compounds that contain the same aromatics as other common gin botanicals, such as pinene, geraniol, linalool and even limonene. While at this point we're getting down to botanicals that appear in only 10–15% of all gins, nutmeg does still seem to be nearly everywhere.

GIN WITH NUTMEG
G'vine Nouaison (page 120)

Cubeb

Tailed pepper, also known as cubeb, isn't often seen outside of the spirits world. Native to Indonesia, it is still primarily cultivated there. The small black berries are harvested before ripening and then dried. The molecule responsible for this is the aptly named cubebene, which is woody, camphorous and piquant. The cubeb berries themselves have a more complex aroma profile, being simultaneously spicy and peppery with background herbal and citrus notes. Despite this complexity, the berries are still remarkably uncommon.

Cubeb berries likely found their way to gin by way of their brief heyday in Europe during the 19th century as a fashionable remedy for a number of ailments including bronchitis and gonorrhoea. Though in modern times, gin distillers use cubeb solely for its distinctive spicy flavour.

GINS WITH CUBEB BERRIES
Hendrick's Gin (page 110)
and G'vine Floraison (page 120)

Grains of Paradise

Back before the Europeans had easy access to the black-pepper-growing regions of Southeast Asia, they were using the small yellow-orange seeds, taken from the pods of a West African plant closely related to cardamom. Important to West African food cultures for centuries, these small, almost peppery seeds were used for hiding off-notes in wines and other spirits, in addition to being the poor person's pepper.

In modern times, despite their catchy name, they're rarely used outside of traditional African food cultures. They're primarily used in aquavits and gins, and in very small numbers. Grains of paradise have an interesting peppery, slightly reminiscent of cardamom aroma – spicy, hot, and a bit pungent.

GINS WITH GRAINS OF PARADISE
Ginskey (page 145)
and Bombay Sapphire (page 92)

How to Taste Gin

TASTING GIN is quite a different practice from tasting other alcholic drinks. Let me explain.

Often, wine tasting notes, for example, include references to *stone fruit, nutmeg, pear, apricot, chocolate, olive, black pepper* and almost any other fruit, mineral or spice you can think of. Those familiar with the wine-making process know that it involves some grapes, a barrel and a bit of help from micro-organisms who are doing the fermentation. But there is no black pepper or olive in your wine.

Moving along to the world of whisky, no matter where in the world it is distilled and aged, tasting notes read rather similarly to one another. You might see notes that include *ginger, honey, pimento, cocoa nibs, leather, gingerbread, vanilla custard,* or even *autumn produce.* However, to make whisky you need nothing more than a barrel, some flavourful grain-based spirit… and time.

In both cases neither set of tasting notes has a direct correlation with the actual ingredients. Though master sommeliers and whisky tasters can attribute effects to causes and tell you something about how the spirit is made, it doesn't change the fact that when a wine sommelier tells you they taste black olives, this isn't an act of deception. More simply, it's because the products of fermentation and distillation, followed by ageing, can cause a wide array of aromatic compounds to manifest and transform into a complex series of flavours.

Both types of tasters rely heavily on the art of metaphor to describe a particular aroma or taste that comes from the whisky or wine. This metaphor is an attempt to map something concrete to the sensation or aroma that a spirit has created over its journey. No one is telling you that there's *cocoa nibs* in your whisky; instead they are telling you that the chemical interactions have resulted in something that tastes of cocoa nibs. This is where the art of gin tasting differs wildly from both the art of wine and whisky tasting. When a gin taster tells you they taste cocoa nibs, they could be either suggesting that cocoa nibs are a metaphor for the aromas, or they could be postulating, 'I think there might be cocoa in this gin'. A good gin taster does not only master metaphor, but they also understand how certain aromas or tastes are indicative of a certain botanical ingredient and can tell you with a degree of certainty what those ingredients are in the gin.

The Science of Gin

WHEN YOU ARE TASTING ANY SPIRIT (not just gin, but why would you want to taste anything else?) there are three sensory systems that are affected and combine to produce the taste and sensation of the spirit.

The first, and most obvious, is the sense of taste. For gin, and spirits in general, your sense of taste is doing very little work. Your tongue contains taste buds for four basic types of taste, which are sour, bitter, sweet and salty. Gin doesn't contain salt, so the last one's not needed. Most gins aren't sweetened, nor have sugar (notable exceptions include Old Tom and sloe gins, but more on those later). Ethanol tastes naturally bitter to humans, so a lot of what you're tasting (literally tasting) when you sip a spirit is just the bitterness of the very base of the substance you're drinking. Others will postulate that the human tongue has receptors for umami, calcium and even carbonation, but I'd say it's all just your olfactory sense; however, that would be doing a disservice and ignoring another sensory system that's hard at work here.

BELOW LEFT *An illustration by John French dating from 1653 shows distillation using a bain-maire and alembic stills.*

ASTRINGENCY

When we talk about the 'heat' or 'burn' of an alcoholic drink (or a chilli pepper, for example), we're actually talking about a whole different sensory path. Your somatosensory system, facilitated by the trigeminal nerve, sends indications of these sensations to your brain. One of the key sensations we observe with this sense, in particular with gin, is that of astringency. Astringency is more of a texture than an actual taste. The tannic drying sensation isn't caused strictly by tannins in this case, it's actually the sensation of alcohol dehydrating the tongue causing it to feel somewhat 'dried out'.

VISCOSITY

Another commonly discussed texture or sensation is viscosity. While it's not something you taste directly, it's the sensation of a thick, or rich spirit that coats the mouth, or feels deceptively thicker than it is. When a writer describes a spirit as 'thin' they're generally referring to the lack of viscosity.

SMELL & TOP NOTES

The final sense, and the most important one in the case of tasting spirits, is that of smell. The sense of smell is responsible for all that you taste, with the exception of the vague sensations of bitter, sweet, sour, salty, and the texture type feelings described above.

This first 'sniff' type of smelling is where we actively inhale through our nose in order to observe the aromas of a spirit. When smelling a spirit, it's helpful to use the metaphor of perfumery to help us understand what is happening, as functionally the two are identical to one another. The first things you detect with your nose are the delicate, most volatile aromas that readily evaporate. These are small, light and often described as the 'top notes'. These notes are fleeting, and are most readily detectable the instant a spirit is opened or poured.

MID NOTES & BASE NOTES

After those top notes fade away, the next smells we detect are considered the middle or 'mid notes'. These notes make up the body of what we are often smelling, and are generally the most dominant aromas. After those fade away, we're left with the base notes. These notes linger, and endure. To use the perfume metaphor again, these are often the musky, earthy notes that hold the whole thing together. They offer depth while rarely rising to a crescendo of their own accord. You'll often detect subtle aromas of angelica, orris root or other musky, dark spices lingering down here.

SMELLING & SWALLOWING

Smelling actively is only the beginning of how our sense of smell dominates the act of tasting gin. The second and most important aspect is how the act of swallowing triggers smelling with one's mouth. More technically this is referred to as 'retronasal olfaction'. This is why, when you put a piece of food into your mouth, you'll detect a sour or bitter note, but upon swallowing perceive the rich cacao notes of chocolate or bright lemony notes that make a lemon taste of lemon. Because of the importance of this 'second smell', serious gin and spirits critics will not spit when they are compiling their tasting notes.

Although many systems work in concert in order to create the sensation and taste of a gin, it's important for tasters of spirits to acknowledge their limitations. While we have serious chemical analysis that is capable of identifying every aromatic compound which contributes to the flavour of a drink, technology is unable to tell us how good a drink is, or how well it mixes.

We as tasters can identify the latter but we are limited by the apparatus we are given. For example, the average expert taster can only authoritatively tease apart four individual flavours. As the number of components increases, the accuracy drops in relation. Adam Rogers nicely described it in his book as 'gestalt aroma'. This limitation means that we'll never match the aromatic identifying powers of the technology available; however, I think this is where the beauty still lies. Our subjective palates and our perceptions of the way aromas and ingredients combine in novel ways create endless possibilities for distillers. Therein lies the excitement and promise of gin.

Tasting Gin: A Practical Guide

Now that we've got the science out of the way, let's get down to the pragmatics of how to conduct a proper gin tasting.

Getting it ready

Choose a gin, preferably as close to room temperature as possible. Tasting at room temperature will allow more of the gin aromas to volatilise and therefore be detectable.

Don't stress over the glass you use. Your choice of glass shape is more likely to be governed by personal preference rather than actual science. If you want to splurge on bulb-shaped glasses, you're welcome to do so, but be aware that you're likely to be adding to the mystique as much as actually helping the tasting process itself.

1 Sit yourself down in a nice seat. Pour the gin.

2 Immediately, with pen and paper in hand, take the glass about 7.5-10cm (3-4in) from your nose. Keeping your mouth just slightly open, breathe in only a little bit – you don't want to inhale so deeply that you feel alcohol fumes in your nose. Note what you detect. These are the top notes. Pause and write your findings. To clear your nasal passages between nosings, smell the back of your hand or the crook of your elbow. Take a slightly deeper inhale this time, just as we did before. Still don't breathe so deeply that you detect ethanol fumes in your nose. These are your mid and base notes. Don't stress if some of the notes are hard to pick out. This will come with practise. There are aroma kits available to help you hone this skill, though the best way is to practice with many different gins. Also don't be shy about looking at botanical lists to help you identify what you're nosing at this stage.

3 Okay, once you have the nose notes, we're on to the tasting. Take a first small sip and hold it in your mouth for half a second before swallowing. Observe the texture: does it feel thick? Does it feel thin? Is it drying your tongue? Do you feel any burn? What is your tongue telling you: is it sweet? Sour? Bitter?
Hint It's probably telling you bitter, because the tongue perceives ethanol as bitter. Sour is likely your second option, and sweet only when you're dealing with Old Tom or cordial gins.

4 Take a second sip and swallow, breathing out deeply as you swallow. Notice the initial flavours. Is it similar to what you wrote down for your initial nosing? Does it differ?
Hint It's sometimes very different. It doesn't have to be the same. Observe the way the flavour changes as you get further out from swallowing. Do you start to detect more juniper? Some citrus? Or do you start to get spice-cake notes

1

2

3

4

like ginger or cinnamon? Observe the final condition of your mouth. What notes remain? What is the sensation of your palate? Is it dry? Is it souring? Do you want more? Does it linger long after? Is it short?

5 Take a third sip and pay attention once again, breathing out as you swallow. Especially when you're just learning how to pick up aromas, I find the third taste to be very helpful. Once you've decoded that first set of tastes, you often are able to look a layer deeper or pick up on background notes. Again, don't be shy about looking at the lists of botanicals that distillers put out. Remember, sometimes you might taste lemon cake because of olfactory metaphor and analogy; sometimes you taste lemon cake because there's cinnamon, lemon and ginger notes at play. There are real ingredients in here. Take your time, and learn to identify their hallmarks.

6 Fortunately for aspiring gin critics, the world of gin is a little more accessible to the novice taster. Ingredients are often disclosed and the aromas they have, from gin to gin, are often similar enough to be learned. Though there's a lot of room for creativity and putting yourself into it, we tread on slightly more objective ground because of the nature of botanicals and distillation. From here, we're going to take a look at those botanicals and understand a little bit of why it's possible to learn/understand how they contribute similar aromas to vastly different gins.

Types of Gin

Contemporary and Classic Gin

PERHAPS YOU KNOW SOMEONE who upon tasting a gin declared it to 'not be gin' while hastily casting it aside. Perhaps you know someone who purports to 'hate gin' because it 'tastes like pine needles on fire', only to be surprised upon trying a new gin. Perhaps you're either the first person or the second person and you've gone to your local adult beverage retailer and attempted to purchase a gin. You might try something new and hope for the best. Or maybe you're reaching for an old standby.

If ever you or a friend has experienced the above dilemma, then you already know both the difference between classic and contemporary styles of gin, and why there's a need for clearer stylistic differentiations between these two styles.

LEGALLY, WHAT'S IN A GIN?

We would not need two stylistic terms if not for the quirk in the definition of gin that allows a wide range of latitude to distillers. Unlike most spirits, where the name of the spirit is derived from the base spirit, gin is defined by the flavour profile of the drink. It doesn't care what the base spirit is. If the main characteristic flavour is derived from 'juniper berries', then it can be gin. Taste is somewhat subjective, and this is where the difference lies. A gin can have a characteristic taste of juniper, while doing nearly anything else it wants, yet still be gin.

In the United States, the legal definition of gin says about flavour: 'It shall derive its main characteristic flavour from juniper berries', and may be created with 'juniper berries and other aromatics' in combination with other 'extracts-derived infusions, percolations, or macerations of such materials'. The European Union defines gin a little more specifically, calling out a specific species of juniper: Gin must be flavoured with 'juniper berries (*Juniperus communis L.*)' and may contain other 'natural botanicals provided that the juniper taste is predominant'. The name most commonly associated with gin, London Dry, is actually a further style of gin regulated to a more exacting letter. London Dry gin cannot have any sweetening beyond 0.1g of sugar nor colouring, and the flavour (which still must be predominately juniper) is solely the result of the redistillation of 'ethyl alcohol in the presence of all the natural plant materials' in 'traditional stills'.

So where's the confusion? It really all hinges on the subjectivity of taste and aroma. Even the term 'London Dry gin' doesn't guarantee much about the overall flavour profile of what you're getting. The regulations are designed to ensure that drinkers get a high quality product – and London Dry is perhaps the most strict of these – but it doesn't guarantee a strong juniper-forward profile.

However, one of the oft-repeated fallacies around gin is that the term 'London Dry' guarantees you're getting a gin like one of the big names such as Tanqueray, Beefeater or Gordon's. This is not true. Take for example Bloom Gin, a London Dry gin made by G & J Greenall's, one of the most esteemed and long-lived distillers in the world, having been making gin since the mid-18th century. Bloom Premium London Dry Gin is by legal definition both London Dry (high quality, natural botanicals, distillation) and gin (yes, there's juniper); however, it is not juniper forward. That is to say that most tasting notes might lead with 'camomile' or 'honeysuckle'. It's a floral gin (and a really nice one at that), and most would say it bears only a passing resemblance to its forbears. But what gives? What's a drinker to do?

Let's take a closer look at the two emergent styles of gin available around the world today.

THIS PAGE *At Sipsmith, gin bottles are sometimes dipped in wax. Originally this was done to keep the spirit fresh and to prove that it had not been tampered with.*

Classic Gins

Classic gins are often what we imagine when we think of the archetypal idea of what gin is: heavy juniper notes, a little bit of supporting citrus and spice, but not too much, all with an astringent drying finish. These gins are among the biggest-selling gins in the world. Many of these gins are London Dry gins, because they've been made to an exacting standard of quality over their long histories.

Classic gins are characterised by being juniper forward. Some might even describe them as 'piny' or 'sharp'. Classic-style gins often have supporting botanicals, but they are just that. Angelica, orris root, some sort of citrus, cassia or grains of paradise are often among the background notes present, but their role is not to take centre stage. They stay in the background, colouring in the scenery. They are what differentiates Tanqueray from Gordon's, Beefeater's from Greenall's; it's really all about the juniper.

Though many of the big names hail from London and the UK, this is more an accident of gin history, London being the centre of gin production for so long. There is very little about the standard botanical bill of gin that is unique to England. Juniper is grown around the world; nearly all of the supporting botanicals come from Asia via the spice trade. To associate a style so strongly with a region would be to do a disservice to the diversity of takes on this classic gin formula that are being distilled around the world today.

For example, in the Pacific Northwest of the United States, Bluewater Organic Distilling creates its classic-style gin called Halcyon. Mile High Distilling in Denver, Colorado makes its Denver Dry Gin in the classic style. In short, Europe, the UK and London do not have a monopoly on classic-style gin. It is being distilled globally. Though the term London Dry still has an important place in history as a designator of quality, for the sake of all those who are distilling gin in the classic style, it's important that we find some way to share a common terminology so that lovers of Gordon's can try something new, or that a new American-distilled classic gin can turn someone on to the world of Tanqueray and Beefeater.

Contemporary Gins

Perhaps one of the greatest fallacies that seems to have been passed along through gin marketing in the early 21st century is the notion that American gin is a gin style all by itself. In a nation as wide as the United States, with so many different climates, the notion that a single stylistic tendency or flavour profile is dominant is absolutely off the mark. 'American gin' has been placed on many a bottle to capitalise on the desire to 'buy local'. However, with the explosion of craft gin – there are hundreds in the United States alone and seemingly more being produced every week – this term is as meaningless as it was the first day it was put on the bottle. American gin is distilled in the United States. That's all, and it tells you nothing about its flavour. Just as the American distilled gins described in the example on page 66 embody a style often thought to be specific to London, it should be noted that the Bloom London Dry Gin (above) would fit squarely in this category of contemporary gins.

Contemporary gins have juniper among their primary flavours, as required by law; however, the range they can exhibit is quite wide. A common gin that has whet the palate for gins of this style is Hendrick's, whose addition of rose and cucumber created a sensation and helped cultivate a following for gin among those who wouldn't normally try gin. But the range of these gins is far wider than just Hendrick's. The challenge is helping would-be-lovers of contemporary gin to identify spirits on the shelf that might be more to their liking. Dorothy Parker Gin from Brooklyn, New York, is floral forward with notes of hibiscus and sweet fresh berries. Port of Dragons 100% Floral Gin from Spain has a bright bouquet of fresh flowers and gentle spices, with just a touch of juniper. The style is neither unique to America, nor Spain, nor even London or anywhere. It simply is, under both continents' definitions of gin. Contemporary gin is certainly gin, but it offers a different take on it.

Styles that are Places

There are, inevitably, some terroir designations that are particular to gin. Many of these are more 'one-off' styles made by a single distillery than a regional trait. Despite that, the regional names have endured and subsequently been codified into law as protected stylistic designators, at least in the European Union.

Plymouth Gin is the most widely available and well-known of the protected styles of gin. Plymouth has been distilling gin since 1793, and is probably most well known for having been the distillery that supplied officers of the Royal Navy in the 19th century. For many years, Plymouth gin was protected as if a style of gin unto itself. Another of these formerly protected gins is Vilnius Gin, a gin made in Lithuania since the 1980s. And finally there was Gin de Mahón, of which Xoriguer was the best known. These gins were made on the island of Menorca as a way of profiting from British occupation. The most notable characteristic of this gin is that its base spirit was distilled from wine, and it was rested in oak barrels. Although both characteristics are becoming

more common among gin, neither the style, nor the geographic indication are still protected, even though gin is still made on Menorca.

Places that aren't Styles

By using the name of a place to describe a gin, it creates a sense of 'false terroir', and inappropriately confuses people by tying a style characteristic to a region. This false equivalence is why some consumers in the United States have 'sworn off American gin' because it didn't match their expectations for what gin should be. It wasn't a region, à la wine, that they disliked, it was the style of the gin they disliked. Certainly if someone offered them a range of styles from a single region, they might come back around and try something else again.

The second reason why we prefer not to use regions is because it takes away from genuine terroir considerations. Might there actually be a style of gin emerging in British Columbia, based on local botanicals and local juniper? Or might the American southwest be developing a gin profile that embodies the sage scent of the desert? Or could there be an alpine style of gin emerging in eastern and northern Europe? If we use regions to describe styles we confuse the message about what is actually coming from where a gin is distilled and what's coming from the type of gin.

Because of that, I think there's a strong argument to cast aside broad regional designations where not already protected. Classic-style gin is a worldwide spirit that is being distilled on both sides of the Atlantic; contemporary gin is being made anywhere.

21st-Century Gin

I think if we were to take the idea of 'classic' versus 'contemporary' gin to the shelves of liquor stores and bars around the world, we'd truly move gin forward into the 21st century. Bartenders could use new gins in the ways they're best to be used (square peg in round hole?) and people who like one style or another can expand their horizons without risk of being burned. On board? In the next chapter we'll include tasting notes for gin that will say whether they are classic or contemporary styled, followed by a section of cocktail recipes for each type of gin.

Genever

JUST TO BE CLEAR, GENEVER IS NOT GIN. The two are
intimately related, though. Genever was the drink
which later begat gin. Genever was the predecessor
of gin, but not all genever became gin. Far from it;
as gin branched off from genever, this Dutch spirit
thrived, declined and rose once more. Genever is
most definitely still its own thing. For most of gin's
history, maybe up until the era of Old Toms in the
19th century, but definitely until dry gin caught on,
the spirits we were talking about had much more in
common with genever. You can see it in many old
cocktail books that call for Dutch gin or Holland
gin by name.

Modern-day genever is often described as a cross
between 'whisky and gin'. It is actually much more
complicated than that. A whole book could be
written on the spirit, (in fact one has been), so this
whirlwind tour isn't meant to be exhaustive, but
simply provides some context to understand how the
two styles have diverged in the last 200 years.

The base spirit is grain, and because of unrefined
distilling techniques at the style's genesis in the
16th century, it was flavoured with juniper (widely
available) and other spices (common in the
Netherlands due to the Dutch nation's extensive
spice trade networks). Although distilling techniques
have vastly improved, the base spirit is still grain,
but of a much higher quality, and flavoured with
additional botanicals. Unlike gin where the primary
flavour comes from the botanicals, genever derives a
lot of its character from the malt wine, or fermented
grain mash, that forms the base spirit.

Though there are 11 protected geographic
appellations for genever, the styles can be generalised
to fit into a few broader categories.

The first one is the heaviest. Korenwijn is an aged
spirit that contains at
least 51% malt wine.
Additional sweetening
is permitted, though
overall the tastes
of these spirits are
breadier, richer,
grainier and somewhat
rarer than the other
categories of genever.

It's likely that these modern-day genevers might be
the closest to those that were being drunk more than
200 years ago.

The next two styles of genever are characterised
by the relative proportions of malt wine in their
mixes. Oude contains at least 15%, while jonge can
contain no more than 15%. Consequently, your jonge
genevers are going to be much lighter with a lot less

LEFT *Contemporary Bols genever bottles.*

emphasis on the malty, grainy flavours of the oude. Oude doesn't have to be aged, though it often is.

An important aspect of genever is that it is protected. Distilling is restricted to only a few countries, namely the Netherlands, Belgium, France and Germany. Only spirits made in these countries (and sometimes in specific regions within them) can be named as genever and sold as such. That

doesn't mean that distillers aren't experimenting with the idea of genever. In the United States you'll see spirits marketed as 'genever-style gins' or 'ginever'. While not subject to the same strict regulations that govern the style when distilled in the EU, many of these play with grain, malt and botanicals in a way that draws more from the genever tradition than modern-day gin. The style is still alive and kicking.

ABOVE *Classic genever bottles were often depicted in Dutch paintings.*

Sloe Gin and Cordial Gin

A LIQUEUR OR CORDIAL is not defined by a set of strict boundaries. They're generally thick, sweetened (more than 2.5% sugar by volume), and are often at a lower proof (30-60°, or 15-30% ABV) than other spirits. A gin liqueur uses a gin, usually a dry one, as its base and then flavours are added through infusion and further sweetening. When you speak of gin liqueurs, you're usually speaking solely about sloe gins and other sloe-like gins. Examples include Greenhook Ginsmiths Beach Plum Gin Liqueur, Hayman's Sloe Gin or Sipsmith Limited Edition Sloe Gin.

To make Sloe gin, the sloes' leathery skins are pierced before they are placed in the gin. They are then left there, with only occasional disturbance, such as shaking or turning, for somewhere between three and six months. Once a satisfactory sloe infusion is achieved, the plums are then filtered out. The resulting liqueur may be filtered through a cheesecloth or decanted to remove all sediment and cloudiness. Modern-day sloe gins are often clear, with no debris.

The origin of sloe gin as a quintessentially British liqueur has its origins in the settling of the British countryside. Sloes were a common hedgerow crop in rural Britain. Dense, thorny and a touch weedy, they were ubiquitous and simultaneously helpful for delineating property lines, while quarrelsome when they grew into dense, brambly groves. The fruits themselves didn't win a lot of fans. They were tough and not particularly good to eat on their own. No one was deterred, though, from finding uses for the plums. In quantities with other ingredients, including sweeteners, sloes could be made palatable. There's a tradition of sloe wines, jellies and, of course, sloe gins. With a little bit of care and attention, they can be made to produce a liqueur or gin that is something quite delectable indeed.

Though recipes exist going back into the 18th century with sloes being macerated in wines or brandies, sloes in gin came into fashion in the mid to late 19th century. Recipes for sloe gins appeared in women's homemaking publications in the 1870s, while they appeared on domestic shelves later the same decade.

Sloe gin would have many names, including 'Hips' and 'Snag Gin', and while sloes would have taken top billing, other local varieties of plum were used as well. It was marketed by some brands as a hunting spirit: the 'sportsman's favourite liqueur'; hunters supposedly would carry a large bottle of it when they left and drank it as they hunted. For the most part, sloe gin lived on as a traditional countryside spirit, with many families having heirloom recipes that were passed down through tradition and fireside sipping during cold British winters.

Nowadays, there are two main types of sloe gin out there. The first is the one mentioned above, one in which plums are macerated in gin and the resulting spirit is sweetened and served. The second type, and perhaps more prevalent before the late 2000s, are the inexpensive sloe gins that contain neither sloes nor gin. They're in fact neutral spirit liqueurs that are artificially flavoured and sweetened. Chances are if you had a Sloe Gin Fizz during the 1970s, you were probably drinking something closer to that.

Fortunately, sloe gin, as well as damson and other similar macerated gins, is making a comeback. Plymouth and Hayman's both make traditional sloe gins using the real fruit. Many smaller distilleries are experimenting with seasonal sloe gins or embarking on creating their own. Though far from as popular as contemporary or flavoured gin, sloe gins is back, as is the Sloe Gin Fizz, but this time with real sloes.

Aged Gin

THERE WAS ONCE A TIME when all gin was what we modern gin drinkers call 'yellow' or 'aged'. To a spirits drinker of the 18th or early 19th century, the fact their gin had a colour would not have even been worthy of remark. Nearly all gins had some degree of ageing because most spirits (liquids and dry goods) were shipped in barrels. Often gin historians point to the British 1861 Single Bottle Act as the turning point for yellow gin. The act allowed distillers and winemakers to sell their wares in glass bottles rather than barrels for the first time. Though this act was specific to the United Kingdom, it had the effect of transforming the nature of gin, since the UK was at the centre of gin production.

Gins were aged not for taste or creative reasons; it was a matter of economy and reality. A gin was aged primarily because the barrel was the only method of transporting the spirit to market. These barrels weren't of the high quality we think of today. Firstly, they were often re-used over and over. Barrels max out after a certain number of uses, when they no longer affect the final product as intensely. Secondly, as the barrels were shipping vessels only they therefore wouldn't have been charred. Although much gin undoubtedly did take on some character from the barrel, it's highly unlikely that the gins of yesteryear had the same range and depth of notes that could come from intentional use of the barrel for enriching flavour.

That's what differentiates it from the next wave of aged gins: here, the barrel was treated as a key component and ingredient of the gin, and the object was manipulated to improve the gin inside. Among the earliest well-known expressions of this style was Booth's (a different Booth's from the one that's available today) but it is no longer around. The widely available Seagram's rested its gin in barrels. This under-reported fact is highlighted by how little it was promoted. Very quietly, it was noted on the bottles and with little fanfare the formula was changed in the early 2010s. Seagram's still has its signature light-straw hue, but it's no longer created in whiskey barrels.

Despite the examples lost to history, we have seen something of a renaissance of the style in the last decade or so. Lots of credit has been given to Citadelle, whose Citadelle Réserve was among the first widely available example on the market. However, the real growth areas in aged gins has occurred in the United States where there's approaching nearly 100 different bottles available; most of them, though, have only a regional reach and therefore you're unlikely to see a shelf-ful of them in any local US liquor store.

But why the rapid expansion in the States? One theory is tied to the challenges of running a small distillery. Many of the distilleries that released a gin during the craft spirits boom did so because it was a spirit they could sell right away, while their whiskey spirit was ageing. This meant that there was a large number of distillers experimenting with gins alongside their whiskies, so they had barrels available. This mutual intersection created a climate where putting gin in a barrel was something you almost had to do!

Among the styles of aged gin that have emerged, there is a wide range that spans new barrels, used barrels, blends of differing gins aged for different lengths in barrels, or experiments with climate and seasonality. In short, it's a category that is rapidly expanding, in large part due to the fact that whisky takes time to mature, but gin does not. Gin drinkers are benefiting greatly from this proliferation, in spite of the fact that the United States liquor regulatory process prevents distillers from making age statements about gin. As of 2015, this is the case, although one hopes that this will change in the future.

Filliers creates its aged gin by means of French barrels that were originally used for Cognac.

The Problem with Yellow Gin

The challenge with the term 'yellow gin' is not that it is an inaccurate way to describe what an aged gin looks like, but that there are also actual yellow gins out there. While aged gins do have a lovely straw colour, with some variations radiating bright gold, shimmering deep bronze, or even darker, the problem is there are gins in other styles that also boast a gold hue.

Take for example Ungava from Quebec, Canada, which is canary yellow, the most 'yellow' of all yellow gins. It is a yellow gin and and not an aged gin.

So for the sake of accuracy, I think it's important to describe aged gins by what their defining characteristic is. They're aged or rested in barrels, where the wood marries with the spirit inside to create something new. That they happen to be yellow is delightful to the eyes, and creates a fantastic connection with the drinking world of Hemingway. But yellow gin is something of a misnomer. Aged gins aren't always yellow; yellow gins aren't always aged. I'm suggesting we should move forward and retire the term and start to call aged gins 'barrel-aged gins' instead.

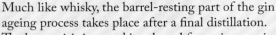

How they're Made

Much like whisky, the barrel-resting part of the gin ageing process takes place after a final distillation. The base spirit is rested in a barrel for a given period of time, generally much shorter than that of the average whisky. Some gins on the market are rested for three months or less, though there are some exceptions to the rule: a handful of barrel-aged gins that have spent 10 or even 13 years in a barrel.

There is no hard and fast rule about the type of barrel, and in fact quite a wide range has been use to great effect. Pierre Ferrand, makers of Citadelle Réserve, use new charred French oak barrels for its gin, as you might expect from a distillery that specialises in Cognac. Southern Artisan Distillery from North Carolina uses new American oak barrels so that the wood interacts with the gin without any outside influences. Corsair Distillery in the United States and Dictador Rum Distillery in Colombia use used rum barrels. New Holland Brewing ages Knickerbocker Gin in used whiskey barrels, while both Distillery No. 209 in California and Painted Stave Distilling in Delaware have released a duo of gins, one aged in a former red wine barrel and another in a white wine. Burrough's Reserve Gin uses barrels that once held the aperitif Jean de Lillet, while Smooth Ambler Spirits in West Virginia use more than one type of barrel, then blends the contents.

Challenges and the Future of Aged Gin

One of the biggest problems facing this growing category is that although I refer to this type of gin as 'aged', it is not legally possible to use the term 'aged gin' on a bottle in the United States, where this style is exploding. Distillers have resorted to all kinds of tactics to get around it, borrowing terms like 'reposado' from the world of tequila or referring to it creatively using other words like 'barrel rested' or 'barrel reserve'. Even as they dance around the way of describing the character, they're prevented outright from saying things like '1-year', '2-year' or '6-month' aged. It makes the act of comparison between gins hard, and often comes down to either checking websites or talking to the distillers themselves. As the style continues to expand, this legal question of how the spirits are labelled will continue to be a thorn in the sides of the creative men and women ageing their gin.

A second challenge facing aged gin is one of 'what do I do with it?' For whisky drinkers, aged gin is a natural next step, combining many of the best parts of both worlds. For gin drinkers, it poses a question. Aged gin doesn't generally work as well in a tonic as a dry gin might, nor as well in a Tom Collins (page 213) or an Aviation (page 208). That's why you'll find cocktails recipes included in this book specifically to help get your aged gin off the shelf. Sure it's good neat, but it's even better mixed.

The barrel-aged gin produced by Four Pillars Distillery in Australia is markedly different in colour to its other gins.

Old Tom Gin

THE OLD TOMCAT NAME used in connection with gin dates back to the origin of the spirit itself. Steeped as the meaning of the term 'Old Tom' is in myth, misinformation and the shadow of history, it's unlikely we'll ever know authoritatively how the association of an Old Cat came to be connected with gin. But that hasn't stopped cocktail historians from mining some interesting theories in old British newspapers.

Perhaps the front runner and most often cited case hails from *The Life and Uncommon Adventures of Capt. Dudley Bradstreet* of 1755, which tells the story of how, at the height of the gin craze, one ingenious property owner sought to get around Prohibition. Underneath a sign depicting a cat, a pipe was installed. A person desiring gin would deposit a coin and say 'Puss, give me two Pennyworth of Gin'. On the other side of the wall, safe within the building, the gin pourer would reply and pour a small measure of gin. The drinker put their mouth on the pipe and thus would be served. This is perhaps the first instance of a cat and gin being tied together in the literature on the subject.

The question about Old Tom was being asked in the 1870s. The above story was posited as being the origin of the term by at least 1873, though the editor of *Notes and Queries* suggested that 'old Tom Hodges' would probably object to that. The tone in which he suggested that seemed to indicate probably the origin was not in as much doubt as it seemed. An 1881 edition of the above-mentioned *Notes and Queries* says that 'Old Tom' was named as a compliment by Thomas Norris to his former Master Thomas Chamberlain, who, it is said, originally invented the gin. By 1885 the term Old Tom was so well known as another word for 'gin' that it was used as a punchline to a comic just on its own.

An 1844 bulletin in the London *Police Gazette* tells the story of a theft where one of the items was 'three painted liquor keys, having the letters "R", "B" and "G"– the gin key having the word 'Old Tom" on it.' Whether or not it was widely known at the time as a term for gin, it was significant enough to be called out specifically in the piece and the connection of 'Old Tom' and 'gin' in the same sentence ranks among the earliest examples of this term in print in the London papers. Before this, when 'Old Tom'

appeared in print, it was referring to a man who had gone by that name. This gives sufficient evidence that the prefix 'Old' before a person's name was sufficiently commonplace to be a likely explanation for the name. But the juxtaposition of the cat remains somewhat more controversial.

Ads for Old Tom Gin were commonplace by the 1890s and whatever the origin of the name, it was being referred to as 'Old Tom' in Sierra Leone and Kenya. It was also being used to describe gins that were made by several companies. Old Tom had become the general name for a large swathe of gins.

What is the flavour profile of this Old Tom gin that people were drinking in this era?

James Mew and John Ashton's 1892's *Drinks of the World* goes on to say, 'Gin has had many popular names, but why gin should be called Old Tom by the publicans and lower orders of London has sometimes puzzled those (who care to look into it).' Mew and Ashton saw it as a general term for gin at the time, so when we look back at trying to revive Old Tom, all we're really trying to do is re-create the general gin available at the time.

Drinks of the World describes the strength of gin as being somewhere between 44 and 96 proof, with a whopping sugar rate of somewhere between 2 and 9 per cent. For comparison, the current London gin specification mandates no more than 1/10th of a gram of sweetening per litre (2 pints). At this time, gin was clearly a much sweeter drink than the one we know today. British gin was notably differentiated from the higher class Holland/Dutch gin, and it was pointed out that the spirit was adulterated with cake, cinnamon, cayenne or even liquorice, the latter being a trick of the trade used even by modern distillers to re-create the gins of this time. The quality of the base spirits, while far better than they had been at the height of the gin craze, were still a bit lacking, so distillers had to sweeten them or more interestingly, use botanicals, to create a palatable product.

The Old Tom style of gin likely originated at a time when gin was primarily transported in barrels primarily, thereby meaning gin would have had a slight 'ageing'. Although not meant to enhance the taste, it would have been part of the character of the resulting spirit, depending on the age of the barrel.

Tastes would soon change, and the Old Tom style,

even if it was only a name for gin at the time, came to be replaced with the new 'dry' moniker. These dry, or unsweetened, gins make up the vast majority of all gins on the market today. As tastes changed, old recipes fell out of fashion and the Old Toms that were advertised on the pages of newspapers around the world became a quaint historical footnote in the evolution of Madame Geneva.

The fact that we don't have an authoritative source telling us which gin was *the* Old Tom gin at the time, leaves cocktail historians combing through notes, journal entries and old recipes for clues. This has led to a really interesting environment where distillers are innovating and drawing from their own historical sources and knowledge of distilling to create gins that are 'in the spirit of' the late 19th-century Old Tom.

The range of Old Toms is probably best seen in

BELOW *Old Tom gin was traditionally sweetened with either sugar or botanicals to make it more palatable, while bathtub gin was seen as an inferior distillation.*

the products of two of the first distillers to revive the style: Hayman's in the UK and Ransom Spirits in the US. Hayman's Old Tom is clear, like a dry gin, but with a noticeably sweeter profile owing to the addition of sugar. It is clear and completely unaged. Ransom's Old Tom is a pot-distilled corn and barley spirit with a simple botanical bill (juniper, citrus, angelica, cardamom and coriander), which is then aged in wine barrels. Both recipes lay claim to being distilled based on an era-appropriate recipe, and therefore can legitimately claim to be 'historically accurate'. It's a long way, though, from defining what exactly Old Tom gin was.

Perhaps it's best to look at Old Tom gin through modern-day eyes. Just as the range of gins on the shelf today is truly diverse, perhaps the gins of yesteryear were equally as individual and unique. Surely, this might take some of the fun out of digging through the cocktail archives, or, is perhaps a warning to cocktail historians of the 23rd century trying to re-create a genuine 21st-century contemporary gin.

ABOVE *Vintage Old Tom advertising posters are nowadays highly sought–after and collectable.*

Flavoured Gin

STRICTLY SPEAKING, all gin is flavoured. Flavoured vodka, even. But when I talk about flavoured gins I'm drawing a line in the sand. Gin is flavoured by adding ingredients and distilling; flavoured gin is created by adding flavours afterwards, often to something that is already considered a gin. This now gets a little tricky. Is Hendrick's technically a flavoured gin because it has rose petals and cucumber added after distillation? Okay, yes, that's technically flavoured. Generally, though, I'm talking about the addition of some sort of flavourant after distillation to an existing product. This isn't a clear stylistic differentiation; however, you usually will know it when you see it.

Once quite popular, particularly in the early 20th century, many flavoured gins were gone from store shelves before the vodka trend took hold in the 1950s. However, perhaps buoyed by the wildly popular and still growing flavoured vodka trend that has endured through the 2010s, we're starting to see a revival of traditional flavoured gins re-emerging from hibernation.

Gordon's, whose flagship gin is among the bestselling gins in the world, especially in its home country the United Kingdom, released a collection of flavoured gins in the early 2010s, including Gordon's Crisp Cucumber Gin and Gordon's Elderflower Gin. Essentially they are just Gordon's Gin with

ABOVE *Elderflower and cucumber are popular flavourings for gin and tend to be less sweet than strong fruit adjuncts.*

elderflower or cucumber added at the end of the distillation process. They're not new to the game either. Gordon's used to have a Lemon Gin and an Orange Gin in the earlier half of the 20th century. Though out of production by 1952, collectors can still occasionally find a bottle (still with gin inside!) on websites catering to collectors.

In the United States, perhaps the best example of flavoured gins might be those from the iconic and bestselling Seagram's brand. In its portfolio you'll find an array of flavoured gins such as Seagram's Apple Twisted Gin, Peach Twisted Gin, Pineapple Twisted and Lime. These gins are flavoured and slightly sweetened to appeal to a wider audience.

Gordon's and Seagram's are well situated atop their respective ladders and may be free to experiment; however, they're not the only ones. Baffert's Mint Flavoured Gin is an extant example of a style once epitomised by Piping Rock in the 1930s and 1940s. Warner Edwards make an elderflower-infused variant of its gin. Perhaps the most interesting stories of flavoured gin only exist in memory. In the 1900s, a company in San Francisco, California, made an asparagus-flavoured gin, while a distillery in Buffalo, New York, made a maple-flavoured gin. These long gone but somehow not forgotten spirits remind us of the range and potential of this growing sub category.

ABOVE *The US brand Seagram's is an old established brand that has recently explanded into sweetened and flavoured gins in a big way.*

Non Gins

Not gin, but sort of like gin. The first of these non gins is called Steinhäger. In the Westphalia region of Germany, the village of Steinhägen was once host to a booming gin industry. Sources say there were as many as 20 distilleries in the region that were making this type of gin as late as the 19th century. Other gin scholars claim that its origins go back to at least the 15th century, and you'll also see references suggesting its origins date back even further, to the 12th century. The style is on the verge of extinction now though, with only two distilleries still making the style. The torchbearer is HW Schlichte, whose distillery has been in continuous operation since 1766 and produces the most widely available of the two Steinhäger gins that are still marketed today.

To make a Steinhäger, fresh juniper is fermented and distilled to make a mixture called juniper lutter. It is then mixed with a neutral spirit and distilled again. The resulting distillate may be flavoured with a 'small amount of juniper berries' and water only. The resulting spirit is bottled to at least 38% ABV. It is often listed as a juniper schnapps as well, though it is technically a gin.

Karst gin is a geographically protected indicator for a specific kind of juniper brandy that evolved in Slovenia. The juniper berries are cleaned and then fermented with yeast to create a mash over a period of at least four weeks, and then distilled twice in copper stills to create a brandy. The resultant spirit is colourless and smells brightly of juniper. Karst gin is a kind of *brinjevec*, which is the more general term

ABOVE *Steinhäger Schlichte gin has been in production since the 19th century and is a form of juniper schnapps rather than a gin, while Karst is a juniper brandy.*

for juniper brandy that is made throughout Slovenia and neighbouring countries. Nearby variations include *klekovača*, a Serbian speciality, which is made from plum brandy aged in oak with juniper berries. *Borovička* is another brandy from the region, which has been drunk there since possibly as early as the 14th century. Though all derive their primary flavouring from juniper (and therefore may possibly be considered gin), these schnapps and brandies involve juniper at differing parts of the process and differ in slight ways from the gins we know today. Many are also traditional spirits (with medicinal origins) and therefore endure by their regional names rather than being lumped in with the larger category of gin. Despite gin's lax categorical and legal definition, it's likely that if these spirits were

invented today, they would all fall somewhere within the category of gin.

Botanical spirits such as Art in the Age's Sage, and Square One's Botanical Vodka, have been referred to as garden gins. This emphasises their commonality with many gins. Take for example Sage, whose botanical list includes rose, cubeb, orange peel, liquorice, sage, angelica and lavender. Square One Botanical Vodka includes camomile, lemon verbena, lavender, rosemary, coriander and citrus peel. Notice what's missing? It's juniper. Both are not gins in any sense of the word; however, botanically and inspirationally speaking they borrow greatly from the gin tradition, and the resulting spirits are actually rather good and work well in many gin cocktails, if only crying out for a little bit of juniper.

ABOVE *Sage is a garden gin, while Navip Klekovača from Serbia is more of a plum brandy, flavoured with juniper berries in the bottle.*

The
Tasting
of Gin

So you're a gin lover...

You've got this far, so I'm hoping that you've found some gin you like and even love. You may now want to share your new-found gin with friends. And listen, we've all got friends like the types listed opposite. Everyone's got their tastes – and that's cool. I'm not looking to turn everyone into a gin lover (well, I might be), but at the very least, by knowing the taste preferences of your friends and the range of gins available it will be easy to find something to suit everyone's gin palate.

Your whisky-loving friend

Lovers of dark, aged spirits can find something to like in the world of gin, especially now there is a proliferation of aged gins out there. But to pull them over to the world of gin, let's consider an aged gin with a base spirit that they're familiar with. Few Barrel Gin (page 152) takes a gin built on a warm, base of white whiskey, adds botanicals, and is then aged in oak. If this sounds familiar you might see why this is a perfect starting point for your whisky-loving friend. Serve it neat, or in whatever style he or she prefers. Once they're sold on it, Few American Gin (page 152) is the next step.

Your vodka-loving compatriot...

This might be a harder transition, since a vodka lover may not be used to taste. If they're a more adventurous vodka drinker, try them first on a vodka with character: once they're sold on the idea that liquor should have some flavour, start them on some accessible, smooth gins. Audemus Spirits Pink Pepper Gin (page 120) might seem exotic to classic gin aficionados, but is smooth, flavoursome, and should not be too far out of a vodka lover's comfort zone. Or try a more subtle gin: Sunset Hills Virginia Gin (page 161) or even Plymouth (page 100). Start with cocktails and work your way up to some of the bolder stuff. Baby steps; taste is a hard thing to get used to.

...and what about citrus-flavoured vodkas or mezcal?

If your friend is drinking citrus-flavoured vodkas, start with something really citrus forward like Larios 12 Botanicals, then level up to Bluecoat Gin (page 144) or Pinckney Bend (page 158). If you get this far, spring for Chase's Seville Orange Gin (page 109). If you get them on board with citrus flavour, congratulations, welcome to the world of gin.

For your mezcal-loving amigo this is almost too easy. It's a mezcal with botanicals. Pierde Almas '9' Botanicals Mezcal (page 172) is where you absolutely should start. If you know fans of smoky tastes, try them next on Corsair's Steampunk (page 148).

A rum type of person?

For a rum lover there's no better time to showcase the world of gin than the present. Dictador's Colombian Treasure (page 173) is a gin from a rum distillery, taking some of the best elements of both. Though its flavours are unique among gins, Monkey 47 (page 122) uses French molasses distillate as a base. That's sure to get any rum aficionado's attention. And although it's not quite a rum by any sense of the word, Waterloo Antique Barrel Reserve Gin (page 162) calls to mind comparisons to rum without literally taking any cues at all from the world of rum.

In short, there's something out there for everyone. So the next time someone regales you with a tale of that time in college they had pine-needles-on-fire and then never touched the stuff again, take a look at their tipple of choice and make a well-considered decision on how to show them the other side of gin.

Cheers!

Tasting Notes
Europe

A DISCERNING
TASTING SURVEY

UK & Ireland

The birthplace of 'mother's ruin' and the place where genever turned into gin. What more can you say? For nearly 300 years, if it happened in gin, it happened here. Gin could best be described as a few centuries of British culture expressed in a single sip.

For a long time, British gin was dominated by the same names our great-great-grandparents knew: Gordon's, Beefeater, Tanqueray and Greenall's. And to be sure, they're still making great gins. Things are slightly more complex now, with small gin distillers emerging everywhere you look. London, Scotland, Wales, Cornwall, Northern Ireland, and everywhere in between. The ingenuity of the British is once more iterating on the spirit they perfected a while ago, and they're ready to do it all over again.

BELOW Bloom Gin (see page 92) echoes the delicacy of its gin on the neck of its distinctive bottle.

England

Adnams Copper House Distilled Gin *40% ABV*
THE COPPER HOUSE DISTILLERY, SOUTHWOLD, ENGLAND

Distilled

The nose has the thick pine-laden air of savoury rosemary. Grain and barley-like creaminess are evident as well, with citrus and floral touches operating on the periphery. The palate is smooth and straightforward, with hibiscus and citrus notes coming on towards the end. Tightly integrated with a high-quality base spirit, this gin is unique and quite nice.

Adnams Copper House First Rate Gin *48% ABV*
Distilled

Adnams First Rate Gin starts from a blend of 13 botanicals. The resulting spirit begins with the creamy rich impression of grain on the nose. Vanilla, light grain and intimations of a white whiskey with a light juniper lift. The overall quality of the spirit is excellent, with a warm silky mouthfeel. The juniper that hits you on the palate is both resinous and piny, with cardamom and spice following in quick order. Coriander, cinnamon and liquorice follow on the finish.

Adnams Copper House Sloe Gin *26% ABV*
Cordial

Luxurious touches of sloe on the nose. Cherry and stone fruit as well, with hints of marzipan and almond. A well balanced sloe gin with sweet and sour held in equal esteem. The gin-like character underneath builds and supports the luscious fruit, spice, and juniper structure that makes this jammy sloe gin work so well. Excellent in a Fizz.

Beckett's London Dry Gin Type 1097 *40% ABV*
KINGSTON DISTILLERS LTD
KINGSTON UPON THAMES, ENGLAND

Classic

This exquisite gin, distilled and bottled in London, has a refreshing, zesty flavour; creamy yet sweet, with a taste that is warm and aromatic, with a slightly cool finish. It is the only gin in the world that is infused with English juniper berries and the finest of botanicals to give a nose that's meadowy and whisky-like with soft citrus and juniper notes. A smooth gin that finishes with a small hint of mint. Based in Kingston upon Thames, Beckett's uses berries that are hand-picked on Box Hill in Surrey.

Beefeater Gin 40% ABV

BEEFEATER DISTILLERY
LONDON, ENGLAND

Classic

Launched in 1876, this is rightfully one of the most revered brands in the gin world. The palate is fresh pine-note-accentuated juniper, but some citrus zest rises from the low notes to give it some colour. The palate begins with some citrus again, bold juniper mid palate pulling no surprises, with a warm, earthy texture and spicy literal coriander seed. The finish is moderate-long, with a warm coriander tone.

Beefeater Burrough's Reserve

43% ABV

Aged

The French oak barrels that Burrough's Reserve gin is rested in used to hold Jean de Lillet, a particularly high-end aperitif from the people behind Lillet Blanc and the extinct Kina Lillet of James Bond Vesper Lore. Warm and floral on the nose, there are lemon, orange and camphorous herbal notes that call to mind pine and rosemary. Lemon peel, then a more traditional mid taste give rise to comparisons with more classic gin, just before vanilla, citrus and a warm, bright oak finish.

Beefeater Summer 40% ABV

Contemporary

The nose on this seasonal gin is somewhat fruit forward with hints of strawberry and hibiscus. The taste is ripe with intimations of pomegranate and a slight elderflower top note. There's plenty of the traditional Beefeater taste characteristics here as well, with fresh juniper leading a finish that veers only slightly from the beaten path. This is fantastic when accompanied by tonic or soda.

Beefeater 24 45% ABV

Contemporary

Beefeater 24 has grapefruit and a couple of kinds of tea added to the Beefeater formula. So-called 24 because Beefeater steeps its botanicals for 24 hours before the final distillation run. Grapefruit zest and green tea notes on the nose. A very smooth, very creamy gin with a rich assortment of citrus, juniper and pine, and a spicy, herbal tea note. Moderate-length finish with a surprising sweetness. Wonderful for mixing in delicate gin-forward cocktails.

Beefeater London Market

40% ABV

Contemporary

Floral high notes with lime, and then lemon and orange. The nose finishes with a brief hint of classic Beefeater. The palate is rife with lemon and lime, in equal parts shedding their zest. The juniper is on the rise in the mids, tapping its evergreen side, before finishing with accents of liquorice and angelica. Warm and bright, you can leave the lime out of your next G&T. The London Market's got it covered.

Beefeater Winter 40% ABV

Contemporary

The nose isn't as wintry at first as one might expect. A bright floral note hits you first, before giving way to warming cassia and nutmeg notes. The palate shows the man behind the curtain was indeed Beefeater, with some more traditional juniper, citrus and coriander notes revealing themselves. The finish is rife with clear nutmeg and a baking spice lift. Great in a Negroni, but you have to turn up the volume. Try two parts gin to one each of Campari and sweet vermouth.

Berkeley Square Gin *40% ABV*

G & J DISTILLERS
WARRINGTON, ENGLAND

Classic, Recommended

Striking nose, with bright lemon and juniper, as well as some floral notes, orris and lavender chiefly. However, the taste veers right back towards the classic: juniper, accompanied by a robust earthiness at the front. Warming in the middle, it brings a bit of heat, before gently fading with herbal citrus. Quite refreshing, and good just on its own. Try it on the rocks.

Bloom Gin *40% ABV*

G & J DISTILLERS
WARRINGTON, ENGLAND

Contemporary, Recommended

A great gateway gin. Honeysuckle and citrus on the nose mean it doesn't immediately register as a gin. The spirit is luxurious and rich with an oily, thick mouthfeel. Juniper registers early to mid palate, with honeysuckle, bright citrus and peppery tea. Towards the finish there are camomile notes. A long, somewhat dry finish has pine-accentuated juniper. Perhaps best described as a 'floral take on London Dry', try it in a French 75 cocktail.

Bombay Dry Gin *37.5% ABV*

LAVERSTOKE MILL
WHITCHURCH, ENGLAND

Classic

Built off a straightforward 18th-century gin recipe consisting of juniper, lemon, coriander, angelica, liquorice, cassia, almonds and orris root, Bombay Dry Gin embraces the classic. The nose is thick with juniper. Tasting it, subtle complexities emerge with the juniper taking on a sharp astringent character, lemon zest and coriander as well. A nicely made classic gin that mixes well. The US version comes in at 43%.

Bombay Sapphire [UK Strength] *40% ABV*
Classic

The UK version of Bombay Sapphire is bottled at a slightly lower strength than that of the US. Nice and similar, although it's not as rich in coriander and spice at points, while, the smoother, lower ABV seems to allow for more of a lavender tinge to the floral finish.

Bombay Sapphire [US Strength] *43% ABV*
Classic

The gin that launched a thousand ships in a manner of speaking. When it launched in 1987, it was really pushing the envelope. The nose, with intensely aromatic, albeit fleeting top notes, gives credit to the carterhead method of vapour infusion. Citrus, coriander and a touch of spice on the nose. When you sip, vivid fresh juniper needles, lemon and coriander swirl, delicately shifting towards a finish enhanced with a peppery lift with just the slightest floral touch. It provides a nice upgrade to a Vesper or French 75 cocktail. It's not as radical today as it was when it was released, but the distinctive aroma and all those it influenced live on.

Bombay Sapphire East *42% ABV*
Contemporary

Bombay Sapphire East's botanicals were influenced by the sights, sounds and foods of Southeast Asia. The novel additions in this case are lemongrass and black pepper. Lemongrass rules the day, contributing a herbal, citrus-tinged character to the nose. The palate is dominated by notes of freshly cracked black pepper with the *mise-en-scène* played by juniper, lemon zest and fresh cut lemongrass. One of the best gins for Basil Smash, or use it in a Gin Bloody Mary.

Brockmans Gin *40% ABV*
G & J DISTILLERS
WARRINGTON, ENGLAND

Contemporary

Bright and floral on the nose with strawberry, hibiscus and a touch of raspberry. On tasting, there's a bit of ginger up front, before raspberry, lemon cake, ripe blackberry and coriander notes. Juniper comes on towards the finish, which is surprisingly dry. A very contemporary-styled gin that is definitely not for everyone. Good in a Bronx cocktail or for a Gin and Tonic that resembles a Blackberry Bramble.

Bulldog Gin *40% ABV*
G & J DISTILLERS
WARRINGTON, ENGLAND

Classic

From its London roots, Bulldog Gin looks 'East' for influence from Asian food cultures. It includes poppy, lotus leaves and longan fruits. On the nose, an Asian influence isn't immediately evident, with juniper and lime up front, and cinnamon cake with a pungent low note in the background. The palate is brightly juniper led, with earthy, spicy notes. The Asian flavour is integrated into a well-balanced palate. Smooth enough to be an everday gin.

Chilgrove Dry Gin *44% ABV*
THAMES DISTILLERY
LONDON, ENGLAND

Contemporary, Recommended

Distilled from a base spirit of grapes, with mineral waters from the chalk hills around Chilgrove, West Sussex, this dry gin uses 11 botanicals including an unusual wild water mint with a distinctive lemony odour when rubbed. A ripe, fruity and floral nose, with evidence of the grape base gives way to a smooth, clean, palate of juniper, coriander and angelica, plus subtle citrus and mint notes. A long lingering finish with mint and pine. Well-balanced.

Broker's Gin *47% ABV*
LANGLEY DISTILLERY
LANGLEY GREEN, ENGLAND

Classic, Recommended

Broker's Gin might also win the prize for best dressed gin with its absolutely dapper bowler hat. The spirit inside exceeds even the headgear. A flavoursome aroma is sweet, bright citrus with a heady dose of green, piny, robust juniper. The palate is shimmering, with green juniper and orange peel. A light orris flavour complicates things a bit. The finish is pine accented, held in place with a melange of dark, earthy spice. Exquisite.

Butler's Lemongrass and Cardamom Gin *40% ABV*
BUTLER'S GIN
LONDON, ENGLAND

Flavoured

Butler's Gin starts as a simple distilled gin with only the one required botanical. Further notes are added via infusion. On the nose, it is bright and floral with cardamom, mostly. The palate shows the botanicals building slowly, one over another: first anise, then cinnamon and cardamom, all before juniper hits mid palate. The finish has a creamy richness wherein vanilla, orange, lemongrass and fennel merge in a rich custardy melange before finishing slightly dry, with green notes.

Cotswolds Dry Gin *46% ABV*
COTSWOLDS DISTILLING COMPANY
STOURTON, ENGLAND

Contemporary

Using a combination of maceration and vapour infusion, Cotswolds works with a botanist to get the most out of its botanicals. Nose has mentholated herbs, grapefruit rind and orange blossom. Extremely lively; it jumps out of the glass. Pine cone and woody, resiny juniper jumps out, citrus, with celery on the palate. Then laurel, lavender and clean sheets. A cool minty finish has a touch of peppercorn. Like drinking a Kandinsky: vivid and unconventional.

D1 Daringly Dry Gin *40% ABV*

D.J. Limbrey Distilling Co.
London, England

Contemporary

D1 has a relatively classic-looking botanical bill (juniper, coriander, citrus peel, angelica, cassia, almond and liquorice), but then kicks it up with the addition of tea-quality nettles. The nose is aromatic, subtle with juniper, citrus and angelica. A silky smooth mouthfeel and a taste of coriander and pine at first, while the middle rounds out with herby touches and a pepper and menthol finish. Mixes well to makes a crisp Martini or a dry Negroni.

Durham Gin *40% ABV*

Durham Distillery
Durham, England

Contemporary

The nose is lovely and floral, with elderflower and pink peppercorn. There's some fennel in the lower notes as well, plus some resiny juniper. Ginger, anise and cardamom forward on the palate. Juniper and coriander follow soon after. Some hints of chai with grains of paradise and lemon. A medium-long, warming, peppery finish with a slight vegetal background note. A good bridge gin between the classic and the contemporary.

Gilpin's Westmoreland Gin *40% ABV*

Thames Distillery
London, England

Classic

Classic on the nose, with lots of juniper, plus lemon and spicy coriander as well. The palate is strongly coloured by juniper, but bitter citrus zest is working alongside it to keep things at just the right balance. The finish is earthy and astringent, with juniper and angelica. Clean and crisp, it makes a superb cocktail: in particular, a Martini, a dry Negroni or a clean, juniper-tinged Aviation.

Dorset Dry Gin *40% ABV*

Conker Spirit
Christchurch, England

Contemporary

The first gin distilled in Dorset, so the folks at Conker Spirit have shared with us a bit of their local flora: elderberry, samphire and gorse flowers. A gentle foresty aroma with a touch of mint and lemon oil. Smooth on the palate, with a slow build. A little bit of coriander and angelica spice on the edges as the resiny juniper note builds. Rich and warming with a slight menthol note. Tight mint and vegetal notes on the finish.

Fifty Pounds Gin *43.5% ABV*

Thames Distillery
London, England

Classic

The 1736 Gin Act attempted to prohibit gin through a punitive £50 annual licence. So-named for one of gin's darkest times, Fifty Pounds Gin is a modern-day classic-style gin. Nose is soft and lemony, with peaks of lime and juniper. Sipping it, juniper on the tip of the tongue, with lemon in mid taste and a cool anise cookie denouement. Long, palate-cleansing finish. Refreshing with tonic or a 20th Century cocktail.

Greenall's Gin *40% ABV*

G & J Distillers
Warrington, England

Classic

Founded in 1761, the oldest continuous producer of London Dry Gin in the world has 250 years of history behind it. The nose is mild and classic, with a bright juniper bouquet greeting you right from the bottle. On its own, a bit more nuance colours in the blank spaces. Hint of spicy citrussy coriander, with a citrus lift of lemon peel. The finish is medium in length and not as astringent or dry as other classic gins. It's a good mixing gin, but the mild flavours mean it can get overpowered.

Greenall's Wild Berry Gin
37.5% ABV
Flavoured

....

More the result of flavouring post-distillation than a long steady infusion, the final gin still has juniper on the nose, along with blueberry. Sipping it, you get a peak at the gin before the blackberry and raspberry flavour hits. A nice citrus and slight spruce background note grounds all of this as a gin. Mixes nicely with tonic. A good entry point to get flavoured-vodka drinkers into gin, though there may be too much blueberry for many.

Hammer & Son
Old English Gin *44% ABV*
LANGLEY DISTILLERY
LANGLEY GREEN, ENGLAND

Old Tom

....

Hammer & Son uses an 18th-century formula for its Old English Gin. It's pot distilled, sweetened and sold in champagne-style bottles to hearken back to the days of 'Old Tom'. The nose is pungent and musky, with hints of rainy autumn days and juniper as well. The palate is creamy with juniper and citrus rind up front, and nutmeg, cloves and orris at back. Smooth and sweet. The finish is long and peppery. Try it in a Tom Collins or a Martinez.

Hayman's Family Reserve
41.3% ABV
Classic

....

An updated variation of the Hayman's 1850, Family Reserve takes the gin and rests it in Scotch whisky barrels for only a short couple of weeks. Despite that, the gin is not about the wood; in fact, on both the nose and palate the wood notes are sedate and kept to the last rows. Coriander and juniper come to the fore on both the nose and the palate, with the finish highlighted by a touch of lemon, orange and pepper.

Greenall's Sloe Gin *26% ABV*
Cordial

....

A rich shade of Tyrian purple in colour, the nose is rife with sugar-drenched fresh sloes. At first taste, poignant ripe sloes in shades of raspberry, with a low note of cinnamon, then juniper, lemon peel and a slight spice coming in on the back of the throat. Nicely balanced and pleasantly sweet. This sloe gin is stellar in a Blackthorne Cocktail or simply drink it neat.

Hayman's London Dry Gin
40% ABV
HAYMAN DISTILLERS
ESSEX, ENGLAND

Classic

....

Aromatic and classic, there's strong juniper at the forefront, backed with an earthy, warm, background rife with angelica, coriander and some citrus. The palate is a bit peppery at first, with intimation of grains of paradise and pepperberry. Crisp juniper beset with a floral/citrus backing. Long, thick and pine beset finish. Nice in a Bronx Cocktail, but classic enough for a Martini, too.

Hayman's Old Tom *40% ABV*
Old Tom

....

Based on a family recipe dating back to the 1870s, Hayman's Old Tom is designed to be a true-to-the-era re-creation of the of gin being drunk at that time. Heavy on the botanicals and only lightly sweetened, it is bold and punchy up front with juniper, citrus, coriander and angelica. The taste is just as vivid: a spicy sweetness, light floral tinges at the front and citrus come together for a well-balanced and tightly integrated palate. The finish is long and dry, with pine-forward juniper notes.

Bermondsey Distillery

Sometimes you can tell a lot about a distillery just by seeing where it's located. The Bermondsey Distillery is to be found in a railway arch close to and just south of London Bridge and Tower Bridge. There's something about the exterior that takes you back about a century or so. Not so coincidentally perhaps, that is the same time period invoked by Jensen's Bermondsey Dry Gin and Jensen's London Distilled Old Tom Gin.

Bermondsey Distillery
55 Stanworth Street
London SE1

www.bermondseygin.com

Notable Gins

Jensen's Dry Gin
43% ABV

Jensen's Old Tom Gin
43% ABV

Inside is a modern distillery replete with a laboratory out the back where new ideas are being put to the test. On a rainy afternoon, Hannah Lanfear and Dr Anne Brock, distiller of Jensen's Gin, showed me around their space.

Dr Brock's pathway to the world of distilling is somewhat unusual. She was a synthetic organic chemist by education, with a PhD from Oxford. Distilling, at its very heart, is all about chemistry: keeping track of boiling points and pressure while delicately managing the molecules that give gin its character. In everyday work at the distillery, 'It's more than just the chemistry side,' she says, 'It's the practical side too. Moving liquids between places. Machinery, pressurised systems.' After years of working in an organic chemistry laboratory, distilling is clearly second nature to Brock.

Bermondsey Distillery makes two gins, both of which are rooted in history.

The first, Jensen's London Distilled Bermondsey Dry Gin, evolved from a recipe that came out of 'IT-professional-by-day' Christian Jensen's quest for a forgotten gin. Christian was inspired by a long-out-of-production gin he once had in a Martini. He collected vintage bottles and recipe books, looking for and eventually finding, the recipe. The 'personal hobby' continued to evolve. He worked with master distiller Charles Maxwell of Thames Distillery fame to re-create the gin. This was back in 2004. Impressively, this means that Jensen's Dry Gin is already a veteran of the modern distillery explosion in the UK. The operation was never meant to be a commercial enterprise, but the 'no-longer gin' spoke for itself and won over bartenders around Europe. In 2013 the distillery moved into its Bermondsey space in Southwark, London, underneath the railway line.

Dr Brock continued to explain how the passion for 'forgotten gins' evolved. 'Christian sought to recreate another recipe: an Old Tom, from an 1840 recipe found in an Old Distiller's handbook. The style differs from many other Old Toms on the market in that it is "botanically sweetened", using liquorice instead of an overt sweetening agent like sugar or honey. It's a true-to-recipe re-creation of the spirit produced by one distillery, and is designed to be as historically accurate as a modern Old Tom can be.'

So it doesn't seem much of a coincidence to discover that when you walk by the arch where the distillery is located, the space itself tells the same stories as the gin. Behind something that's over a century old – both the recipe and the space – there's a modern distilling laboratory with a sense of experiment alive and well behind the label. Christian and Dr Brock are putting together something that embodies the best spirits of today and the past.

OPPOSITE Distiller Dr Anne Brock inspects the gleaming still set in a laboratory-like environment in Bermondsey.

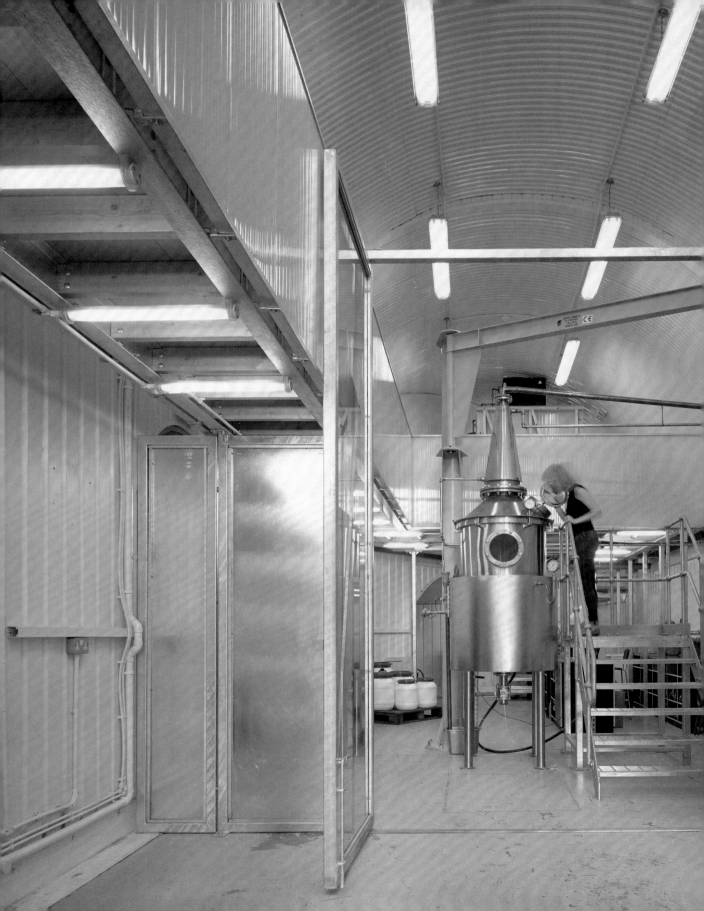

Hayman's Royal Dock of Deptford 57% ABV
Classic, Navy Strength

One of the most important dockyards for the British Royal Navy located on the River Thames, the Royal Dock was actively used from 1513 until its closure in 1961. The nose here is simplicity itself: pine-forward juniper. The palate is smoother and sweeter than you might expect from the first nose. Primarily orange citrus, angelica and orris. White pepper and juniper on a long, warm finish. An exquisite mixing gin, try it in your next Bramble.

Japanese Gin 42% ABV
CAMBRIDGE DISTILLERY
CAMBRIDGE, ENGLAND

Classic

This gin includes Japanese botanicals shiso, sesame and yuzu. Each is individually vacuum distilled at low temperatures and subsequently blended. A mild nose with juniper and a faint spiciness leads to an aromatic burst on the palate. Resiny, herbaceous juniper, pink peppercorn and a sweet cucumber. It offers a long finish with toasted sesame and juniper. Excellent in a Negroni, it also brings a unique touch to an Aviation.

The Lakes Gin 43.7% ABV
LAKES DISTILLERY
COCKERMOUTH, ENGLAND

Classic

Juniper, coriander, angelica and citrus on the nose with a herbal lilt in the lower notes. A rich, thick mouthfeel supports a clean, crisp flavour that hits many of the expected marks in a classic gin. Tightly integrated, the flavour profile comes across as singular. Though juniper is clearly leading the charge, the profile is fresh and bright, something that is often lacking in the resinous/sappy juniper character often found in other gins. Remarkably accessible and delightfully well balanced.

Hayman's Sloe Gin 26% ABV
Cordial

A traditional sloe gin liqueur made from wild sloes harvested shortly after the first frost. The fruits are then macerated for several months with Hayman's Gin before additional sweetening is added. Hayman's Sloe Gin has a lovely cordovan hue. On the nose, ripe fruit, strawberries, orange and spice in the lower notes. The palate is rife with plum, grilled cherry and pink grapefruit. The palate intensifies, terminating with a complex citrus and nutmeg finish. Excellent in a Sloe Gin Fizz or on the rocks.

Jensen's Dry Gin 43% ABV
BERMONDSEY DISTILLERY
LONDON, ENGLAND

Classic, Recommended

Using a more traditional botanical arrangement, the London Dry still manages to be floral without breaking convention. Heavy on the coriander, notes of orris, piny juniper add depth. The palate is smooth, complex juniper up front, true to the nose lavender, violet and sedate coriander occupy space on the side. Jensen's London Dry Gin is great in a Martini, while the Old Tom is great in a Martinez.

Lord Astor London Dry Gin 40% ABV
LANGLEY DISTILLERY
LANGLEY GREEN, ENGLAND

Classic

Crystal-clear juniper on the nose, pine forward and brisk. On tasting, it's straightforward and clean; two-thirds juniper and the other third is a clean but very classic combination of coriander, angelica and citrus. The finish is pithy, but carries the requisite juniper and pine nuance that a good classic gin should always provide.

Martin Miller's Gin 40% ABV
LANGLEY DISTILLERY
LANGLEY GREEN, ENGLAND

Contemporary

Martin Miller's is distilled in the UK, but it hangs its hat on the mystique of Iceland as well. It's not just the spirit or the botanicals, but also the water whose provenance is clearly called out on the bottle. Orange zest on the nose with juniper berry backed up with a slight hint of liquorice. Orange zest and cucumber notes at first give way to pine-forward juniper. Medium-length dry finish with peppercorn, orris and vegetal after-notes.

Martin Miller's Westbourne Strength Gin 45.2% ABV
Contemporary, Recommended

Like the original, but dialled up a notch in strength. In my opinion this is the superior gin because of how much better it works in cocktails. The orange and cucumber, which seemed so strong on the original, tastes better integrated, with the juniper packing a little more punch. Still impressively smooth, with a long crisp finish. Try this with tonic for a very crisp G&T, or in a French 75 cocktail.

Mayfair Dry Gin 40% ABV
THAMES DISTILLERY
LONDON, ENGLAND

Classic

A classic nose with woody juniper and lemon, plus coriander notes hovering in the background. Green juniper hits immediately on sipping, with resiny and earthy notes coming later. In the middle, bitter cinnamon is followed by a herbal hoist, then savoury tarragon notes followed by more juniper. The finish is long, with subtle, earthy angelica. Best in a Tom Collins or a Gimlet with their citrus counter notes.

Mombasa Club Gin 41.5% ABV
THAMES DISTILLERY
LONDON, ENGLAND

Classic

Kenya was a British protectorate in the 19th and 20th centuries, and this gin is named after a famous social club in Mombasa, whose members imported gin from half a world away. This gin could begin with 'inspired by a true story...' The nose is deciduous forest with aromas of bark and soil, beset by orris and lemon. The taste is complex with lime, green juniper, spiced breads and nutmeg. Long piny finish. A really surprising, complex gin.

Opihr Oriental Spiced Gin 40% ABV
G & J DISTILLERS
WARRINGTON, ENGLAND

Contemporary

Opihr Gin aims to reconnect modern gin with a previous era of spiced botanicals, when exotic spices made their way from the orient to Europe via the spice trade, overland and across seas. Savoury spices, some local (caraway) and others distant (cardamom, cumin and cassia) on the nose. The palate is smooth, with dry juniper and coriander complementing a spicy profile. A good example of a spice-forward contemporary-styled gin.

Oxley Gin 47% ABV
LAVERSTOKE MILL
WHITCHURCH, ENGLAND

Classic

One of the earliest vacuum-distilled gins on the market, it sought to use lower temperatures to preserve some of the more delicate aromatics in its botanical mix. The nose is bright with orange and juniper at the forefront, strongly so. The palate is still expressive pine-note and green juniper, with lemon and grapefruit flourishes. Nice in a Martini, with tonic in a G&T or dolled up in a Corpse Reviver #2 cocktail.

Plymouth Gin

For quite some time, the name 'Plymouth Gin' was protected by the European Union as if it were its own style of gin. Lighter than most London Dry gins, until the recent explosion of more contemporary styles, it certainly convinced many that it might have legitimately been its own thing.

Plymouth Gin
Black Friars Distillery
60 Southside Street
The Barbican
Plymouth, Devon PL1 2LQ

www.plymouthdistillery.com

Notable Gins

Plymouth Gin
41.2% ABV
Plymouth Navy Strength Gin
57% ABV
Plymouth Sloe Gin
26% ABV

But in 2014 Pernod Ricard, the owner of the Plymouth brand, decided that it might not be in the brand's best interest to continue forth as a protected style. The name will remain protected, but the days of Plymouth Gin (along with Vilnius Gin, and Gin de Mahón from Menorca, Spain) being a brand that represented an entire style in itself, were over. That doesn't take away from Plymouth and the Black Friars Distillery as being an important part of gin's heritage.

The distillery in Plymouth is over five centuries old, and records suggest gin and other spirits may well have been distilled on this site since 1697.

Plymouth Gin itself was first produced in 1793. Its legend has grown in recent centuries as it was the place from which the Pilgrims took off for America aboard the *Mayflower* in 1620. It began when Mr Coates joined an existing distilling business run by Fox and Williamson. Soon his name took top billing. It stayed until 2004.

The gin rose to fame, especially throughout the 19th century when the distillery supplied the Royal Navy with gin. The 57% or navy-strength version arose out of this partnership. Plymouth supplied the navy, and they in turn carted gin all over the world. In terms of volume, it was among the world's largest brands of gin. It was mentioned by name in many cocktail manuals of the early 20th century.

Plymouth today not only makes its main gin and navy strength variations, but also a sloe gin liqueur. For quite some time Plymouth was the only distillery making an authentic sloe gin. Based on an 1883 recipe, it was in the late 2000s the go-to sloe gin for bartenders looking to recreate authentic sloe gin cocktails, and remains so today for many.

Though no longer specifically protected, the Plymouth distillery is one of the oldest landmarks in the gin distilling world, a testament to the brand and the spirit's lasting influence.

ABOVE Tucked away in the Barbican, the distillery is a popular mecca for gin tourists.

BELOW The distillery offers a master distiller's tour during which you can create your own gin recipe.

The Plymouth Gin distillery has been in existence since 1793.

Plymouth Gin 41.2% ABV
BLACK FRIARS DISTILLERY
PLYMOUTH, ENGLAND

Classic, Recommended, Top 10

Plymouth is a fantastic classic gin. A gentle nose with pine-note emphasised juniper, coriander and orange oil. The taste is sublime, with juniper and citrus holding hands. It's creamy and confident. The finish is gently sweet with a clear note of coriander, elongated with aromatic highlights and a touch of anise. An exquisite gin for mixing or for sipping on its own.

Sacred Gin 40% ABV
SACRED SPIRITS COMPANY
LONDON, ENGLAND

Classic

The nose is gentle, but mostly led with fresh juniper and pine aromas that are like fresh pine carried on the wind from quite some way away. The palate has juniper and coriander up front, liquorice and a subtle anise sweetness in the mid notes, with violet notes and pepper on the finish. Long and dry, the finish is quite peppery with oily/resinous juniper.

Sacred Gin (Coriander)
43.8% ABV
Classic, Recommended

Of all the gin botanicals, I think coriander sometimes ends up getting the least credit relative to the effect it has on gin. The nose of Sacred's Coriander Gin showcases perfectly the exotic aromas that it can produce in gin. The palate showcases the way it can colour gin with a bright, citrussy spice that only coriander can deliver. Such a complex and misunderstood botanical, laid naked for all to appreciate. Recommended for a Gin and Jam or Bronx Cocktail.

Plymouth Navy Strength Gin
57% ABV
Classic, Navy Strength, Recommended

This is *the* navy strength gin. It is the gin that was drunk regularly by officers in the British Royal Navy. And as hard as it is to improve upon the original, the added ABV muscle here makes it an even better choice for cocktails. Aroma and palate-wise, it's like the original with a bit more oomph. The citrus notes are brighter, the juniper is sharper.

Sacred Gin (Cardamom)
43.8% ABV
Classic, Recommended

I've heard some say that cardamom is nearly everywhere in modern-day gin (truth be told, it's in somewhere closer to 25% of gins, but I digress). But really when we get down to it, why not? This wonderful spicy, floral aroma, with its woody, camphorous and exotic character leads to a palate where woody/floral tones harmonise with the juniper and pine. Try this gin in an Alexander or Ramos Gin Fizz and you'll see just what cardamom is capable of doing to gin.

Sacred Gin (Grapefruit)
43.8% ABV
Classic, Recommended

Lime is often added to the G&T. Lemon and orange are in nearly three-quarters of gins. So what does grapefruit have? Sacred highlights this ingredient and you start to wonder how it ended up outside the medal position. Faint citrus in the top notes, with a bit of juniper underneath that. Sipping, after starting with herbaceous juniper, fresh white grapefruit bursts out. The finish is slightly more ruby red: long, fresh and citrus forward. Love this in a Tom Collins.

Sipsmith London Dry Gin
41.6% ABV
SIPSMITH DISTILLERY
LONDON, ENGLAND

Classic

....

With 10 botanicals built on a base of wheat and London water, the gin itself is mild, but assertive. Bright, robust juniper on the nose, if only a touch piny, with a dash of lemon behind it. The palate is ripe with dry, crisp juniper, bitter orange zest, a gentle touch of lemony sweetness and a crisp, dry finish. Well-balanced gin with a quality base spirit and a well-curated botanical blend. Great in a French 75 or a Gimlet.

Sipsmith VJOP *57.7% ABV*
Classic, Navy Strength, Recommended, Top 10

....

VJOP stands for Very Junipery Over Proof. Juniper is added in three stages: at maceration, then in the still, and then even more juniper through vapour infusion. The result is a bold juniper-forward nose with hints of pine and wood. The palate is the fullest representation of juniper I've ever tasted, with its pine aspects, woody aspects, herbaceous and oily sides fully expressed. It sings on the palate, with a long finish of some earthier notes to round things out. Absolutely beautiful.

Tarquin's Dry Gin *42% ABV*
SOUTHWESTERN DISTILLERY
ST ERVAN, ENGLAND

Contemporary

....

An intriguing nose with lemon sherbet and pear candy, followed by juniper and fresh citrus. On the palate, dry juniper gives way to bright citrus, which segues into a floral burst. The finish is slightly savoury with a touch a saltiness, calling to mind visions of the Cornish coast. Tarquin's Gin straddles the line between classic and contemporary.

Sipsmith Sloe Gin 2013
29% ABV
Cordial

....

Rich on the nose, with aromas of dark cherry, fresh picked berries and a touch of gin-like juniper, citrus and cinnamon. Nicely spiced and quite inviting. The palate is robust and jam-like, with the sloes coming on most strongly, and baking spices chiming in only late and softly. The finish is ripe with more berry-like notes. Makes a great Sloe Gin Fizz, but honestly it's good enough in its own right out of the bottle. Fresh and honest, this is a top-notch sloe gin.

South Bank London Dry Gin
37.5% ABV
THAMES DISTILLEY LTD
LONDON, ENGLAND

Classic

....

The nose is quiet, with whispers of juniper, citrus and a hint of sweet spice. Cassia and orris present as well, but only faintly. It's as if everything is dialled down as low as it can go, yet can still be heard. Notes of spiced orange blend into a piny green juniper finish on the palate. The juniper fades quickly into a slightly warming, albeit short, finish. South Bank London Dry Gin is a good mixing gin with a clean, classic profile.

Two Birds Gin *40% ABV*
UNION DISTILLERS
MARKET HARBOROUGH, ENGLAND

Classic, Recommended

....

Two Birds Gin is a well-balanced traditional gin with fresh, green juniper-forward notes. It starts from a traditional launch-off that includes juniper, citrus, coriander and orris. Citrus is present on the palate at first with lemon and coriander adding spice. Juniper adds depth in the mids, with angelica, vanilla cream and candied violets towards the end, then a long, warm finish. Works well in a Martini, though it can be overpowered in more complex drinks.

Sacred

When you walk into Ian Hart's Sacred Microdistillery in Highgate, London, you might be forgiven for thinking you've walked into a mad scientist's lair, or perhaps the backdrop to a children's science TV programme, where condensers, glass bottles and tubes curlicue around one another, and coloured liquids and abstruse controls adorn apparatus that spans the entire room.

Sacred Spirits Company
5 Talbot Road, Highgate
London N6 4QS

www.sacredspiritscompany.com

Notable Gins

Sacred Gin
40% ABV
Sacred Gin (Cardamom)
43.8% ABV
Sacred Gin (Coriander)
43.8% ABV
Sacred Gin (Grapefruit)
43.8% ABV

At first glance Sacred surely doesn't look like any other distillery you might have seen. But that's OK, because Sacred Gin isn't like any other gin you've had and Ian Hart isn't a mad scientist, though he does have a degree in Natural Sciences. He came to the world of distilling through a downturn in the financial markets, which was the impetus that got him exploring the world of distillation. Ian's first experiments were with wine; he had a collection of old wines that he had gathered. Could one remove water and make richer wines? Yes. Richer and commercially viable...? Well, not exactly, so Ian quickly moved on to the world of gin.

But first let's go back to the lab set-up. It's not for show. Sacred Gin is distilled in a low-pressure system that, by trying to distil in vacuum-like conditions, lowers the boiling point. This allows distillation with less heat. In turn the botanicals aren't 'stewed' and thereby some of the more volatile aromatics are preserved and distilled over again.

Ian's distillates are some of the most pure expressions of a single botanical that you will ever taste. In each one you can taste the myriad ways that botanicals come out in other gins, but rarely as bright or as whole as they are here. You can taste the coriander and, say, identify that aspect in the Coriander Gin; but to taste that single ingredient so completely is quite something.

Each botanical in Sacred Gin is distilled individually, using wheat spirit as a base and then blended to achieve the final gin. The botanicals include juniper, the aforementioned coriander, angelica, nutmeg, cinnamon, cardamom, lime, orange, lemon and frankincense (hence, the Sacred). It's more than just a question of scale. The advantages of distilling each ingredient individually is that flavours or aromatics from one ingredient interact with another, sometimes absorbing or otherwise affecting the outcome. It's a conscious design decision that pays off in the end. Sacred's botanicals have unparalleled clarity and precision. They are as truthfully expressed as they can be.

Sacred's line of gins invites experimentation as well. You can purchase a kit that includes individual distillates so you can become a Master Blender. Or put on your Ian Hart hat and try your own hand at creating a gin that meets your exacting needs. For those who want to experiment with the impacts of certain botanicals in a less analytical environment (say a Gin and Tonic?), Sacred's Pink Grapefruit Gin, Juniper Gin, Cardamom Gin and Coriander Gin each take one botanical and accentuate it to make it the focus of the spirit. Sacred's Coriander Gin is indispensable for people learning the ins-and-outs of gin tasting, who want to get a feel for what this common note is, just on its own.

But I digress. Sacred also makes a Rosehip Cup, various vermouths and a line of vodkas, including a London Dry Vodka, re-distilled with seven botanicals (but no juniper).

OPPOSITE Ian Hart's distillery might look like something out of a science programme, but his gin proves it's definitely far more than a show.

LIQUID NITROGEN CONTAINER

CAUTION

Sipsmith

'The dream began — we were drinking gin,' said Sipsmith co-founder Sam Galsworthy, telling of how he and Fairfax Hall came to decide to open the distillery that would become the renowned Sipsmith Independent Spirits.

Sipsmith
The Distillery
83 Cranbrook Road
Chiswick
London W4 2LJ

www.sipsmith.com

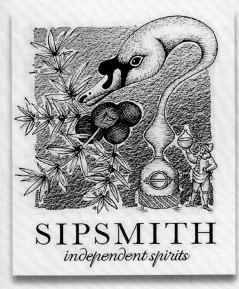

SIPSMITH
independent spirits

Notable Gins

Sipsmith London Dry Gin
41.6% ABV
Sipsmith VJOP
57.7% ABV
Sipsmith Sloe Gin
29% ABV
Sipsmith Summer Cup Cordial
29% ABV

Though in truth, the story begins a little bit earlier. 'Plymouth was my parents' gin,' Sam says, talking of his first encounters with the spirit, 'education was forced upon us. You must learn about it... respect, appreciate that which you were drinking.' The foundation was laid early on for the principles that would underlie the work Sipsmith does at its distillery. But back a little closer to the present.

Sam and Fairfax began what would be a half-decade-long exploration of the spirits scene in the United States. They visited two distillers in the US and took in all that they could. Sam, at the time, was working for Fuller's Brewery and said he learned another lesson. 'Small guys were challenging the big brewers', but it didn't need to be about competition or annihilation. 'On their shoulders we stand,' he said, reiterating the message of respect.

The duo quit their jobs to open Sipsmith in 2007, but it wouldn't be until late 2008 that they would have the licence required to begin making their gin. Sam says they met Jared Brown and Anastasia Miller, esteemed cocktail historians, at a meeting of the Negroni Club in London. This fateful encounter would lead to Jared Brown joining the team, where he is today the Master Distiller. The 'resting on shoulders of giants' approach guided the team's experiments. As they got to know their still (Prudence), they began to craft the recipes that would make up the Sipsmith Gin line.

'Sipsmith is all about classicism,' Sam says. They began with a London Dry style and went up from there. The botanical bill doesn't pull a lot of surprises: juniper, orris root, liquorice, angelica, cinnamon, cassia, almond, coriander and two kinds of citrus. But perhaps the most stunning of their creations, a love song to classicism, turned up as far as the juniper will let you, is the VJOP (Very Junipery Over Proof). 'We do it in three stages: first juniper is macerated in the spirit. Then more juniper is added directly to the spirit when it is moved to the still. And finally, even more juniper is added to a Carterhead.' He describes it as their 'masterpiece'. By adding juniper in each of the three different ways that distillers can add botanicals to their gin, it lets every frequency of the juniper's flavour through to the final product. You get the delicate notes from the vapour infusion, and the robust body that comes from having the berries in the still.

Sam says: 'There are more and more distillers around, it's great', commenting on the recent explosion of small distillers across the UK. Sipsmith was among the first and will be far from the last. 'For these new distillers, it's important for them to "tell the story..." this has changed the market place. People make emotional connections with the story. And that's how you get people calling your name at the bar, "do you have such and such?"'

Sipsmith's story is one of passion, respect for tradition and prudence. When they quit their jobs in 2007, they might not have expected it to take so long before their dream was fully realised. Now that it is though, and speaking for gin drinkers, it certainly seems to have been worth it. Sipsmith also makes Sloe Gin and a Summer Cup Cordial, in addition to its London Dry Gin and VJOP. It also produces a 'sipping' vodka and a Damson-flavoured variant.

OPPOSITE Jared Brown, Fairfax Hall and Sam Goldsworthy were at the forefront of the craft gin distillers' revolution in London. Their gin has quickly become a benchmark for the new generation of artisan gin makers.

Two Birds Speciality Cocktail Gin 40% ABV

UNION DISTILLERS
MARKET HARBOROUGH, ENGLAND

Classic

Designed to be a specifically-for-cocktails version of their Two Birds Gin, the Speciality has a little bit of volume added to the juniper pedal. The nose is bright juniper with a coriander backing. Pleasant and classic. The palate is bright with botanicals, juniper is loud and crisp, but there's coriander, lemon and angelica notes present too. At this proof-point, it certainly is one of the best mixing gins. Try it in... well, cocktails of course.

Warner Edwards Elderflower Infused Gin 40% ABV

Flavoured, Recommended

Taking its excellent Harrington Dry Gin (which already counts elderflower among the botanical bill), the team infuses fresh elderflower harvested from local farms and adds a touch of sweetening. Vanilla, elderflower and baking spice on the nose. The palate overall is a confectionery mix. Warm spice and crème brûlée up front, the finish floral with notes of elderflower and rose. Try it in a Gimlet, or with soda.

Warner Edwards Victoria's Rhubarb Gin 40% ABV

Flavoured

Rhubarb is occasionally present as a botanical in gin, but rarely does it take top billing as it does here. The nose is primed with the summery aroma of stewed rhubarb, with an assortment of traditional pie spices like nutmeg and cinnamon lending it some depth. Rhubarb appears again, recognisable and clear on the palate with its requisite sour tang. Vanilla sweetness and a bit of spice (cardamom, cassia and nutmeg) lend it a gin-like complexity.

Warner Edwards Harrington Dry Gin 44% ABV

WARNER EDWARDS DISTILLERY
HARRINGTON, ENGLAND

Contemporary

When two people who love drinking gin meet at an agricultural college, the result is almost the stuff of gin fairy tales. Made with 11 botanicals and a barley base, many of the ingredients are sourced from their very own farms. Orange zest, baking spice, lavender and a faint intimation of cola. The palate is complex, with warm grain, juniper, coriander, cardamom and an impression of garam masala. The finish is citrus tinged, brisk and dry.

Warner Edwards Harrington Sloe Gin 30% ABV

Cordial

Working with their gin as a starting point, the guys at Warner Edwards add local, hand-picked, British countryside sloes. The resulting Sloe Gin is jammy and bright, with fresh sloe, ripe plum and thick stewed cherry. Quite lovely; try it in a Savoy Tango.

Williams Chase Elegant Crisp Gin 48% ABV

WILLIAMS CHASE DISTILLERY
HEREFORD, ENGLAND

Contemporary, Recommended

Williams Chase turns its apples into cider, which is made to produce cider vodka.It then turns that vodka into Elegant Crisp Gin. It has an elegant spice and a slight fruity, sweet aroma on the nose. Florid juniper leads into a delightful mid palate with notes of walnut brittle, toffee, honey-dipped candies. The finish is long and dry, with juniper and hops lending a crisp, fresh, drying texture with just a touch of orange. A beautiful gin and ideal for your next Martini.

Williams Chase
Seville Orange Gin *40% ABV*
Flavoured, Recommended

The nose is a bricolage of tangerine, bergamot and lemon oil. Intensely and single-mindedly citrus. The palate begins though with a crystallised impression of gin: coriander, juniper, and orris root, before it clarifies the tenor of the citrus, bitter orange, rind and all, fresh and exuberant. Ends with a concise finish of orange and a touch of gin spice. Really lovely stuff, perfect for a Martini, with a tonic, or use in a Fizz, or Collins. This is among the best flavoured gins available.

BELOW Sacred (page 104) pays homage to the science of gin creation by incorporating images of distilling equipment on its cap seals.

Scotland

Blackwood's Vintage Dry Gin (2012) *40% ABV*
DISTIL COMPANY
SHETLAND, SCOTLAND

Classic

Here 'hand-picked Shetland botanicals' mean differences from year to year, according to the climate/terroir of the season. 2012 has juniper, sweet orange and meadowsweet on the nose. The palate is vanilla and meadowsweet, with a berry-like note merging into herbaceous juniper. Slightly sweet, average-length finish. Makes a good Gin and Jam or French 75.

The Botanist Gin *46% ABV*
BRUICHLADDICH DISTILLERY
ISLAY, SCOTLAND

Contemporary

The distillery name catches your attention with Islay being so well known for Scotch. Next, the eye-popping 22 botanicals celebrate the heritage of the island. The nose is floral leaning, with echoes of coriander, lemon verbena, meadowsweet and mint. On the palate, the botanical diversity hums along without a ton of surprises: juniper, sweet herbs and mint. Finish is green in character. Pleasant bright lift, fruits or dry vermouth.

Gordon's Gin *40% ABV*
CAMERONBRIDGE GIN DISTILLERY
WINDYGATES, SCOTLAND

Classic

Gordon's has been around since 1769 and is truly an elder statesman on the dry gin scene. It's widely reported that Gordon's has been the top gin brand in the UK for over a century, where it is available at 37.5% ABV, noticeably weaker and more watery than versions available in the US. Brilliant juniper and crisp lemon zest on the nose, the palate is crisply pine-expressed juniper with accessory cassia, and orange. The finish is relatively tight, but clean and classic all the way through.

Gordon's Crisp Cucumber Gin
37.5% ABV
Flavoured

One of two expansions to the Gordon's product line launched in the 2010s, Gordon's is no stranger to flavoured gins. Collectors have already snatched up many of the extant bottles of Gordon's Orange Gin that was made during the first parts of the 20th century, but I digress. This one has cucumber and lemon on the nose and a palate that is weaker than the classic Gordon's profile, with faint sweet vegetal notes. Inviting, smooth and easy to drink, it works best with just plain tonic water.

Gordon's Elderflower Gin
37.5% ABV
Flavoured

Elderflower has been a hot flavour trend in the early 2010s, with a large number of spirits and cocktails embracing it. This Gordon's has a floral and juniper-led nose, with sweet underlying intimations of violet and camomile. A first sip reveals juniper and wet pine boughs, then citrus rind mid palate. The elderflower comes on strong to finish. Breathe in gently after a sip and the elderflower aroma comes to life, like dry leaves being tossed on a fire. Accessible, it works well in a Martini, though gin traditionalists might disagree.

Indian Summer
Saffron Infused Gin 46% ABV
Duncan Taylor Ltd
Aberdeenshire, Scotland

Contemporary

Saffron is the world's most expensive spice, but fortunately, a little goes a long way. In this gin saffron lends the spirit just the slightest golden tint, but also gives a rich nose that carries the exotic, leathery and unmistakable warmth of this spice. At the first sip there's zested orange, cinnamon and pine-forward juniper. A long aromatic finish sees cinnamon again with black peppercorn and orange zest.

NB Gin 42% ABV
NB Distillery Ltd
North Berwick, Scotland

Classic, Recommended

Small-batch gin with a keen attention to detail. This gin doesn't try anything too crazy. Produced by a husband and wife team, they use the most common gin botanicals but let the process make the difference. Pine, rosemary and tangy lemon on the nose, which evolves as basil and a broth low note emerges. The palate is more traditional. Juniper and lemon at first; while the lemon steps aside, the juniper stays strong, supporting delicate touches of spice. Warm finish.

Hendrick's Gin 41.4% ABV
Girvan Distillery
Girvan, Scotland

Contemporary

The distinctive bottle may make you think of the word 'peculiar', as you imagine some Edwardian dandy with a monocle eating a cucumber sandwich. Hendrick's marketing is ubiquitous and distinctive, but the product also deserves a lot of credit for cultivating a taste for the contemporary with gin drinkers. A fresh, unmistakably gin-like nose with a rose, floral back note. The palate is well rounded with juniper, coriander and a finish of meadowsweet and rose. Great in Gin and Tonic.

Makar Glasgow Gin 43% ABV
Glasgow Distillery Company
Glasgow, Scotland

Classic

The label itself says the words 'superior juniper-led dry gin'. Makar Glasgow Gin is truth in advertising. Sappy juniper on the nose, complemented with fresh spruce. Lively and exhilarating, it's supported by citrus and some ligneous rosemary. Sipping reveals more of the same: strong and bold, practically bursting at the seams with green, resinous juniper. Coriander, dry angelica, citrus and rosemary support the juniper. If you think modern gins are too light on juniper, this is the gin for you.

Pickering's Gin 42% ABV
Summerhall Distillery
Edinburgh, Scotland

Classic, Recommended

Based on a secret family recipe dating back to 1947 and crafted in a copper still. The base spirit is grain, with eight botanicals in addition to juniper: coriander, cloves, anise, cardamom, angelica, fennel, lemon and lime. Herbaceous juniper and coriander on the nose. The palate has pine and lemon zest up front with delicate violets, cracked black peppercorns and fennel seed. Long, dry finish, warm with fennel seed and clove oil. Try it in a Corpse Reviver #2 or Last Word.

Rock Rose Gin *41.5% ABV*

DUNNET BAY DISTILLERY
DUNNET, SCOTLAND

Classic

....

Combines traditional gin botanicals with a couple of local botanicals (sea buckthorn, rowan berries and rose root) to give an impression of the Scottish highlands. The nose is a breezy pine branch with spicy cardamom and coriander. The juniper is herbaceous and green, gently slaking the palate. Towards the end, you'll note a dark outfit of earthy rose, coriander and white peppercorns. Restrained but elegant, an ideal gin for your next Martini.

Tanqueray 10

47% ABV (UK) 47.3% ABV (US)
Classic

....

Don't be surprised when you go to an upscale cocktail bar and notice that the house pour is Tanqueray 10. It's been out since 2000, with its juniper-forward but-wait-that's-not-all-here-comes-grapefruit-and-jasmine nose. The palate is traditional, but noticeably richer with vanilla, lemon and coriander. It's cakey, buttery and really rich. It's a great gin for mixing Martinis, Aviations or Pegu Club Cocktails, which all work very nicely with Tanqueray 10.

Tanqueray Old Tom *47.3% ABV*

Old Tom, Recommended

....

The nose is warm, with creamy juniper, lemon and tightly bound hints of orris and camomile. The palate is pleasingly soft and smooth, with gentle juniper, slowly unravelling to reveal a menthol note, which anchors the finish with its pungent slightly malty, fruity and floral note. The sweetness is only subtle, and this is quite a nice Old Tom style gin, perfect for your next Martinez.

Tanqueray

43.1% ABV (UK) 47% (US)

CAMERONBRIDGE GIN DISTILLERY
WINDYGATES, SCOTLAND

Classic

....

Launched in 1830, Tanqueray is one of the iconic gin names. Its flagship gin has a mere four botanicals: juniper, coriander, angelica and liquorice. They're blended to great effect, and drinkers might be forgiven for thinking there must be more in here. Juniper predominates on the nose, with a citrussy touch. The palate is classic through and through with juniper offset by baking spice notes. Cinnamon? Black pepper? Neither. Try it in an Aviation.

Tanqueray Malacca *47.3% ABV*

Contemporary

....

A limited edition Lazarus of a gin, initially launched in 1997, but taken off the market shortly after the launch of Tanqueray 10. This spirit had something of a cult following. It was clearly ahead of its time, because when it relaunched in 2012, it was right on trend. Citrussy and bright grapefruit on the nose. The palate is citrus led with baking spices and a long finish redolent of crème anglaise. Nice on its own, but for something special, try it in a Clover Club or Ramos Gin Fizz.

Tanqueray Rangpur Distilled Gin *41% ABV*

Contemporary

....

When you hear the word Rangpur Lime, or see a green bottle with a green lime on it, you might think of the small green citrus fruit you see at your grocer. The rangpur is a cross between a mandarin and a lemon. It looks like an orange, but taste-wise, it's similar to a lime. So predictably, Rangpur Gin on the nose and palate reads as tart, bright lime, with a traditional Tanqueray flavour coming through on the palate. Try it in a Gin and Tonic.

Wales

Seaweed Farmhouse Botanical Gin *42% ABV*

DÀ MHÌLE DISTILLERY
LLANDYSUL, WALES

Contemporary

....

A good pairing for seafood, since Newquay seaweed is added to the Botanical Gin. The nose is summer herb garden with lemon verbena, spearmint, sage, fennel and distant flowers. The palate is fresh with spearmint and eucalyptus notes. Unique and bold, try it in a Southside Cocktail or a Basil Smash.

BELOW This bottle of Seaweed Farmhouse Botanical Gin was sealed with wax by the author to survive a transatlantic journey.

Ireland

Dingle *42.6% ABV*

DINGLE WHISKEY DISTILLERY,
DINGLE, COUNTY KERRY, IRELAND

Classic

....

Dingle gin uses vapour infusion to impart the flavours of several local botanicals. This isn't just Irish distillers making gin. It's Irish distillers adding Irish touches to gin. Rowan berry, bog myrtle, chervil and heather are among the botanicals. The nose is slightly jammy with a herbal, mentholated under note and the finish is juniper.

Knockeen Hills Elderflower Gin *43% ABV*

THAMES DISTILLERY
LONDON, ENGLAND

Contemporary, Flavoured

....

Knockeen Hills uses whey base spirit rather than grain for its gin as it also uses it in the award-winning Poitíns. Herbaceous aroma with a slight jasmine low note. Warm, thick mouth-feel with elderflower, lemon and leaves. Green juniper mid palate and a sedate elderflower finish.

Shortcross Gin *46% ABV*

RADEMON ESTATE DISTILLERY,
DOWNPATRICK, COUNTY DOWN
NORTHERN IRELAND

Contemporary

....

One whiff of the nose and you're whisked off to the Irish countryside in spring, with the hedgerows in full bloom: berry, leaves, herbs and floral notes all merge together in a fresh breeze. Slightly lower, vanilla cream and lemon shortbread. The spirit coats the mouth with a rich oily texture and an impressive smoothness uncharacteristic of a 46% ABV gin. Coriander, citrus, berry sweetness, juniper and clover. Long, quite dry finish.

OPPOSITE The bottle design of Martin Miller's gin (page 99) makes a visual reference to the origins of the water that is used to make it.

Belgium

Along with the Netherlands, Belgium can be considered one of the places from which genever evolved, followed much later by gin. Similar to the Netherlands, Belgium's gin selection is a mixture of products from well-established distilleries like Filliers, and newer operations such as Cockney's.

Genever is afforded geographic protection status, which affords Belgium, the Netherlands and only a couple of places in both France and Germany the ability to make genuine genever. The Dutch still partake widely of genever and many Dutch distillers still make the spirit.

That being said, Dutch producers aren't resting on their laurels. Established distilleries like Nolet have been putting out high-quality gins for some time, while new gins such as Goodman's are now appearing on store shelves as well. Gin and genever are both alive and well in the low countries, and there are plenty of great gins worth trying.

BELOW At Filliers, a traditional wooden cap with cork stopper is used as the closure.

Cockney's Gin 44.2% ABV
VAN DER SCHUEREN
AALST, BELGIUM

Contemporary

Based on a recipe dating back to 1838, this purports to be the 'oldest' gin of Belgian origin on the market today. Featuring 15 botanicals, the old recipe was resuscitated and brought to market in 2013. The nose is stark, with notes of orange-flavoured chocolates, while the palate brings cocoa notes to the surface, with a citrus and slightly floral coriander complement. The palate finishes with a drier and crisper impression as the dark chocolate mid notes fade. Bold and memorable, good for summer cocktails.

Filliers Dry Gin 28 46% ABV
FILLIERS DISTILLERY
DEINZE, BELGIUM

Classic, Recommended

The number of botanicals in addition to juniper that are in this gin is 28. Lemon and orange citrus assuage the nose, with a dash of coriander, mentholated juniper and a herbal finale. The next act has orange and lime, with bright chewy juniper-berry notes. Some creamy notes beset with a peppery lift. Rich, palate-encompassing mouthfeel. Moderate-long finish with evolving warm spice for the patient sipper.

Filliers Dry Gin 28
Barrel Aged 43.7% ABV
Aged

The distillers at Filliers Distillery have taken their Dry Gin 28 and twisted it, modified it and bottled it in so many different directions. When you have such an excellent point to launch from, a lot of experimentation really works. Gentle spice and citrus on the nose, the palate sheds light on a rich spice-forward underside. I didn't fully appreciate it until I tried it aged: nutmeg, vanilla and lemon loaf cake. Complex and great sipped slowly or as part of an Old Fashioned.

Filliers Dry Gin 28
Pine Blossom 43.7% ABV
Flavoured, Recommended

The pine that graces this gin is blossom from the Scots pine, which grows right across northern Europe and Siberia. Also used historicially for medicinal purposes, pine blossom gives this gin a creamy, coniferous character resembling on the palate a combination of vanilla and freshly cut pine trees. A stretching, evergreen finish with a slight menthol tinge. Really stunning stuff, good with tonic but best in one of those chilled Churchill-style Martinis, with nothing else whatsoever.

Filliers Dry Gin 28
Sloe Gin *26% ABV*
Cordial

Plum, tomato salsa, cloves, nutmegs and vegetal top notes part ways for a more traditional sloe and cherry sweetness in the lower notes. The vegetal complexity here sets it apart from other sloe gins and will likely determine whether you love it or prefer another sloe gin. On the palate, prune juice dominates, giving way to a sweet cinnamon spice on the finish. Pungent and gently sweet, try it in a Sloe Gin Fizz.

Netherlands

Goodmans Gin *44% ABV*
THE HAGUE, NETHERLANDS
Contemporary

Though Dutch distilled, the inspiration for this gin is many miles away, in the Florida Keys of the United States. The nose is orange and grapefruit peel, with hints of cassia, juniper and grains of paradise. Juniper on the palate, with cinnamon and lemon rind. There's some floral lavender and violet, which opens up brightly with a couple of dashes of cold water.

Nolet's Reserve Dry Gin
(Bottle: 007/998) *52% ABV*
NOLET DISTILLERY
SCHEIDAM, NETHERLANDS

Contemporary

I'd like to keep these notes more about the taste than the price, but it's worth acknowledging. This is the most expensive gin in the world. Coming at around £450 (US$700 or E600), it's designed to be sipped on its own. The nose brings rose, honeysuckle and pine. The palate is complex, as raspberry, oak, saffron and peach lead into a lasting warm finish with lemon cream, iris and juniper.

Filliers Dry Gin 28
Tangerine *43.7% ABV*
Flavoured, Recommended

What do you get when you take the flourishing aroma of a complex gin and add one more component? Fillier's Dry Gin + tangerine = an incursion of key lime on the nose, with juicy mandarins and lemon meringue pie. The palate builds slowly, with crystal-clear tangerine at mid palate. Juniper emerges, with a touch coriander and nutmeg. Stellar with tonic or in a French 75.

No. 3 London Dry Gin *46% ABV*
DE KUPER ROYAL DISTILLERS
SCHIEDAM, NETHERLANDS

Classic

It's not necessarily who a gin is distilled for (in this case Berry Bros & Rudd of London) but where it is. In this case, No 3 Gin is distilled in Holland. So technically, it is a Dutch gin. The nose is classically formed by juniper, backed with lemon and angelica. The palate is quiet at first, with juniper usurping the mid notes. Sweet and bitter oranges in the mid notes, with a pleasant coriander lift. Enduring finish of warm juniper.

Nolet's Silver Dry Gin
47.6% ABV
Contemporary

Nolet's Silver has a long-standing reputation as perhaps one of the most contemporary of the modern contemporary gins. Rose, peach and raspberry grace the nose with a floral effervescence rarely experienced in gin; the palate settles things down with piny, Douglas-fir notes and peppery spice. Keep it simple and try it in a Martini or on its own, on the rocks.

Filliers Distillery

Filliers Distillery is located in Deinze, Belgium, in East Flanders, which is the birthplace of genever, the forerunner to gin as we know it today.

Filliers Distillery
Leernsesteenweg 3
B-9800 Deinze
Belgium

www.filliers.be

The distillery story begins in the late 18th century. The Filliers family were farmers by trade who grew grain through the summers and stored the excess for the winter. Karel Lodewijk Filliers, born in 1792, owned the farm until the early 19th century and decided that he would take whatever surplus grain they had and turn it into genever during the winters, when there was little work to do elsewhere on the farm. Karel was the first Filliers family distiller, beginning a tradition which has lasted five generations and is still alive today.

Although the family was already distilling, the official founding date of the distillery is set at 1880, when Kamiel Filliers, Karel's successor, purchased a steam engine. The distilling operation was transformed overnight from a small-scale farming operation to a serious distillery.

It wouldn't be until the 1920s when Firmin created a gin for an English friend who was visiting Belgium. This gin recipe became part of the Fillier's family lore, but it wasn't commercially made until the 21st century. This recipe was the foundation for Filliers Dry Gin 28.

The distillery today is managed by Bernard Filliers, the fifth generation of the family to stand at the helm of the esteemed institution. Under his watch, Filliers resucitated the 1928 gin recipe and released a line of excellent gins based on that original recipe.

MAIN PICTURE Based on the family farm in Deinze, Filliers was founded in 1880 by Kamiel Filliers.

BELOW The fifth generation of the Filliers family continues to distil fine gins and genevers in traditional copper stills.

The recipe calls for 28 different botanicals. They are macerated and distilled in four separate batches, which are then blended later. Owing to their family tradition as grain farmers, they use grain spirit as the base, distilled in copper pots.

The botanical mixture spans traditions: allspice comes from the Caribbean Islands; cinnamon and ginger from Southeast Asia. Lavender flowers, angelica, hops, coriander, gentian and three kinds of citrus are among the selected 28.

Though Filliers makes an impressive line of handcrafted gins, including both tangerine- and pine-blossom-flavoured varieties, together with aged gins and sloe gins, it is still perhaps best known for its genevers. It also distils Wortegemsen (a genever with fresh lemon pulp), fruit genevers, vodka and its line of Goldlys whiskys.

Notable Gins

Filliers Dry Gin 28
46% ABV
Filliers Dry Gin 28
Barrel Aged
43.7% ABV
Filliers Dry Gin 28
Pine Blossom
43.7% ABV
Filliers Dry Gin 28
Sloe Gin
26% ABV
Filliers Dry Gin 28
Tangerine
43.7% ABV

BELOW The Filliers distillation process is a closely guarded family secret, passed down through the generations from one master distiller to another.

Oliver Cromwell 1599 Gin
40% ABV

UNKNOWN, PRODUCED FOR ALDI STORES LTD, NETHERLANDS

Classic

Gin produced for supermarket chains as branded gin rarely equates to a high-quality gin, but allow Aldi's 1599 Small Batch Gin (distilled in the Netherlands, sold in the UK) a chance to change your mind. Juniper forward, but with ample complexity underneath it, coriander and spice notes, Oliver Cromwell 1599 Gin is not just an acceptable mixing gin – it's a pretty good one. Nice flavour that delivers exactly as promised.

Sylvius Gin *45% ABV*

DISTILLEERDERIJ ONDER DE BOOMPJES SCHIEDAM, NETHERLANDS

Contemporary

You might expect a distillery located in Schiedam to specialise in genever. Onder de Boompjes does do genever, but it also distils Sylvius Gin in the traditional dry gin fashion, using a grain base along with herbs and juniper to create a botanically driven spirit. Caraway, cinnamon and citrus on the nose, then a palate of caraway with juniper leads to fennel seeds on the finish. Modern, spice forward and good in a Martini or a Negroni.

Three Corner Dry Gin *42% ABV*

A. VAN WEES DISTILLEERDERIJ DE OOIEVAA, AMSTERDAM, NETHERLANDS

Classic, Recommended

Can simplicity be everything? Opting for only two botanicals: lemon and juniper, Three Corner Dry Gin is surprisingly deep. The nose is a nicely balanced combination of citrus and juniper; however, there's an interesting underlying floral note reminiscent of orris or coriander. A bright palate has lemon oil up front and pine-heavy citrus. Creamy and rich, you'd swear there was more here. Excellent mixer but great in Gin and Jam.

Van Gogh Gin *47% ABV*

ROYAL DIRKZWAGER DISTILLERIES SCHIEDAM, NETHERLANDS

Contemporary

Van Gogh Gin is among the elder statesman of the gin renaissance. Its origins date from 1999, and although it might not seem too divergent from the norm today, there was a point when this was as wild as it might get. A melded nose of lemon, coriander and liquorice greets the nostrils, while the palate is a lemony blend that combines juniper, cassia and cubeb for a spicy complex mid palate. Ends on a warming note, with an earthy, lengthy finish. A really good cocktail gin.

Zuidam Dutch Courage
44.5% ABV

ZUIDAM DISTILLERS BAARLE-NASSAU, NETHERLANDS

Classic

'Dutch Courage' was the name that English soldiers were said to give to the drink that the Dutch quaffed before heading into battle. British and Dutch tradition again fight side by side as this Dutch-made gin exhibits all of the finest traits from the style popularised in London. Juniper and exotic coriander on the nose. The palate is lemon zest, piny juniper and some warm spiced notes. Has a moderate, very clean, dry finish.

BELOW The distinctive and elegant elongated neck of Three Corner Dry Gin.

France

Key to France's alcohol traditions are wine and Cognac, and they both figure prominently in France's modern gin tradition. Among the best-known French gin brands, two use grape spirits as a base and include grape blossoms in their gin, while other distilleries from the Cognac region use their stills for gin when they're not legally permitted to make Cognac. Overall, French gins are incredibly diverse in character, ranging from the traditional to those that are prominently pushing forward just what a gin can be.

BELOW The frosted neck of Citadelle Reserve proudly proclaims the founding date of the Pierre Ferrand distillery.

Citadelle Gin 44% *ABV*
PIERRE FERRAND DISTILLERY
COGNAC, FRANCE
Classic

....

According to French law, Cognac can only be produced between November and March. Citadelle uses the normally idle copper pot stills during the off-months to produce an exquisite, brightly classic-styled gin. Among the 19 botanicals, violet, sweet orange and coriander alight on the nose. You'll pick up cardamom, baking spices and juniper, then a finish of liquorice and fennel. Good in an Aviation or a Pegu Club cocktail.

Citadelle Réserve Gin (2013) 44% *ABV*
Aged, Recommended, Top 10

....

The first gin to be aged using a Solera method. In brief, it's designed to create a uniform end product by adding new spirit to the top barrels, and as it ages, the spirit 'trickles down', or is moved into the lower barrels containing older spirits. Coriander and cardamom on the nose, with a robust palate, a bright blend of barrel notes like vanilla and cedar, with herbal notes and a dry juniper-led finish.

Diplôme Dry Gin 44% *ABV*
PRODUCED AND BOTTLED
FOR BEBO DRINKS
DIJON, FRANCE
Classic

....

The Diplôme recipe dates from 1945 and was a gin that was served to American soldiers stationed in France. The botanical selection is traditional, based on botanicals widely available in the region at the time: juniper, coriander, lemons, orange, angelica, saffron, orris and fennel. The nose has a hint of juniper and coriander. A rich, soft mouthfeel led by crisp, herbaceous juniper, a touch of fennel seed and citrus. Good for all cocktails.

Gabriel Boudier Rare London Dry Gin 37.5% *ABV*
GABRIEL BOUDIER, DIJON, FRANCE
Classic

....

Makes for a nice Gin and Tonic, and is much more traditional than the Saffron offering (page 120). Warming spices with some bright intimations of fennel complement pine-forward juniper with a hint of citrus backing. It has some spice notes, but the overall profile is purely classic.

Gabriel Boudier Saffron Gin
40% ABV
Contemporary, Flavoured

Vividly coloured, the liquid inside immediately calls to mind the world's most expensive spice: saffron. The saffron is infused post-distillation to give it that distinctive colour. A strikingly traditional nose, with aromas of juniper, coriander and only the faintest hint of saffron. The palate delivers the promise of its colour, but does so with a smooth, sophisticated profile that lingers warmly on the palate. Quite nice on its own, or with tonic or soda.

G'vine Nouaison *43.9% ABV*
Contemporary

More traditional than the Floraison, takes the formula and bottles it at a slightly higher proof with a bit more juniper. On the nose, floral bright flowers, cardamom, but also ginger and juniper. On the palate, juniper comes through much more vividly, with coriander in the mids and a wide range of lower spice notes. Cinnamon, ginger, nutmeg and a light anise/liquorice sweetness. Try it in a Martini or a Gimlet.

Magellan Iris Flavoured Gin
44% ABV
ANGEAC DISTILLERY
ANGEAC-CHARENTE, FRANCE
Classic

Magellan Gin stands out visually. Really, it does. A vivid Tiffany blue, it might raise alarm to purists on its colour alone. The colour is partly due to a post-distillation infusion of iris flower. The nose is far less out-there than the colour, with a classic, clean juniper aroma. The palate is a bit citrussy, with orange zest begetting a warming body of coriander, grains of paradise and cardamom and only a touch of orris. Surprisingly, it is juniper forward.

G'vine Floraison *40% ABV*
EURO WINEGATE SPIRITS AND WINE
MERPIN, FRANCE
Contemporary

G'vine's gins distinguish themselves from others by the two methods that grapes – an important part of the French alcohol tradition – impact the final flavour of the gin. The base spirit is distilled from grapes, then, a grape vine flower is used as a botanical. The nose is incredibly floral and vibrant, with cardamom too. The palate is out there. For the most part lime zest, coriander and liquorice.

Le Gin 1 & 9 *40% ABV*
DISTILLERIE DES TERRES ROUGES
TURENNE, FRANCE
Contemporary

The nose is slightly exotic with liquorice, anise and sweet spice. The palate builds on the nose, with a loud, vibrant character. Green juniper notes build the backbone, which has notes of cardamom, angelica and coriander, with a warm, spiced finish rife with liquorice, fennel and celery salt. The finish is dry and a bit peppery with a sophisticated and spice-forward character. Well suited to a French 75 or Negroni cocktail.

Pink Pepper Gin *44% ABV*
AUDEMUS SPIRITS
COGNAC, FRANCE
Contemporary, Recommended, Top 10

I love the way this gin transforms a Gin and Tonic, or the way it adds a peppery sweetness to a Negroni. But I really love it on its own. The flavour profile, true to its name, accentuates the flavour of pink peppercorns down to a tee: dry and freshly cracked on the nose, the palate is rich and creamy, with peppercorn, vanilla, butter-topped cinnamon spice cake, all with just the right amount of juniper behind it. It's sure to be divisive, but for those who've embraced the 'Wild West' of gin, this is as good as it gets.

Germany

Juniper grows wild across this nation; German food tradition made extensive use of the ubiquitous berry and it is prominently featured in dishes such as *Sauerbraten* (marinated pot roast) or *Choucroute Garnie* (a fancy version of sauerkraut). Additionally, two German federal states with close historical ties to Belgium are able to make authentic genever under EU regulations. That being said, Germany has not had as strong a gin-drinking tradition in modern times as its neighbours; however, things are changing.

Many new distilleries have opened since the mid 2000s and many are creating German expressions of gin. Monkey 47 uses the Black Forest as inspiration, while the distillers behind Ferdinand's Saar Dry Gin combine gin with Germany's strong wine tradition.

ABOVE Dactari is known for the extraordinary insect/woman illustration that appears on its bottles.

Berlin Dry Gin 43.3% ABV
BERLINER BRANDSTIFTER UG
BERLIN, GERMANY

Contemporary

Each bottling of Berliner Dry Gin is limited to 9,999 bottles due to the limited supply of the Berlin-inspired botanicals that go into the gin: elderflower, cucumber, mallow and woodruff. These floral botanicals combine on the nose for a fruit-forward mix of fresh berries and lime. A rich mouthfeel of berry notes leads to resiny juniper, citrus and coriander and a modern, floral finish.

The Bitter Truth Pink Gin
40% ABV
THE BITTER TRUTH DISTILLERY
PULLARCH, GERMANY

Contemporary, Flavoured

The colour is a light hue of pink carnation, true to the name. The nose is an intriguing combination of fruity and floral with juniper, pomegranate and rose notes. The taste is pine-accented juniper, with cherry and apple as well. The finish is astringent and dry, with wormwood and gentian at first. But when those fade, there's a surprising sweet liquorice and caraway/fennel note. Nicely balanced, perfectly suitable for a Negroni.

Dactari Gin 40% ABV
DAC DESIGN AM CHIEMSEE
PRIEN AM CHIEMSEE, GERMANY

Contemporary

Ideal for a Tom Collins or Gin and Tonic. On the nose lemon, orange blossoms, honeysuckle and fresh herbs. Lots of very bright high notes, and not much else. A smooth palate in three waves: lemon and lavender at first, juniper and cedar in the middle, and a finish of candied orange peel and pecans. Has a moderate-length citrus-led finish, clean and fairly dry.

Elephant Gin 45% ABV
SCHWECHOWER OBSTBRAND
SCHWECHOW, GERMANY

Contemporary

Though distilled in Germany, Elephant Gin's inspiration lies thousands of miles south in the African savannah. Baobab, African wormwood and buchu give the botanical bill an African-inspired influence. Despite these exotic additions, the spirit itself is pleasantly familiar: herbal, citrus blossom and zest on the nose, with a hint of lavender. The taste is complex and layered with spice, herbs, pine-forward juniper and fresh cracked black pepper.

Ferdinand's Saar Dry Gin
44% ABV
AVADIS DISTILLERY
WINCHERINGEN, GERMANY

Contemporary

A complex gin with tricks up its sleeve. Thirty different hand-picked botanicals might seem out there enough, but what sets this apart is the addition of German Riesling wine. A floral nose (lavender and rose) and citrus (mandarin and lemon) with hints of grasses and herbs as well. The taste has a lot of lemon rind building to meadowsweet mid palate. A long, cooling juniper and lemon/lime finish. Good in a French 75.

Lebensstern Pink Gin 43% ABV
BAR IM EINSTEIN
BERLIN, GERMANY

Contemporary, Flavoured

Technically this could fall under the category of *pre-bottled cocktail*. Pink Gins work well as gins within their own right if treated like a flavoured gin. On the nose, fennel, peppermint oil and a surprising hint of candy floss. A herb-forward nose with fennel, liquorice and wet juniper. The finish is similar to Angostura bitters. Good on its own or as a bittered touch in a Martini or a Negroni.

Monkey 47 Schwarzwald Dry Gin 47% ABV
BLACK FOREST DISTILLERS
LOSSBURG, GERMANY

Contemporary

Contains 47 different botanicals and a base spirit distilled from molasses instead of grain. The nose is bright with lime zest, complemented by juniper, lemon oil, lemongrass and a hint of coriander. Incredibly complex, it seems like it could be a crap shoot trying to identify everything. The palate is similarly complex, though citrus seems squarely in charge. Lemon flesh, grapefruit rind, cinnamon, Froot Loops cereal long, warm finish.

Granit Bavarian Gin 42% ABV
ALTE HAUSBRENNEREI
PENNINGER GMBH
HAUZENBURG, GERMANY

Classic

From a distillery that specialises in Bavarian products, Granit Gin uses the herbs and roots of the Bavarian forest (lemon balm, baldmoney and gentian), before resting it in earthenware pots and filtering it through granite. A fennel and caraway nose, plus the expected licks of coriander and pine. Herbaceous pine on the palate that lingers on the finish.

Lyonel Dry Gin 50% ABV
WIEGAND MANUFAKTUR
WIEGAND, GERMANY

Contemporary

Bottled at a muscular 50% with 13 hand-picked herbs and copper-pot-distilled over a naked flame, then bottled with a classy design reminscent of Piet Mondrian. A delightful nose comprises well integrated juniper and coriander notes with hints of mint and orris. The palate is assertive with sweet rose and coriander up front, followed by juniper and clear, subtle cumin seed. A dry medium-length finish. Soft and well crafted, try it in a Last Word or Alaska cocktail.

Simon's Bavarian Pure Pott Still – Harvest Gin 47% ABV
FEINBRENNEREI SIMON'S
ALZENAU, GERMANY

Contemporary

The nose is really unique. At first, there's a bit of mushroom and dark notes, but if you're patient and look a bit closer, intense, liquorice and cherry/vanilla jam notes emerge. The palate is clouded with citrus up front, wet leaves and then liquorice and fennel. Long piny-juniper finish, but nonetheless, a somewhat challenging mixer.

Simon's Bavarian Pure Pott Still – Summer Gin 42.5% ABV
Contemporary

....

Vegetal/fruity notes on the nose lead to cucumber, bay leaves, thyme and some herbaceous juniper further down in the mix. The palate has a robust, fresh evolving juniper tone with a nice offset of *herbes de Provence*, before it becomes more mentholated and eucalyptus like. Rosemary and sage on a moderate-length finish. Summer and blossoming herb gardens are an ideal match. Top with soda and lemon.

Vallender Pure Gin 40% ABV
Brennerei Hubertus Vallendar Kail, Germany

Contemporary

....

Piny juniper with liquorice fringe on the nose. Low malted notes with barley and fermented apples. The palate is intense, with thundering juniper and spiced orange cake. Camphorous notes, with fennel seeds and grain in the lower notes. The finish is long and hot with a copious amount of resiny pine sap and juniper.

RIGHT Each Elephant gin label carries the name of past great elephants and tuskers. The distillery partners with foundations currently helping to protect the elephant.

Scandinavia

Scandinavia has been drinking spirits like gin for centuries. But rather than flavouring them with juniper, they used caraway and dill. This spirit is better known as akvavit or aquavit. Aquavit is similar to gin, in that a neutral grain or potato spirit, known to the Swedes as *brännvin*, is infused with herbs and spices. Aquavit is often enjoyed neat in shots called snaps.

This tradition of using local herbs has carried over to the local gins as well. Gin distillers like Hernö in Sweden or Kyrö in Finland are creating high-quality local spins on gin that you can drink in the traditional style or mix up in cocktails. Many distilleries are even adding local berries like cloudberry or the quintessentially Swedish lingonberry to create new things that evoke a sense of the region, no matter how you sip it. Skål!

BELOW Vor Gin wears its country of origin with pride, however discreetly.

Denmark

Mikkeller Botanical and Hoppy Gin 44% ABV
BRAUNSTEIN DISTILLERY
COPENHAGEN, DENMARK

Classic

The nose blooms like a pine forest, with juniper at first, then a touch of earth and fresh leaves. The palate is similar, a warming pine forest, with cardamom and angelica notes ushering in a touch of hops and bitter orange zest. A long, dry finish running on orange fumes and a faint hops aroma. Well balanced for cocktails.

Nordisk Gin 44.8% ABV
NORDISK BRÆNDERI
FJERRITSLER, DENMARK

Contemporary

Nordisk means 'Nordic' in English, and therein lies the inspiration for this gin. Local botanicals like cloudberries and *qajaasat*, mixed with a touch of apple brandy for good measure. The nose is apple strawberry, bright and very sweet. The palate is a little greener, with flower stems and rose building to a piny juniper mid palate. Mint on the loose with a long finish brimming with apple pie and kale. Imaginative and quite contemporary.

Finland

Koskue Gin 42.6% ABV
KYRÖ DISTILLERY COMPANY
ISOKYRÖ, FINLAND

Aged

Created by taking the rye-based Napue Gin and resting it in wood, Koskue has a vivid golden hue and majestic aroma. A warm lemongrass nose with a vivid spruce, wood and eucalyptus palate. Beneath the fresh menthol notes there's grain, caraway, anise and juniper. The finish is slightly sweet with caramel, lemon pepper and spruce. Good in an Old Fashioned or a Negroni.

Napue Gin 46.3% ABV
Contemporary

Rye gin is experiencing a return to form in the last decade. Once a forgotten descriptor seen in 19th-century gin advertisements, several gin distillers around the world have brought new life to it. And what a surprise this is, from distillers whose website boasts 'In Rye We Trust'. Lemon and meadowsweet on the nose, the palate has a warm grainy character with mint, liquorice and a touch of fennel on the finish. Warming, protracted coda. In Rye We Trust, indeed.

Greenland

Isfjord Premium Arctic Gin
44% ABV
ISFJORD, GREENLAND
Classic

....

Made with the water from melted icebergs in Greenland, Isfjord is juniper with salty, savoury notes on the nose, including nutty hints of macadamia, hazelnut, as well as lemon and vanilla. The spirit is smooth, rich and dry, with early coriander as a drying sensation builds. Sweet spice towards the end. The long finish has juniper notes.

Iceland

Vor Gin *47% ABV*
EIMVERK DISTILLERY
GARÐABÆR, ICELAND

Contemporary, Recommended, Top 10

....

The barley, juniper and botanicals here are all Icelandic. Some only grow in Iceland: crowberries and Icelandic moss included. The effect is stunning. Grains, herbs and a touch of liquorice on the nose, while the palate is a wall of juniper, rhubarb, thyme, oregano and mint, with a long, warm finish. A complex gin, good with tonic and in a Negroni.

Norway

Hammer London Dry Gin
40% ABV
ARCUS BEVERAGE
OSLO, NORWAY

Classic

....

Bright, classic, London Dry gin appears right away on the nose. Juniper is the first thing to hit you, but right below that there's earthiness and spice like coriander and rose. But don't get caught up in the details: it's juniper-led on the nose and on the palate. The finish is coriander, citrus and a touch of caraway. Lovely classic-style gin, really good in a Bronx or a Clover Club.

BELOW On the Isfjord Gin bottle you'll find a gentle reminder, if one were needed, that Arctic gins come from somewhere cold.

Nordisk Brænderi

Anders Bilgram is an adventurer. He spent a decade of his life travelling above the Arctic Circle in an open boat, where he met the local people who lived in the regions around the North Pole. These travels would be the inspiration for his gin. But we're getting ahead of ourselves…

Nordisk Brænderi
Hjortdalvej 227
9690 Fjerritslev
Denmark

www.nordiskbraenderi.dk

Notable Gin

Nordisk Gin
44.8% ABV

A little over a decade ago, Denmark, like many other places in the world, was not a place where the decision to open a distillery was an easy one. 'While boating along the Arctic coast I got the idea that it might be possible to get permission from the Danish authorities to actually produce high-quality alcohol for filling the glasses made by my wife…' (Anders' wife was a glassblower.) 'At the time, the authorities told me that it was possible…but it wasn't easy.' Anders finished his expedition in 2008 and when he returned home, he went to work. His efforts paid off and Nordisk Braenderi was born.

He distilled grappa, whisky, rum, fruit brandies and schnapps at first. 'After a few few years I was thinking of making a gin. It had to be a gin where the botanicals are from the Nordic region.' He chose to use *qajaasat* or *grønlandspost*, a low-growing white flower native to Greenland whose leaves are often used as a cooking herb and a complement to savoury meats. He also added Swedish cloudberries, a small boreal plant that produces a salmon-coloured fruit resembling a raspberry or blackberry. Cloudberries are often made into jams and are very difficult to grow commercially. From Denmark, he added sea buckthorn, wild rose flowers and elderflowers. 'My whole life and my own personal story is about the Nordic region,' Anders explains. 'These local botanicals are very tasty, which is why I chose to use them.'

The base spirit for Nordisk Braenderi is a mixture of molasses spirit and apple spirit, distilled from local Danish apples. It is distilled in a Mueller pot still and the botanicals are added via a sieve, a bit like a gin basket, where the vapours pass through. 'I make three different distillates and afterwards I mix these the way I want the gin to taste.'

'I think gin has a great future – this is not a fad,' Anders says, describing the gin renaissance. 'Gin has so many exciting possibilities and I love to see the way it's being used in so many interesting ways and in new cocktails.' He suggests trying his spirit in a Gin and Tonic, but for a Danish touch add some berries or herbs, but omit the citrus.

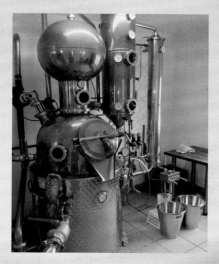

ABOVE The Mueller pot still at Nordisk is used to triple distil the gin.

LEFT Wild rose flowers are added to the still to provide Nordic floral flavouring notes.

MAIN PAGE *Qajaasat* is a plant that grows in the wild in Greenland. The flowers are often used to make tea, but Nordisk adds them to the botanicals in its Nordisk Gin.

Sweden

Hernö Swedish Excellence Gin (Batch 11) *40.5% ABV*
HERNÖ GIN, HÄRNÖSAND, SWEDEN
Contemporary

This flagship gin is distilled in one go with eight different botanicals. It's the lingonberries that make it distinctly Swedish and, while often burdened with Ikea/Swedish stereotyping, they are great here. Bright juniper and astringent berry notes lead to jam and vanilla, then a long finish. Great with Fever-Tree Tonic Water.

Hernö Navy Strength Gin
57% ABV
Contemporary

In short, it's like the Hernö Swedish Excellence Gin, but dialled up a notch. However, the real story is how much brighter its character comes through in cocktails at this strength. It has the power to add a Lingonberry punch to a Negroni. It can add the juniper and vanilla lift to an Aviation. The build is quicker, but the juniper gives way to a buttery richness on the back half with emphasided citrus. One of the best contemporary-styled Navy Strength gins.

Hernö Juniper Cask Gin (Batch 5) *47% ABV*
Aged, Recommended, Top 10

Juniper wood is an important part of Scandinavian tradition, used for making small containers, or even filtering mash for traditional beers. But never before had anyone successfully aged gin in a barrel made entirely out of juniper until Hernö did it in 2013. The experiment alone is worth the price of admission, but the gin exceeds on all counts. Warming on the nose, the palate is intense with juniper, citrus, flowers and spice. Highly recommended, and best drunk neat, by the fire.

Hernö Old Tom Gin (Batch 5)
43% ABV
Old Tom

Take the Hernö standard-issue gin, add a touch more meadowsweet, then sweeten with both honey and sugar. The nose is dialled back with a bit of juniper and coriander. The palate is noticeably bright and floral, with juniper at first, meadowsweet and jasmine flowers in the middle, then Hernö's trademark lingonberry and vanilla finish. The subtle sweetness comes through at the end, imparting a gentle creaminess. Makes a proper Tom Collins or Martinez.

Nils Oscar Tärnö Gin *41.5% ABV*
NILS OSCAR BREWERY
NYKÖPING, SWEDEN

Contemporary

Floral, with a touch of berry, coriander and cardamom on the nose, but not altogether without a slight juniper note. The palate is in the same vein, but there's a bright hit of lemon, enhanced with notes of cinnamon and then a finish ripe with elderberry. Nicely balanced and contemporary, it works well with tonic water or soda water. Bright and easy to drink.

Spirit of Hven Organic Gin
40% ABV
SPIRIT OF HVEN
BACKAFALLSBYN, SWEDEN

Contemporary

Spirit of Hven Organic Gin is unique in that it is intentionally aged with oak before the final distillation run. The nose is lively with lemon zest and freshly squeezed orange oil. The palate begins with a mellow and creamy start, then rises to a roar. Cubeb and grains of paradise mid palate, loud and peppery, are softened by herbaceous juniper and a faint vanilla/cardamom note fading on a dry pepper finish.

Strane London Dry Gin (Merchant Strength) *47.4% ABV*

SMÖGEN DISTILLERY
HUNNEBOSTRAND, SWEDEN

Classic

....

The distillers at Smögen Distillery blend each of their gins from a combination of three distillates: citrus, juniper and herbal. Each of their three proofs of gin are a unique expression. Merchant strength has a bright nose with almond, lemon and cinnamon. The spirit is thick and rich with juniper up front, lemon rind, camomile tea and mint. Try it in a Gin Fizz or a Gimlet.

Strane London Dry Gin (Navy Strength) *57.1% ABV*
Classic, Recommended

....

Bottled at a higher proof, this blend is ideal for almost any cocktail you wish to mix it in. You'll find it perfectly suited to a Corpse Reviver #2, Aviation or Last Word. The aroma is rife with coriander and juniper with lemon zest in the wings contributing a smidge of colour. It sticks fairly closely to the classic formula on the palate with lemon zest, resiny juniper and *herbes de Provence* on the finish, which is dry and short. As a high-proof mixing gin, this is top-notch stuff.

RIGHT The Spirit of Hven gin bottle looks more like laboratory glassware than a traditional bottle.

Hernö Gin Distillery

Hernö Gin Distillery sits in the village of Dala, outside Härnösand, just south of the High Coast, a stunning World Heritage Site awash with cliffs formed by glaciers. It is here that Sweden's first gin-only distillery operates.

Hernö Gin
Dala 152
871 93 Härnösand
Sweden

www.hernogin.com

Notable Gins

Hernö Navy Strength Gin
57% ABV
Hernö Swedish Excellence Gin
(Batch 1) *47% ABV*
Hernö Juniper Cask
(Batch 5) *47% ABV*
Hernö Old Tom Gin
(Batch 5) *43% ABV*
Hernö Blackcurrant Gin
28% ABV

'My interest in gin started in 1999 when I was a bartender in London,' explains Hernö founder and Master Distiller Jon Hillgren, 'my interest evolved during these years.' Then,10 years ago, he began studying gin in earnest. He visited many other distillers and began doing theoretical work. In 2011, he founded Hernö Gin distillery and by 1 December 2012 Hernö Gin was on the market.

Jon thought there was a taste missing from gins that were on the market so when he conceived his Hernö line he thought: 'I wanted a fresh, floral gin with clear notes of citrus.' He says the process took nearly four months of dedicated work to ensure that not only was the botanical mix right, but also the temperature and the pressure. He made sure every detail was properly aligned to reproduce what was in his head.

He uses an organic wheat base with which he does a first pass-off to create what is essentially vodka. 'After this first distillation, I clean out the still and put the vodka in the pot.' The pot in question is a Holstein 250-litre (66-gallon) copper still with column, though by the end of 2015 he hopes to quadruple the size, with the addition of a new 1000-litre (264-gallon) still.

Jon adds the juniper and coriander and allows the spirit and botanicals to macerate for 18 hours before adding the other botanicals. 'I peel the lemons myself,' he says, in addition to lingonberries (a Swedish speciality), meadowsweet, black pepper, cassia and vanilla.

'I think we will see an explosion of new distilleries in the market for quite a few years,' Jon says. 'Local', 'handcrafted', 'organic' and 'bio' he cites as among the things that people are looking for. 'The market is huge, there is still room for many small distilleries and probably a few medium ones as well, without the big ones being threatened.'

Hernö makes an array of gins using Jon's certified list of organic botanicals. Handcrafted? Check. Organic? Check. There's his Hernö Gin, as well as a navy strength variant and, in 2014, he put out an Old Tom alongside a Blackcurrant Gin, the Swedish answer to British hedgerow cordials. And then there's the ultimate in Scandinavian culture meets gin: juniper-cask-rested Hernö Gin. Rested in a cask made from juniper wood, it's an update on the trend of ageing gins that's strongly rooted in northern European cultures who historically worked with the wood for weaving. They even used it in the process of making other traditional drinks, such as the Finnish beer Sahti.

While the Hernö distillery wears its Swedish heritage on its sleeve, it does focus only on gins. It's hard to go wrong with any of its offerings. Jon suggests enjoying his gin 'neat, at room temperature', but 'for hot summer days, a Gin and Tonic or a Tom Collins is great too'.

MAIN PAGE & RIGHT Sweden's northernmost gin-only distillery in midwinter, and surrounded by meadowsweet, a key botanical, in spring.

Spain

For many people, Spain's contribution to the world of gin is the national fascination or obsession with the Gin Tonica. This style of preparation, replete with the detailed study of gins, aromatics, garnish and presentation has elevated a simple mixed drink to the world of craft.

But that's not all. While many were talking about bold gins which emphasised botanicals other than juniper, and looking for a new name for them – new American, new Western – they needed only look east, or south, to a place where gin creativity was thriving across the country. Spanish gins range from the more typical to some of the boldest, brightest and most surprising. Contemporary gin is truly the world's playground and Spain might have been first to the top of the slide.

BELOW The complexity of this gin calls for a 'sip and savour' approach to tasting.

69 Brosses Desig Gin Destilado
37.5% ABV
69 BROSSES
VALENCIA, SPAIN
Contemporary

A delicate sweetness, means 'handle with care' here as heavy mixing will diminish this gin. It might be best enjoyed simply over ice. Soft and sweet on the nose, with intimations of talcum powder, Imperial Leather soap, violet sweets and light raspberries. The palate is a perfumed, floral medley of fruity sweetness. A slow, dry end with juniper as a background note; very short finish.

69 Brosses Clàssica Triple Distilled *37.5% ABV*
Contemporary

A clean, classically styled nose with juniper, angelica, coriander and a background note giving it some structural fruity sweetness. The spirit itself has a soft, water-like texture. Gentle, it might be the perfect match for something spirit forward such as a Martini. It hits all the marks as gin, barely whispering, but they're all there, along with a delicate violet sweetness.

69 Brosses Mora Silvestre
37.5% ABV
Contemporary

Intensely perfumed with floral coriander, rose and citrus blossom bursting forth on the nose. The palate is incredibly floral with notes of potpourri, Parma Violet sweets and even some blackberry. the perfume touches tend to overwhelm any of the gin-like character that may be present.

69 Brosses Naranjha Navelina
37.5% ABV
Contemporary, Recommended

Vibrant, with the zest practically singing on the nose. Exciting and stimulating to the senses even at the pouring stage. The palate reins in the orange notes by a fraction, giving way to some more traditional gin notes to come through towards the finish. The bright citrus flavour is distinctive and memorable as it is accommodating. Hot Toddy? G&T... or even a Spanish Gin Tonica? It works well in a wide range of drinks. Really quite nice.

Cool Gin 42.5% ABV

BENVENTO GLOBAL SL
GRANADA, SPAIN

Contemporary

....

This purple-wisteria-coloured spirit is definitely eye-catching. The colour looks as though someone dissolved Parma Violet sweets in a gin. And that may well be the truth behind it. Fake violet, aka the aforementioned sweet is on the nose at full volume. The palate has a surprisingly robust gin-like texture, with juniper, citrus and coriander in the background. Sugar-cinnamon and violet at the end. Can replace crème de violette in an Aviation.

NUT Gin 45% ABV

ARVENIG
L'EMPORDÀ, SPAIN

Contemporary

....

Light ligneous, savoury spices on the nose, with a minimum of sweetness coming out in the lower notes. The spirit has a lush mouthfeel. Vanilla, cinnamon, nutmeg and ginger all come through. The finish is more spiritous with a dry sprinkling of angelica. The finish is long and warming. Try NUT Gin in an Alexander; it seems custom-built for this cocktail.

Xoriguer 41% ABV

M. PONS JUSTO
ILLES BALEARS, SPAIN

Classic

....

Geographically protected, gin de Mahón is distilled from grapes, then rested in oak before bottling. It evolved when local distillers tried to meet the needs of the British when they occupied the island of Minorca. Gentle resiny and pine juniper on the nose, the palate clearly lets you know this isn't standard grain-based gin. Herbaceous juniper, with hints of basil and thyme, cracked peppercorns and meadowsweet on the finish. Lovely stuff in a Martini or a Negroni.

Ginself 40% ABV

CARMELITANO BODEGAS Y DESTILERÍAS
BENICÀSSIM, SPAIN

Contemporary

....

Citrus hits you right away on the nose, with all aspects recognisable: zest, peel, oil and blossom. But despite this, there's complexity in the mix of citrus, with even nutty notes of biscuit underneath. Thick, rich mouthfeel, redolent of orange shortbread, and marmalade. The palate ends with a bit of juniper and angelica poking through. The finish is somewhat long with bitter citrus notes lingering on.

Santamanía Reserva 41% ABV

DESTILERÍA URBANA
MADRID, SPAIN

Aged

....

A limited edition of only five barrels aged in French oak, then rested in a stone cellar that's over 500 years old. Lemon chiffon cake in colour, the spirit also has a grape base. With lemon and candy on the nose, the woody, earthy note deep down throws a slight contrast. The palate begins softly with fire-like juniper, oak and angelica. Sweet-tinged finish smacks of liquorice, juniper bark and fresh cracked peppercorn. Dry profile with a warming character. Lovely in a Negroni.

BELOW Hiding discreetly on the frosted surface of 69 Brosses's Mora Silvestre gin are the names of the many botanicals that make up its unique and aromatic flavour.

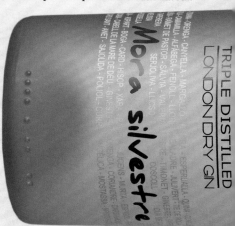

Switzerland

The land that brought us absinthe thanks to a French doctor living in Couvet, which is situated at the crossroads of central Europe, seems an apt place for another herbal spirit to undergo a transformation.

Local Swiss distilleries have combined local touches with Alpine water and herbs such as edelweiss, plus high-quality distillation to create Swiss expressions of gin that are as classic as they come, or are Swiss interpretations of where gin might be headed.

BELOW Xellent Gin is made from local rye and botanicals in Willisau, Switzerland.

Nutmeg Gin 44% ABV
OLIVIER MATTER
KALLNACH, SWITZERLAND

Contemporary

Unsurprisingly, nutmeg is one of the first notes present on the nose, but coffee and pipe tobacco hover in the background, as well as hints of wood and leather. Sipping, citrus and coriander shine brightly at the fore, while cosy warm touches coddle the palate as the flavour evolves. Ligneous spice and sylvan touches of leather and tobacco usher in a finish with vegetal and briny characteristics. Complex, well balanced and unique among contemporary gins.

Studer Original Swiss Gin
40% ABV

STUDER & CO. AG
FREIHEIM, LUCERNE, SWITZERLAND

Classic

Angelica and violet notes rise to the fore on the nose, while the gin itself begins with a pronounced dryness. Sweet cinnamon and orris root present in the background, to give the spirit sweetness following a more traditional gin character. The overall impression is reminiscent of a liqueur, but the sweetness doesn't overwhelm in a negative way. Citrus and warm spice to end. An interesting take on a classic gin.

Studer Swiss Gold Gin 40% ABV
Contemporary

You'll notice that there are minute flecks of gold leaf floating around in Studer Swiss Gold Gin, but gin drinkers will likely be more entranced by the unique aromas and palate. Herbal notes dominate on the nose, with additional aromas of dill and parsley. There's a slight note of brine as well. Lots of lemongrass on the palate, but citrus peel and coriander lend some depth, rounding out the perfumed floral notes with some warming spice.

Studer Swiss Classic Gin
40% ABV
Contemporary, Recommended

Resinous nose with green, leafy, herbal notes including fresh garden basil. The palate begins with a fiery kick of ginger at the front that complements a note of lemongrass. Fresh green and leafy notes, as detected on the nose, come on late, with citrus and subtle pine-accented juniper. Excellent gin with a nice balance to it.

Xellent Gin *40% ABV*

DIWISA DISTILLERIE
WILLISAU, SWITZERLAND

Classic

....

Made with local ingredients indigenous to Switzerland, from the rye base to the woodruff and lemon verbena found among the botanicals. The nose has warm hay, as well as a touch of anise and herbaceous juniper. Creamy and well-balanced on the palate, it's less about what stands out and more about how well it blends together. Floral hints and juniper are evident but understated. Try it in a Rickey or a Pink Lady.

BELOW Studer has been making gin in Switzerland for over 130 years.

Austria

Hiebl Destillerie Gin No. 1
40% ABV

HIEBL DESTILLERIE
REICHHUB, AUSTRIA

Contemporary

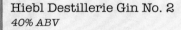

The nose is bright with lots of pine-note-accentuated juniper. The punchiness is complemented with creamy citrus notes. The nose's low notes invoke the feeling of terroir, conjuring an image of an alpine forest floor. Earthy herbs and floral notes abound. The palate is strong and loudly coloured by coriander, but those same perfumed floral notes, citrus bitterness and herbal, earthy character are present as well. Menthol notes on the finish.

Hiebl Destillerie Gin No. 2
40% ABV

Contemporary

....

Perfumed nose with bright, floral-accentuated coriander seed on the nose. The notes also call to mind raspberry, blueberry and violet, with citrus pine and sappy wood. The palate is similarly floral, with notes of talcum powder, violet, lavender and mountain meadows. The finish is boreal with pine forest, blossom and all the magic of the crisp winter air.

Monopolowa *43.5% ABV*

ALTVATER GESSLER -
J.A. BACZEWSKI, GMBH
DEUTSCH WAGRAM, AUSTRIA

Contemporary

....

Distilled from potatoes rather than grain, Monopolowa has a reputation for being rather inexpensive for the quality it has. The nose is lemon heavy, with a resiny pine back note. Fresh lemon notes lead into orange peel. There's anise hovering just outside the field of view, with a resiny, thick, but low-in-volume juniper note that comes on late. Good in a Last Word or Corpse Reviver #2.

BELOW The tall neck of the distinctive bottles from Hiebl reveal the nifty bottle forming the 'i' of the company logotype.

Czech Republic

OMG Gin *45% ABV*
ŽUFÁNEK, BORŠICE U BLATNICE,
CZECH REPUBLIC

Contemporary

Just when you think you've mastered all of your internet acronyms, LOL, someone comes along and turns it into a gin pun. 'Oh My Gin' is what it stands for and it includes 16 botanicals. Coriander and woody spice on the nose, while the palate is loud. Liquorice, violet and berry notes with a long finish.

OMFG Gin *45% ABV*
Contemporary

Where the F stands for 'finest'. OMFG adds one new botanical to the OMG formula. Damiana, a camomile-like aromatic with scientific papers attesting to its aphrodisiac quality (in mice at least). The nose is nutty, with accents of root and pine. The palate has a pronounced botanical sweetness to it; coriander and orris predominate at the expense of the other botanicals. Dry gin character on the finish, with juniper and spice.

Liechtenstein

Telser Liechtenstein Dry Gin *47% ABV*
TELSER DISTILLERY
TRIESEN, LIECHTENSTEIN

Classic

Alpine inspired reinterpretation of gin replete with local camomile, lavender, elderflower and three types of citrus. Coriander, lime and ginger on the nose. Warm, thick mouthfeel, with crisp juniper berry and neroli oil. Elderflower towards the finish with notes of fresh pollen, lavender and a bit more coriander. Good with tonic.

Lithuania

Vilnius Gin *45% ABV*
OBELIAI SPIRIT DISTILLERY
ROKIŠKIO, LITHUANIA

Classic

The nose leans towards lemon rind and sweet orange, with a vague fresh, grassy tone. It's quite dry and straight-forward at the front, with a juniper-like astringency manifesting even before the pine flavour really kicks in. On the mid palate citrus, with a slight soapy note, right before a finish with a hint of dill and celery. Relatively long, dry finish heavy on heat and pine. It mixes nicely, however, bringing punch to cocktails.

ABOVE On gins from Žufánek, the distillery that produces OMG Gin in the Czech Republic, there's a different kind of proof indicator, to show what the acronym OMG stands for.

Russia

Veresk Dry Gin 1898 *40% ABV*
VERESK KASHINSKY DISTILLERY
KASHIN, RUSSIA

Classic

....

Cardamom at first, with green juniper needle and then coriander in the lower notes. The palate starts off with green, fresh juniper, then resinous and sappy notes in the middle. Cardamom is present and centre stage once again; notes of lemon rind build into a finish that is a tad hot, but overall surprisingly smooth and balanced. It acquits itself quite nicely in mixed drinks, the cardamom note being welcome in drinks like the 20th Century or the Bronx Cocktail.

Slovenia

One Key Gin *40% ABV*
BIO-SAD D.O.O
ZGORNJI JAKOBSKI DOL, SLOVENIA

Contemporary

....

The only gin that you could seriously lose the key to, by design. Elegant on the shelf, the square design and peculiar pour spout arrangement is a tad unpractical. Nose is slightly heavy on the citrus, with ginger and juniper underneath. The palate is saturated with light citrus, lemon rind, candied orange, citrus hard candy. A slightly spicy juniper finish, however, largely one-note. Brings a citrus perspective to a Gin and Tonic or a Gimlet.

RIGHT Is it a glacier? Is it a mountain? The simple yet effective adaptation of the traditional dimple at the base of Studer bottles (page 134) is striking – especially when surrounded by gold snow.

Tasting Notes

The
Americas

A DISCERNING
TASTING SURVEY

USA

What the US has done with gin is as diverse as the nation itself. Old traditions are being executed faithfully, or being cast aside in search of something new. No matter what your tastes are, there's an American gin to suit them.

For the better part of the last century, it was the big British names that dominated American cocktail craft. It was in the mid 2000s that craft and small-scale distilling caught on, thanks to the government casting aside some Prohibition-era impediments. The number of gins proliferated from only a handful of American-distilled creations as recently as 2006 to hundreds by 2015. They continue to proliferate. Gin has never seen an explosion like the one happening across the US in the past decade. And it has spawned new craft spirits movements in the UK, Australia and elsewhere too.

BELOW Beehive Distilling's Jack Rabbit Gin shows its provenance on the neck label.

Abernathy Gin 43% ABV
TENN SOUTH DISTILLERY
LYNNVILLE, TENNESSEE
Contemporary

Tenn South Distillery uses vapour infusion and a mix of nine botanicals in its Abernathy Gin. The nose is a pleasant, and slightly traditional citrus with a dry spicy coriander aroma. The palate leads with a warming astringency and a hint of citrus, heavy with coriander on the palate. A medium-length finish has a dusty, spicy character. Adds a lively touch with added tonic, but I liked the way it worked in a Negroni.

ADK Gin 47% ABV
ADIRONDACK DISTILLING COMPANY
UTICA, NEW YORK
Contemporary

Made grain-to-glass with corn spirit and local bilberries — wait, what? They're small, dark in colour and though closely related to blueberries, are quite different, and native to Europe. The nose is quite fruit forward with boysenberry and cardamom notes. The taste, though, is up front, with a lemon balm herbal note, coriander, lemon zest and a delicate background of juniper. A slightly jammy finish with a touch of berry and lemon. Served with tonic, this is a beautiful gin.

Aria Portland Dry Gin 45% ABV
BULL RUN DISTILLING COMPANY
PORTLAND, OREGON
Classic, Recommended

Classically styled with an immense fresh juniper nose, Aria is like freshly picked and finely chopped berries. Soft and full-bodied, the palate sings with juniper at first, with oranges, cardamom and cassia mid palate, then coriander and peppery notes on the finish, with crisp piny juniper alighting on the tips of the tongue. A long, classic-style gin finish is perfectly suited to cocktails. Try it mixed up with lemon zest. Makes a fantastic Martini.

Austin Reserve Gin 50% ABV
REVOLUTION SPIRITS
AUSTIN, TEXAS
Contemporary

Bottled at an incredibly assertive 100 proof, Austin Reserve Gin is a great mixing gin (try it in your next Southside or Alaska Cocktail). With a strong contemporary perspective from the nose of rosemary to the crisp palate of juniper, fresh rosemary branches, followed by a floral note somewhere on the plains between lavender and orris root, and tart citrus rinds and back to the finish, which is long, resiny and piny with rosemary notes lingering on the back of the palate.

Back River Gin *43% ABV*
SWEETGRASS FARM WINERY AND DISTILLERY, UNION, MAINE

Contemporary

....

Owing to its proud Maine Heritage, Back River is inspired by its London roots but adds organic, local botanicals, the most surprising of which is the Maine blueberry. A hint of berry on the nose, along with resiny juniper and tarragon leads to a palate that is boldly contemporary and generally floral/fruit forward. The finish is bright cinnamon stick, freshly stirred with apple cider, citrus and a faint fruity note. It may easily be the most contemporary gin in the bunch, but also makes one of the best Gin and Tonics.

Back River Cranberry Gin
40% ABV
Flavoured

....

There is clearly cranberry here, but also tart cherry and orange zest on the nose. The taste is sharp, with a pronounced tartness again, which is quite clearly cranberry, but there are intimations of spice and citrus playing in the sides as well. This is spirit food for mixing, so try it with tonic or sodas, with added herbs and fruits. A Basil Smash or a Southside Cocktail are good starting points.

Barr Hill Gin *45% ABV*
CALEDONIA SPIRITS
HARDWICK, VERMONT

Classic, Top 10

....

A beautiful, simple expression of juniper berry, sweetened with raw local honey just before bottling. Though not technically an 'Old Tom' in name, it is similar in style because it's sweetened. The base spirit is thick and rich, the juniper expressive and bright, but what's most exciting is the way that the honey imparts floral notes that conjure up jasmine, tulips and sagebrush. Be literal and mix up a fantastic Bee's Knees. Or make an outstanding Martini. Hard to classify, but easy to enjoy.

Barr Hill Reserve Tom Cat
43% ABV
Aged, Recommended

....

Shimmering gold in colour, this gin takes Barr Hill's juniper + honey gin and rests it in American oak casks. The nose is equal parts juniper and fresh-cut wood. The palate is as smooth as gin gets: vanilla custard and pecan pralines dazzle. Bushy juniper rides in shotgun from start to finish, which is where it comes through most clearly. The finish is tight, but it doesn't detract from the beautiful flavour profile. This isn't aged gin for mixing, it's for sipping neat.

Black Button
Citrus Forward Gin *42% ABV*
BLACK BUTTON GIN DISTILLING
ROCHESTER, NEW YORK

Contemporary

....

The label says citrus flavoured gin, but I respectfully disagree. It's more a citrus-forward contemporary gin than a flavoured gin. While there's a hint of fresh mandarin on the nose, plenty of grain and hay notes add colour. The palate has got a peak of pine-forward juniper at the front, but it quickly moves to the background. Fresh orange juice, lemon zest and spearmint round out a clean, refreshing taste. Delicious with tonic.

Blaum Bros. Gin *45% ABV*
BLAUM BROS. DISTILLING CO.
GALENA, ILLINOIS

Contemporary, Recommended

....

Historic Galena, Illinois, was the site of a mineral rush in the 19th century. The mineral? Galena, of course, and it's a lead sulphide, one of the most important sources of silver. Blaum Brothers uses a different local resource: farmers and their grain. Each botanical is distilled separately and blended. Peppery and dry coriander on the nose, with a robust palate that is incredibly bright with fennel, candied orange, pine branch and a long, dry, slightly floral, slightly spicy finish. Exquisite in a Negroni.

Black Button Distilling

Jason Barrett, head distiller of Black Button in Rochester, New York, first learned the craft of alcohol production in the home-brewing world, in common with many other distillers. 'I became an avid home brewer in college and spent many years with that as my main hobby.' It was a visit to Washington DC that opened his eyes to the world of distilling. Having his MBA in hand, he noticed that gin was a less mature market and therefore might be a better personal fit for where he could make his own way and establish his own business.

He openly admits that he's a bourbon fan first, but that doesn't mean that gin is an afterthought: 'Gin is my second favourite spirit, it offers just as much as bourbon in terms of true craftsmanship plus the opportunity to deliver a unique product to the market.'

Enter Black Button Distilling, the first grain-to-glass distillery in Rochester, NY, since Prohibition. Jason and his team produce white whiskey, bourbon and vodka in addition to their Citrus Forward Gin, with more gin variations to come in the near future.

The gin uses their wheat-based vodka as a starting point. 'When I drank Gin and Tonic I would always ask the bartender for extra lemon or lime wedges...I found it was orange peels that worked best for me and my still.'

Black Button Distilling
85 Railroad Street
Rochester, NY, USA

www.blackbuttondistilling.com

Notable Gin

Black Button
Citrus Forward Gin
42% ABV

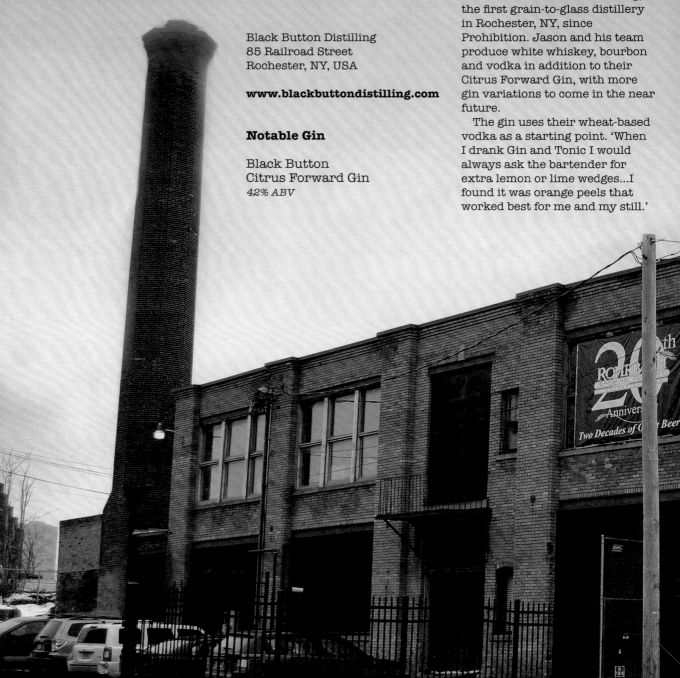

While the inspiration for the Citrus Forward Gin was rooted in personal preference, the rest of the botanicals draw from his experience in both brewing and classically styled gin. Juniper, coriander, cardamom, grains of paradise, angelica, fennel, cinnamon and two kinds of citrus make up the classic influences. Jason also adds Cascade hops to the mix. 'We steep the botanicals in the still pot overnight in giant tea bags and in the morning haul the bags out and put them in our gin box where we re-distil the base spirit, forcing the ethanol steam through the gin box...'

His hope for gin, though, rests not just on his own tastes, but also on his business acumen. He sees customers looking to gin for new experiences, and well-made gins will help win drinkers back over from vodka.

Using the lessons he learned at his grandfather's button factory (hence the name), Jason, along with assistant distiller Derek Carlson, production distiller Tom Stock and the rest of the team, is helping to bring distilling back to upstate New York. But more than that, Black Button offers courses and classes to inspire those who are looking to bring their own visions to reality.

Jason suggests trying his gin in a 'Gimlet on the rocks', but skipping the Rose's and going for 'freshly squeezed lime juice'.

ABOVE Based in Rochester, New York, Black Button Distilling produces small-batch gin that is distilled, bottled and hand-labelled on site.

MAIN PAGE The Black Button distillery, founded by Jason Barrett when he was only 24, welcomes visitors on a regular basis.

Bluecoat Gin 47% ABV

Philadelphia Distilling, Philadelphia, Pennsylvania

Contemporary

What once might have seemed audacious nowadays passes as a tad more traditional than we thought at first glance. The vibrant nose, swimming with mandarin and Meyer lemon notes hides, but doesn't obscure, a hint of coriander and juniper that's always been there. The palate is as citrus forward as ever, but still the juniper comes through brightly with a prickly and sharp character. The finish seems thick with angelica, pine resin and lots of citrus. Great in a Vesper or dolled up with a spoonful of jam in a Gin and Jam cocktail.

Boreal Cedar Gin 45% ABV

Vikre Distillery, Duluth, Minnesota

Aged

Infused with cedar, this gin evokes the feeling of the northern Minnesota woodlands through the company's choice of botanicals and flavours for their spirit. The nose is somewhat spice forward as cardamom, coriander and cinnamon greet the drinker. The palate begins with a hint of wood, as well as the spice from the nose. Juniper builds on the palate, tart berry towards the finish (black currant perhaps?). A long astringent finish reveals clear notes of cedar. Warm, and a touch spicy, definitely a gin that warms you.

Boreal Spruce Gin 45% ABV

Classic

...but it's not the spruce you get first on the nose. It's rosemary. The palate is an intense hit of evergreen forest, with rosemary, piny juniper, camphorous sage and damp spruce buds (likely the spruce?). Rather heavy and laden with evergreen, the finish is green, without being prickly or hot. It's a different expression of the pine side of juniper, and it works quite nicely. Try it in a Pegu Club or Moonlight cocktail.

Blue Line Gin 40% ABV

Lake Placid, New York

Classic

The 'Blue Line' is a boundary of the Adirondack Park in upstate New York; Blue Line Gin is an ode to the inspiration of this vast wilderness. A sedate nose has faint intimations of pine and pepper. But the pine isn't just metaphor — here the shoots of the Adirondack White Pine are used in the gin. Peppery, with notes of coriander, cardamom and pine/juniper as well on the palate. A long, juniper-laden finish is warmed with cardamom and cassia, too.

Boreal Juniper Gin 45% ABV

Classic

Designed to be a bit more traditional, the nose has juniper, yes, but also white cardamom. The palate still has a signature Vikre warmth to it (the base spirit is malted barley) and a camphorous, slightly herbaceous juniper note. Bright and evocative of pine without actually being pine-like. The finish has a touch of pie (like garden-grown rhubarb) and pie spice. Long, slightly herbal finish with a tinge of tarragon. Beautiful on its own, but this is also the best Martini gin of the American bunch.

Botanica Spiritus Gin 45% ABV

Falcon Spirits Distillery Richmond, California

Contemporary

Small batch Botanica Spiritus imparts its aromatics through vapour infusion. But when the spirit is diluted down to bottling strength, a water infused with Persian cucumbers is used. This is evident right away on the nose, with lots of vegetal cucumber notes. Lemon and Parma Violet notes on the nose, then restrained juniper with a holiday wreath-like note plus a crackle of coriander at the end. Finish is fairly long, with violet and angelica hues.

Bourbon Barrel Gin 44% ABV

WATERSHED DISTILLERY
COLUMBUS, OHIO

Aged

After resting its Four Peel Gin in barrels formerly used to hold bourbon, the gin takes on a Stil de grain colour. The nose is slightly citrussy with dry cassia in kind. The palate has cinnamon at the forefront, juniper berry and dried citrus zest in the mids. The finish is dark and peppery, with a good deal of cassia. A medium-length finish, dusty with baking spices. Try it in an Old Fashioned or a Negroni, but the Toddy was where it stood out most for me.

Bulfinch 83 Gin 41.5% ABV

WISHKAH RIVER DISTILLERY
ABERDEEN, WASHINGTON

Contemporary, Recommended

Zested citrus and lemon oil on the nose, augmented with green-note accentuated juniper as well. The taste begins quietly but rises steadily: initially citrus zest, cardamom and juniper with fennel notes crystallising into black liquorice towards the finish. A medium-long, warming finish with lemon and cardamom. Nicely balanced, with enough flavour to hold its own in a Negroni or mixed with a tonic syrup.

Candy Manor Gin 40% ABV

PAINTED STAVE DISTILLING
SMYRNA, DELAWARE

Contemporary

Prohibition-era lore runs deep in this country. The Candy Manor is so named for the local candy store, which was also a brothel. Order the 'Candy Special' to find the key. That key opens the door to... The nose is bright and floral, lavender, orris and a touch of coriander. Very floral and perfumed. The palate is brightly floral, with orris, honeysuckle, lavender, the finish taking on a creamy slightly citrus, but heavy orris flavour. Floral contemporary with a heavy hand, but quite nice, especially with tonic or in a Moonlight cocktail.

Big Gin

47% ABV

CAPTIVE SPIRITS
SEATTLE, WASHINGTON

Classic, Recommended

The flavour is big, but 'Big' was also the nickname for distiller Ben Capdevielle's dad. Juniper and peppery, warm spices hit you on the nose, while the palate remains big without being overbearing. A slight sweetness underscores bright herbaceous and resiny juniper notes, spiced orange and peppery notes ringing clear with grains of paradise and pepper berry. Really fantastic stuff, try it in a Martini or Clover Club. It's hard to go wrong here. Try also the Bourbon Barreled Big Gin.

Bummer and Lazarus 46% ABV

RAFF DISTILLERIE
SAN FRANCISCO, CALIFORNIA

Contemporary

The base spirit is distilled from Californian grapes, beginning its life as brandy before becoming gin. Lemon candy, berry and sweet herbs are on the nose. Mysterious and captivating, citrus and floral in nearly equal parts. The palate brings in lemon, a dash of juniper, sweet cinnamon, Concord grape, Parma Violets and Seville orange rind. A longish finish, generally dry and quite warm. Try this with tonic and a small dash of lemon and lime.

Cardinal Gin 42% ABV

SOUTHERN ARTISAN SPIRITS
KINGS MOUNTAIN, NORTH CAROLINA

Contemporary

From the foothills of the Blue Ridge Mountains, Cardinal Gin uses only organic botanicals. Camomile flowers, orange blossom, spearmint and the slightest hint of fennel seed. The overall profile leans towards a herb-forward contemporary style, but a hint of liquorice, herbaceous and resiny juniper in the middle leads to a heavy dose of freshly picked spearmint to finish. This makes a stellar Gin and Tonic, the mint hinting at a Southern Cocktail.

Vikre Distillery

Emily and Joel Vikre were working in global health and academia respectively when they decided it was time to 'make something'. Emily says, 'basically the whole pat urban-hipster-becoming-an-artisan thing'. Inspired by the story of some Swedish guys travelling in Scotland, where they heard the distillers boasting of their water, grain and peat. All of those things are common in Sweden as well, so they went home to make a whisky.

Vikre Distillery
525 Lake Avenue South
Suite 102
Duluth, MN 55802

www.vikredistillery.com

Notable Gins

Boreal Cedar Gin
45% ABV
Boreal Juniper Gin
45% ABV
Boreal Spruce Gin
45% ABV

It's been said that Northern Minnesota was settled by immigrants from Sweden because it was so similar to their native country. Emily recounts just how true this was: 'Minnesota has the best water in the world, we grow amazing grain here, there are even peat bogs in Northern Minnesota. So why isn't anyone making a Minnesota whiskey?' The idea of using distilled spirits to embody the terroir of Northern Minnesota was born.

'Even though the idea for the distillery came from whiskey, my preferred spirit for drinking and for cocktails is gin,' Emily says. The feelings and atmosphere of the place they moved back to for their distilling inspired the design decisions that went into crafting Vikre's line of gins. 'I became excited about using gin as a creative avenue to explore the traditional flavours of gin in combinations with more local and regional flavours and particularly other evergreen flavours.' The botanicals aren't strictly local, though the feeling they're meant to evoke is, for sure.

With the three Boreal Gins, each tries to highlight a different aspect of the north. 'Juniper is a little more...I sort of want to say domestic.' It's the addition of rhubarb that sets it apart. They use both local and imported juniper ('we haven't been able to pick enough volume of local juniper here'). The spruce seems rather straight- forward, as one might imagine it would smell like to stand in a boreal pine forest. 'It's meant to be evocative of standing in a glen in a pine forest. Dark, with a few rays of sun dappling through.' Cedar is a little more woody and evocative of a night out camping. Emily says a friend put it best, describing it as 'a breeze over the temperance river'.

Each gin is made from a base spirit created out of a distiller's beer made from 100% malted barley, in partnership with some friends at a nearby brewery. The base spirit is distilled four times; the fourth being the one where a gin basket is added to vapour infuse the gin as it condenses. This is all done in a 945-litre (250-gallon) pot still.

There's both a pragmatic and artistic side to the choice of gin. Sure, whiskey takes some time 'so people go around looking for something to make in the short term. Some make white whiskey or very short-aged whiskey, some turn to vodka, white rum or other unaged spirits, but many go for gin.' She adds: 'But you can also decide to make gin because it is a remarkable spirit for its beautiful complexity and history and the room there is in the definition of gin for experimentation.' Interest in craftsmanship, local economies and the heightened esteem in which artisans are held are all part of what makes gin distilling so attractive and why it's likely to continue to grow in the future.

Vikre, true to its Scandinavian inspiration, also makes an un-aged and aged aquavit, too, but it is also being patient with its whiskeys. For now though, it's the gins that are the stars of the show, and it's not by accident. Evocative and unique, they not only add something new to American gin, but you can taste the Northwoods, albeit different aspects of them, in each individual gin.

OPPOSITE The base spirit is distilled from local Minnesota grain at Vikre distillery.

Barrel Rested Cardinal Gin
42% ABV

SOUTHERN ARTISAN SPIRITS
KINGS MOUNTAIN, NORTH CAROLINA

Aged

The nose is a well-balanced blend of oak and spearmint leaves. The floral notes of the former are a little blunted here, with only camomile coming through in the early and mids. Oak and wood notes are strong, with a touch of vanillin. The finish is characterised by a blossoming spearmint flavour emerging from the oak tones and rising to a crescendo on the finish. Nice on the rocks or in an Alexandria.

Corsair Genever *44% ABV*

CORSAIR DISTILLERY
BOWLING GREEN, KY/NASHVILLE, TN

Holland Style

The nose is rich with malted grain. Intimations of hay, grass and then a surprising dash of ginger on the edges. Gingerbread anyone? Early on you get grain, primarily with yeasty, bread-like notes; the palate emerges with lemon rind, cardamom, cinnamon and the slightest hint of juniper. Warm and inviting, it works well in all the drinks that Holland Gins would normally be part of.

Counter Gin *40% ABV*

BATCH 206 DISTILLERY
SEATTLE, WASHINGTON

Contemporary

Albanian juniper, local cucumber, local lavender, infused and re-distilled from Batch 206 Vodka. The nose is a quiet split between the floral and herbal. For your orange and lavender, there's a tarragon and rosemary note. Juniper and a hefty hit of orange on the palate, with cucumber and lemon verbena hovering on the edges. A dry, 'green'-tasting finish; herb forward without ever being brothy. Nicely balanced, try it with tonic or mixed simply with juice. Sophisticated, but handles casual gin drinks with an effortless ease.

Coppers Gin *42.5% ABV*

VERMONT SPIRITS
QUECHEE, VERMONT

Contemporary

This features a little touch of Northern Vermont terroir, using local hand-picked wild juniper along with a few other traditional gin botanicals. The nose is built on gentle spice: coriander, cardamom and even a slight tinge of angelica. Heavy, multifaceted taste, with a touch of spice segueing into crisp orange peel. A background note of brown sugar, with a medium-long finish that's slightly celery, slightly pine. Fascinating and crisp, skip the Martini and go for the Alaska.

Corsair Steampunk *45% ABV*
Flavoured

Steampunk is unlike any other gin you are likely to have tasted, ever. It's either a smoke-flavoured gin, or one of the most contemporary gins you are ever likely to encounter. The smoked grain gives it an intense, barbecue-flavour profile, while the hops contribute a gentle bittering coda. But it's all about knowing what to do with it. Try it first in a Red Snapper or a Negroni cocktail.

Counter Old Tom Gin *40% ABV*
Old Tom

Take the standard issue, and already outstanding, Counter Gin and then pour it into a Hungarian oak Chardonnay barrel and leave for six months. That's how you get Counter's Old Tom-style gin. Rosemary and other herbal nuances with a slight whiskey colour on the nose. The barrel puts a really different spin on the spirit compared to the standard issue: cinnamon, and orange chocolate on the palate. Dry cocoa notes usher in a long, also dry, but quite smooth finish. Nice on the rocks; smooth, but not sweet.

Crabby Ginny 42% ABV
HARDWARE DISTILLERY CO.
HOODSPORT, WASHINGTON

Contemporary

....

Designed specifically to be enjoyed with crab, it is unusual in another facet, which is that its base spirit is derived from pear. The nose betrays that, with a crystal-clear pear brandy aroma. The palate begins with Calvados and pear, then hay and minty herbaceous juniper. The finish is a little bit briny, with hints of soil, mushrooms and other umami flavours. Fascinating and unusual, it shines in a Pink Gin or a Martini with a dash of bitters.

Dancing Dog 40% ABV
FLOOD FOX DEN DISTILLERY
FOREST GROVE, OREGON

Contemporary

....

The label of Dancing Dog Gin ranks among my top labels. Gin-wise, there's juniper, sitting crisply atop a subtle nose with cinnamon and lavender down in the mix. Once you sip it, Dancing Dog shows off its floral side in more detail. Yes, lavender is among the loudest notes, with orris and a tender touch of lemon rind, all setting it up for coriander then cardamom on the finish. A medium-long, warm finish with a bit of bite (no pun intended).

Death's Door Gin 47% ABV
DEATH'S DOOR DISTILLERY
MIDDLETON, WISCONSIN

Classic, Recommended

....

Juniper. Coriander. Fennel. If you are new to gin and are looking for a gin on which to hone your palate, this one might be it. And it's delicious in cocktails to boot. Juniper hits at first, sharp and evergreen, but although a dull pine note lasts throughout, it's not overwhelming. On the mid palate, coriander adds an exotic brightness that could easily be misread as cardamom or vanilla. The finish is crisp and warm, like your breath after chewing a fennel seed.

Crater Lake Handcrafted Estate Gin (2013) 42.5% ABV
BENDISTILLERY, BEND, OREGON

Classic, Aged, Recommended

....

Made with hand-picked Sierra juniper (*Juniperus occidentalis*), the Crater Lake Estate Gins capture the essence of any individual season: 2013 features lime basil, lemon balm and juniper before being aged briefly in oak. The nose is delicate, with the lemon balm of my childhood vivid on top. The palate is incredibly smooth, a gentle juniper made more herbaceous due to the backing notes. The finish is clean and creamy, with hints of walnut brittle, vanilla cream and pine cones. Lovely stuff.

Darjeeling Gin 44% ABV
CALIFORNIA DISTILLED SPIRITS
AUBURN, CALIFORNIA

Contemporary

....

The first legal distillery since Prohibition is in Placer County California, just north of Sacramento. It looks westwards towards India for the inspiration for its flagship gin. Flavoured with Darjeeling tea as the name might indicate, the nose is fragrant with toasted tea leaves and coriander, among other spices. The spirit is smooth, while green juniper, citrus rind and mint provide a bright lift. Earthy and warming, the menthol notes provide a long, bright finish. Best with tonic.

Denver Dry Gin 40% ABV
MILE HIGH SPIRITS
DENVER, COLORADO

Classic, Recommended

....

Sometimes the most humble of aspirations can result in the most extraordinary of creations. Nothing ostentatious, a modest-proof gin with a classic botanical mix – and the result is an American distilled product that can rival the big names around the world. Bright juniper-led nose, with a hint of coriander and lime, the palate rounds things out with just the right amount of earthy spice and a clean finish. A fantastic gin that works in any cocktail you want, perhaps a measly 5% ABV away from being among the very best of the best.

Captive Spirits Distilling

Captive Spirits is led by Ben Capdevielle, a third-generation distiller who fell in love with the creation of gin by way of his dad. 'He taught me the basics and I fell in love with it. I feel like distilling chose me.' Located in the distilling hot bed of the Pacific Northwest, in Seattle, Washington, Captive had its work cut out for it to make a mark. But stand out it did, and quickly, on the strength of its single-minded focus on superlative gin.

Captive Spirits Distilling
1518 NW 52nd Street
Seattle, WA 98107

www.captivespiritsdistilling.com

Notable Gins

Big Gin
47% ABV

Bourbon Barreled Big Gin
47% ABV

'Why gin? We drink gin. We only make gin at Captive Spirits and we do that because gin is a spirit that can be produced quickly, at world-class quality, with our signature on it.' The signature is as concise as it is bold: Big. Ben says: 'It's all about botanical quality and balance.'

Making a gin that lives up to the name might seem like a challenge. Big sets a lot of expectations. Ben first takes a corn base that he describes as a 'blank canvas of sorts'. He adds juniper ('Lots of juniper. That's what Big Gin is all about'), coriander, angelica, grains of paradise, cassia, cardamom, orris, bitter orange peel and Tasmanian pepperberry. The precise quantities were chosen because of how 'they make a juniper-forward, spicy-in-the-finish and complex-in-the-middle gin'. It mixes well. It's good on its own.

Captive Spirits makes its gin in 378-litre (100-gallon), stainless steel and copper, direct-fired Vendome pot stills. The stills' names? 'Phyllis and Jean, named after some of our favourite grandmas.'

There's also a barrel-rested variation of its Big Gin, which is placed into bourbon barrels. It maintains all of the bigness that defines Big Gin, but adds a creamy, slightly oaky, caramel and vanilla profile that brilliantly complements the spicy juniper of the original.

'As our gin-loving elders leave us and cocktail culture continues to thrive, I think gin has a chance.' It's going to be gins like Big Gin that evolve and expand the notion of what gin is, that help gin thrive and grow moving forward. Big Gin is on the forefront of the new wave of gins. Ben says that he enjoys his gin in 'cocktails that make me feel good', citing everything from the Ramos Gin Fizz back to the Martini. It goes 'mixed up with vermouths and bitters and everything nice'. Try it in whatever way you like, Big Gin has already become entrenched as a Big part of the gin renaissance. Right now Captive produce just two gins, Big Gin and Bourbon-barreled Big Gin, but with gins of such stature, you don't need many to really stand out.

MANUFACTURED BY

Vendome COPPER & BRASS WORKS

LOUISVILLE, KY

ABOVE The labelling line at Captive Spirits.

MAIN PAGE The pot stills at Captive Spirits are named after the founders' favourite grandmas – in this case, Grandma 'Jean'.

Dorothy Parker 44% ABV
NEW YORK DISTILLING COMPANY
NEW YORK, NEW YORK

Contemporary, Top 10

Dorothy Parker Gin is a triumph of contemporary-style gin. The nose is brilliant with juniper co-starring besides hibiscus, elderberries and cinnamon, almost as if a floral tea. The palate strikes the middle path of expressive juniper, with the elderberry, citrus and hibiscus evoking images of cinnamon-tinged cranberry sauce and candied citrus rinds. The finish is pleasantly long with lavender, elderberry and juniper nuances dazzling long after the sip passes. One of the best. Makes a wonderful Aviation.

Few Barrel Gin 46.5% ABV
Aged

If you age a gin with a white whiskey base, does that make it just a plain old whiskey with juniper? Perhaps, but the botanicals are the star here, make no mistake. Orange peel and creamy vanilla-tinged liquorice are all part of the nose. The barrel really adds a lot of character here, the finish is a stunning textural Bavarian cream, with intonations of juniper, fennel seed and even banana. Long finish reminiscent of banana cream pie with black pepper. Intriguing; sip it neat, or mix it in an. Alexandria.

Four Peel Gin 44% ABV
WATERSHED DISTILLERY
COLUMBUS, OHIO

Contemporary, Recommended

The four peels in question are lemon, lime, grapefruit and orange. A citrus melee flashes on the nose, though I picked up tangerine and key lime mostly. Lovely, well-integrated blend of the citrus zests. The palate is surprisingly balanced: herbaceous, slightly minty juniper, bright citrus and spiced notes of cardamom and coriander. The finish is long and slightly peppery. Beautifully balanced, Four Peel Gin transforms a Gin Rickey into something special.

Few American Gin 40% ABV
FEW SPIRITS
EVANSTON, ILLINOIS

Contemporary

Using white whiskey as the base for its gin might seem unconventional at first, but like many genevers or Holland gins, the base spirit is so much part of the taste: it truly makes Few Gin. Lemon zest and creamy vanilla/anise on the nose. The flavour is uncommonly smooth. Herbaceous juniper, cherry jam, vanilla and cream, coriander and angelica late. Though it's not as grain heavy as other gins of this style, try it in a Holland Fizz cocktail.

Fleischmann's Extra Dry Gin
40% ABV
FLEISCHMANN DISTILLING COMPANY
LOUISVILLE, KENTUCKY

Classic

America's first gin... first dry gin at least, having been distilled since 1870. The brand has changed hands many time in the ensuing century and a half, but the formula remains the same. Juniper and dusty coriander on the nose, celery and pine a bit lower. The palate is quiet at first, before juniper weighs in mid palate, with fresh grated coriander seed. There's a slight twist of lemon before a medium-long crisp finish. A classic gin but best when not mixed.

Genius Gin 45% ABV
GENIUS DISTILLER
AUSTIN, TEXAS

Contemporary

Using a half hot/half cold technique whereby half of the botanicals are infused in the spirit and removed before distillation, and the other half are added via gin basket and vapour infusion. The spirit is malty, with cardamom and zest on the nose. A warm, creamy palate with lime, juniper and cardamom. The spirit quality is thick, and it clings to the tongue, giving it a long, rich finish. Try it in a Gin and Tonic, where the citrus side rises unexpectedly.

Genius Gin Navy Strength
57% ABV

GENIUS DISTILLER
AUSTIN, TEXAS

Contemporary, Navy Strength

Here is everything great about the regular Genius Gin, kicked up to a stronger ABV. The bright flavours of the gin come through in the most demanding of drinks. Warm spice colours the first impressions of a Negroni. Adds a malty, spiced-orange rind depth to a Bronx Cocktail, or adds a touch of exotic spice to a Singapore Sling.

Glorious Gin *45% ABV*

BREUCKELEN DISTILLERY
NEW YORK, NEW YORK

Contemporary

The first gin distillery of the gin renaissance to set up shop in Brooklyn. The base spirit is local wheat with botanicals ginger, rosemary and two kinds of citrus. Still as distinctive today as it was then, juniper and herbs predominate on the nose, while rosemary and ginger complement a relatively mild juniper flavour on the palate. Grapefruit and ginger combine for a long, warm finish. Try it in a Tom Collins for a glorious spin on the classic cocktail.

Green Hat Ginavit Fall/Winter
45.2% ABV

NEW COLUMBIA DISTILLERS
WASHINGTON, DC

Aged, Contemporary, Recommended

Gin (juniper) + Caraway (aquavit) = Ginavit, roughly speaking that is. The nose is caraway, lemon, juniper and baking spices. Spices a plenty when sipped, orange and cinnamon, then floral mid-palate notes that call to mind the standard issue gin. Caraway notes come on in a little past the halfway pole, with fennel, fir trees and the slightest oaky sweetness from the apple brandy barrels Ginavit is aged in. Well balanced and memorable.

Gilbey's Gin *40% ABV*

W&A GILBEY LTD/BEAM SUNTORY
FRANKFORT, KENTUCKY

Classic

Yes, originally a gin distilled in London, the 40% version is distilled in the United States overseen by Beam Suntory. So it's technically now an American gin made under authority of the original Gilbey's (founded 1857). Technicalities aside, the nose is heavy with juniper and citrus. The palate is crisp with heavy pine-laden juniper, while the end is short and astringent. Ideal for mixing.

Green Hat Gin *41.6% ABV*

NEW COLUMBIA DISTILLERS
WASHINGTON DC

Contemporary, Recommended

The classic, the original. Green Hat Gin might be divisive, certainly if you're expecting only traditional gins, but among those who appreciate the merging of tradition with contemporary sensibilities that push the envelope, Green Hat Gin is it. The nose bursts with fresh orange, fennel seed and thick coriander. The palate colours in the herbal with cassia, dusts of ground coriander, celery seed and cardamom. Earthy, herbal, slightly exotic, but familiar.

Green Hat Gin Navy Strength
57% ABV

Contemporary, Navy Strength, Recommended

Dialed up to a robust 57% flat alcohol by volume, Green Hat Navy Strength is the amped up contemporary gin that cocktail aficionados have been waiting for. Equally flavoursome in a Singapore Sling or an Aviation, it can stand up to anything you throw at it. The nose is juniper, candied lemon rind and an iota of celery. Powerful on the palate, bristling with juniper and a strong peppery close with peppercorn, grains of paradise and an exceptionally long, hot, bright finish.

Green Hat Gin
Spring/Summer 45.6% ABV
NEW COLUMBIA DISTILLERS
WASHINGTON DC

Contemporary

What's more representative of spring in DC than cherry blossom? Millions attend the annual festival every April in the nation's capital. Juniper and an intimation of cherry jam adorn the nose. The palate is well balanced with orange candies, cherry/vanilla jam, *herbes de Provence* and pepper on the finish. Perfect for summer, this does it all: Gin Rickey, Gin Brambles, Gin Fizzes and most definitely a Gin and Tonic. Lovely.

Greenhook Ginsmiths Beach Plum Gin Liqueur 30% ABV
Liqueur

Beach plum is America's answer to the sloe. From the Canadian Maritimes south through Maryland, beach plums grow wild in windswept dunes. The small fruits aren't often eaten on their own, but when they are, they're quite sweet. The fruits have been used in wine, and now in gin. Specifically, Greenhook Ginsmiths in combination with its vacuum-distilled standard gin. Oxblood in hue, the nose is lemon lime, camomile, ginger and stewed raspberry. The palate has rich plum and cherry notes. Drink it on the rocks.

Greyling Modern Dry Gin
41% ABV
TWO BIRDS ARTISAN SPIRITS
MADISON, WISCONSIN

Contemporary

The name itself refers to a colourful bellwether fish of the Great Lakes eco-system, the gin uses local red winter wheat distilled on a copper pot and local botanicals imparted via vapour extraction. The nose is fresh with fragile pine-accented juniper and a hint of lavender. Nicely balanced. Juniper at first on the palate, coriander, hints of lavender and jam, and a crisp, long, dry finish. Enjoy it in a Gimlet or a Martini cocktail.

Greenhook Ginsmiths Gin
47% ABV
GREENHOOK GINSMITHS
BROOKLYN, NEW YORK

Contemporary, Recommended

Greenhook Ginsmiths uses a vacuum to achieve distillations at lower temperatures to better preserve some of the more volatile aromatics present in its ingredients. Noticeably vibrant nose, the taste is camomile and cinnamon at first, juniper with a piny oily character, then ginger, and a finish of berry and sharp coriander. Long crisp finish. Exotic and untraditional, it makes a vibrant but-not-your-grandfather's Martini.

Greenhook Ginsmiths Old Tom Gin 50.05% ABV
Liqueur, Recommended

Greenhook Ginsmith's Old Tom is pot distilled, sweetened and aged until it's a lovely straw colour. The nose is crisp juniper, cassia and walnut. The quality of the base spirit is exceptional, rich and oily, as the palate is generally spice forward. Ginger, nutmeg, almond, cinnamon are all present, as is a slightly citrussy lift at the end. Fresh cedar blocks and lavender on the finish. Only a touch sweet, perfectly suited for the Martinez or Tuxedo cocktail.

Halcyon Gin 46% ABV
BLUEWATER ORGANIC DISTILLING
EVERETT, WASHINGTON

Classic, Recommended, Top 10

Bright classic-style nose, with juniper, coriander and some citrus. The palate is warmly classic, with piny and green juniper, rich coriander sliding into a spicy/citrus note as the finish wraps up, complemented by baking spice and just a dash of orange zest. Long, warm finish with prominent juniper. Classic gin at its best, on par with the big names like Gordon's or Tanqueray. Halcyon is just the right proof to work in a Martini, with tonic, or indeed in any other cocktail.

Hat Trick Botanical Gin 44% *ABV*

HIGH WIRE DISTILLING COMPANY
CHARLESTON, SOUTH CAROLINA

Contemporary, Recommended

Lovely contemporary nose with traditional gin nuance: plenty of coriander, cardamom and citrus. Rich, full-bodied palate with piny juniper, a dash of lemon and bright pronounced spearmint. Long warm finish with a resinous character; juniper and rosemary notes lifted with a slight touch of angelica. Good with tonic, in a Martini, or a Negroni, or a Tom Collins. Versatile, stand-up contemporary-style gin with a slightly herbal edge to it.

Imperial Barrel Aged Gin (Ginksey) 47% *ABV*

ROUNDHOUSE SPIRITS
BOULDER, COLORADO

Aged

Golden brown in hue, Imperial Barrel Aged Gin (now Ginksey) has been rested in oak for at least 10 months. The nose is sweet, with hints of caramel and candied orange rind. Camomile, violet, cloves, nutmeg, allspice and cinnamon all clear and present up front on the palate. The oak contributes a warm baked pastry note on the back end. One of the most accessible aged gins. Perfect for a Negroni or Varuna cocktail.

Koval Dry Gin 47% *ABV*

KOVAL DISTILLERY
CHICAGO, ILLINOIS

Contemporary, Recommended

A delicate nose that calls to mind summer gardens: there's a herbaceous, slightly minty note of juniper, but additionally an almost spectral song of lavender and leaves. Tasting, you get lemon on the tip of the tongue, muted juniper and cardamom on the edges, but a peppermill full of spicy, snug black peppercorns. The finish is medium length with pepper, maple bark and baking spice. Swap in Koval Gin for your next Bloody Mary, or try it in a more traditional dry Martini.

Hedge Trimmer Gin 42% *ABV*

SUN LIQUOR
SEATTLE, WASHINGTON

Classic

Hedge Trimmer has a classic profile, but you can't help but notice one exotic botanical. The rind of locally grown cannonball watermelons grace this gin. The nose is citrussy with lemon, a hint of spice and a hint of bright hibiscus. The palate is wet with foresty, green juniper, offset by a balancing spice contributed by angelica and coriander. A little sedate in heavy cocktails, it shines brightest when combined with tonic water or soda water.

Jack Rabbit Gin 45% *ABV*

BEEHIVE DISTILLING
SALT LAKE CITY, UTAH

Contemporary

Beehive Distilling is the state of Utah's first modern-day distillery, and its signature gin takes inspiration from the desert, adding rose and sage to otherwise fairly traditional botanicals. The aroma is noticeable at once, with rose water, coriander and even a smidge of mint. Sipped, juniper and lemon rind emerge before the rose again. Basil and sage highlight the finish. This refreshing, contemporary gin is best with just tonic and ice, but is also good in a Gimlet.

Lockhouse New York Style Fine Gin 41.5% *ABV*

LOCKHOUSE DISTILLERY
BUFFALO, NY

Contemporary

Having grown up in Buffalo, NY, it is with great pride I cover a Buffalo area gin. Sage is strong on the nose, then the palate colours in the edges with some additional complexity. Fresh orange, then sage, spruce and pine-forward juniper grace the palate; the finish is clean and warming with lemon and background intimations of coriander and the slightest hint of anise. Although good with tonic, this gin works really well in drinks like the Aviation or Last Word.

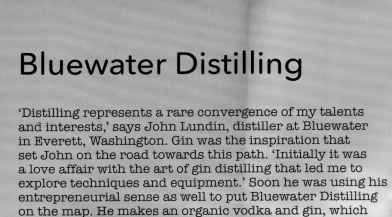

Bluewater Distilling

'Distilling represents a rare convergence of my talents and interests,' says John Lundin, distiller at Bluewater in Everett, Washington. Gin was the inspiration that set John on the road towards this path. 'Initially it was a love affair with the art of gin distilling that led me to explore techniques and equipment.' Soon he was using his entrepreneurial sense as well to put Bluewater Distilling on the map. He makes an organic vodka and gin, which represent the ideals he had when he set out 'to forge spirits from a responsible foundation, creating something unique both in terms of tasting and sustainability'.

Bluewater Distilling
1205 Craftsman Way, Ste 116
Everett, WA 98201

www.bluewaterdistilling.com

Notable Gin

Halcyon Gin *46% ABV*

MAIN PAGE Beautiful and traditional pot stills are used to produce the small-batch Halcyon that is a great classic gin, in the style of a Tanqueray or a Gordon's.

BELOW John Lundin, co-founder of Bluewater Distilling, recommends Halcyon for a perfect Martini, combined with orange bitters and garnished with an orange twist.

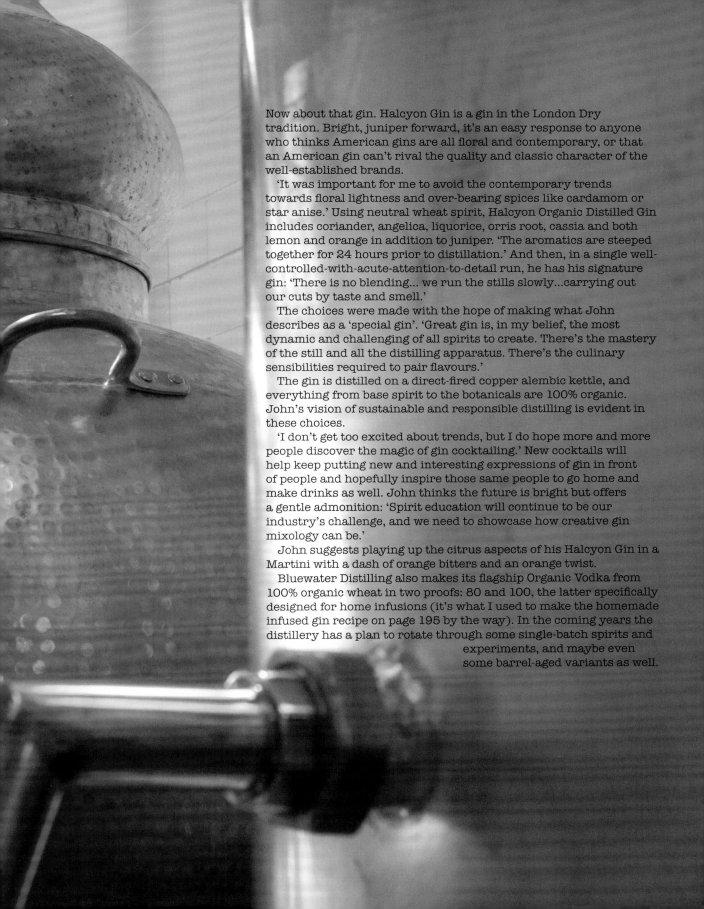

Now about that gin. Halcyon Gin is a gin in the London Dry tradition. Bright, juniper forward, it's an easy response to anyone who thinks American gins are all floral and contemporary, or that an American gin can't rival the quality and classic character of the well-established brands.

'It was important for me to avoid the contemporary trends towards floral lightness and over-bearing spices like cardamom or star anise.' Using neutral wheat spirit, Halcyon Organic Distilled Gin includes coriander, angelica, liquorice, orris root, cassia and both lemon and orange in addition to juniper. 'The aromatics are steeped together for 24 hours prior to distillation.' And then, in a single well-controlled-with-acute-attention-to-detail run, he has his signature gin: 'There is no blending... we run the stills slowly...carrying out our cuts by taste and smell.'

The choices were made with the hope of making what John describes as a 'special gin'. 'Great gin is, in my belief, the most dynamic and challenging of all spirits to create. There's the mastery of the still and all the distilling apparatus. There's the culinary sensibilities required to pair flavours.'

The gin is distilled on a direct-fired copper alembic kettle, and everything from base spirit to the botanicals are 100% organic. John's vision of sustainable and responsible distilling is evident in these choices.

'I don't get too excited about trends, but I do hope more and more people discover the magic of gin cocktailing.' New cocktails will help keep putting new and interesting expressions of gin in front of people and hopefully inspire those same people to go home and make drinks as well. John thinks the future is bright but offers a gentle admonition: 'Spirit education will continue to be our industry's challenge, and we need to showcase how creative gin mixology can be.'

John suggests playing up the citrus aspects of his Halcyon Gin in a Martini with a dash of orange bitters and an orange twist.

Bluewater Distilling also makes its flagship Organic Vodka from 100% organic wheat in two proofs: 80 and 100, the latter specifically designed for home infusions (it's what I used to make the homemade infused gin recipe on page 195 by the way). In the coming years the distillery has a plan to rotate through some single-batch spirits and experiments, and maybe even some barrel-aged variants as well.

Merrylegs Genever Style Gin
40% ABV

Oregon Spirit Distillers
Bend, Oregon

Holland Style

Strongly influenced by the tradition of genever, the nose is rich with fragrant grain. Malt comes to the forefront, and it wouldn't be a stretch to compare it to the nose of a white whiskey, if not for that liquorice note hanging on the edges. The palate is like drinking an anise cookie. A dash of floral rose at the front, spicy citrus and coriander towards the end. Long, chewy liquorice to finish. Try it in the Improved Holland Gin Cocktail.

New Amsterdam Gin *40% ABV*
New Amsterdam Spirits Company
Modesto, California

Contemporary

A gin brand that is widely available Stateside, it has unabashedly embraced the notion of gin leading with something other than juniper. Sedate citrus-forward nose that calls to mind a citrus-flavoured vodka more than a gin. The palate is primarily citrus forward as well. Juniper up front, but it fizzles out. A creamy finish is reminiscent of orange sherbet more than gin. Juniper makes it technically a gin; this is sure to be divisive among gin aficionados.

Perry's Tot *44% ABV*
New York Distilling Company
New York, New York

Contemporary, Navy Strength

Commodore Matthew C. Perry (after whom this gin is named) was the commandant of the New York Navy Yard in Brooklyn, hence the eponymous Perry's Tot. The gin itself is softened with the addition of upstate New York wildflower honey. Evident in some floral tones on the nose. On the palate, there is juniper starboard, grapefruit windward, with spicy coriander in the keel. Ahoy! Makes a great Last Word cocktail as well.

Mohawk London Dry Gin
40% ABV

Heaven Hill Distilleries
Bardstown, Kentucky

Classic

With juniper and ethanol on the nose here, the palate is sharp with citric hints of soapy lemon. Juniper is found in the mids, but presents as somewhat flat and inexpressive. Finishes quickly on a sour note, with lemon, alcohol and heat. Rather bland and the quality of spirit overall is quite harsh.

PathoGin (Batch 14) *48% ABV*
Stay Tuned Distillery
Munhall, Pennsylvania

Contemporary

100% barley base spirit, non-chill filtered, PathoGin is a locally styled Pennsylvania craft gin that embraces seasonal variability. Batch 14 is eminently Batch 14, with its own unique character on the same base/botanical blend. Mint and liquorice on the nose, the palate is robust with herbaceous juniper in the mids. The finish is exceptionally long, with anise notes and a warm grain-like character. Beautiful stuff, recommended in a Negroni or on the rocks.

Pinckney Bend Gin *46.5% ABV*
Pinckney Bend Distillery
New Haven, Missouri

Contemporary

Each botanical is treated separately with the respect its due. Some are macerated and distilled; others are suspended and infused in a vapour column. Delicate juniper graces the nose, but the mixture of those three different citruses come through most clearly. Orange and lemon notes upfront, crisp juniper next, but enduring through the finish along with dashes of liquorice and angelica. A clean, long and warm finish bridges the worlds of contemporary and classic gin.

Prairie Organic Gin *40% ABV*

Ed Phillips & Sons
Princeton, Minnesota

Contemporary

The nose is a bit floral here, with perfumed touches. Cardamom, spearmint and the slightest hint of herbaceous juniper are all present. The palate is soft, juniper up front and piny, but barely whispering. Cardamom and white pepper, leading into some coriander follow. The finish is peppery and herbal, and although long and warming, it isn't bursting with flavour. Restrained and slightly contemporary, it rests on its organic and handcrafted backstory.

St. George Botanivore Gin *45% ABV*

St George Spirits
Alameda, California

Contemporary

A captivating nose that is herbal, floral and yet still has the signature of juniper (pine note accentuated) written right across it. It begins with a rather traditional burst of crisp juniper and citrus, but it begins to evolve: spruce branches, cardamom and coriander. The finish is equally complex, with cracked pepper and fresh fennel lingering long and gently on the palate. Good in a Tom Collins, but also great in a herbaceous Martini.

St. George Terroir Gin *45% ABV*

Classic, Top 10

With a nose thick with juniper, pine, spruce, pine cone, pine resin and freshly picked pine buds, it famously smells like a pine thicket and tastes like a Redwood forest smells. Thick Douglas Fir envelops the palate, coating it with a thick layer of wilderness: bay leaf, oily sage leaves and sharp juniper round things out. There is nothing else quite like this gin out there. Many gins purport to taste of a place, but this one really does. Stunning with tonic; distinctive in a Martini, or utterly idiosyncratic in a Negroni. You can't go wrong.

R Gin *42% ABV*

Hardware Distillery Co.
Hoodsport, Washington

Contemporary

This seasonal offering is designed to be paired with oysters, but the oysters make an unexpected appearance in the gin as well. The barley used to make the base spirit was actually smoked in an oyster smoker. The nose is dark, with grain, mushroom and a hint of ripe cherry. Tasting wise, you get a hefty hit of grain at first, with pine-accented juniper that ushers in a long, dry finish with angelica and ginger, as well as a smoky spectre. Try it in a Negroni.

St. George Dry Rye Gin *45% ABV*

Holland Style, Recommended

Among the finest of the style, the pot-distilled rye shines through, branding this gin something unique and special. The palate is vividly coloured with tons of brisk, green juniper up front, caraway and mentholated liquorice, and then coriander and cracked black pepper on the finish. Warm and smooth, if you're on the fence about rye gins in general, this is the one to decisively put you on the 'I'm in' side of the fence. Drink it neat, or if you absolutely must mix, make it a Negroni.

Seagram's Extra Dry Gin *40% ABV*

Pernod Ricard, Indiana Distillery
Lawrenceburg, Indiana

Classic

Though moving on from the 'barrel mellowed for smoothness' tagline after its early 2010s redesign, Seagram's still maintains the signature light-straw coloration. The nose is slightly citrussy, with juniper and flourishes of coriander and angelica. Juniper, lacking edge, dominates early, but candied citrus rind, cardamom and cinnamon sticks and a fairly long crisp finish round out Seagram's. It's an ideal gin for mixing in any cocktail.

Seagram's Apple Twisted Gin *35% ABV*

PERNOD RICARD, INDIANA DISTILLERY
LAWRENCEBURG, INDIANA

Flavoured

Perhaps the most challenging of the Seagram's Twisted series for mixing beyond the Gin and Tonic. It adds a green apple candy note, apparent on the nose as well, to anything you mix it with. Paired with elderflower liqueur in a Spring Orchard, it makes for a rather interesting, if decidedly untraditional, flavoured gin drink.

Seagram's Lime Twisted Gin *35% ABV*

Flavoured

Lime and other citrus-flavoured gins were once fairly common. Gordon's and Beefeater are just two of the bigger names that have tried their hand at this style in the past. Designed to be ready to mix in drinks like the Gin and Tonic, it works well and there is no need to cut a lime. The nose has a touch of juniper offset by sweet lime, the palate coming off as key lime pie, lime-flavoured gelatin and candied lime.

Seagram's Peach Twisted Gin *35% ABV*

Flavoured

Although relatively sweet, and seasoned sweet eaters might recognise the flavour of peach rings chewy sweets, there's some juniper and citrus on the edges. Try a beach party drink of equal parts Peach Twisted Gin and lemonade. Sure, it's not the kind of thing you'd find at a speakeasy, but Seagram's Twisted Gins aren't trying to disguise anything. They're exactly what you think they are, and if that's what you're looking for, the peach one works quite well.

Seagram's Pineapple Twisted Gin *35% ABV*

Flavoured

Twisted gins work well as the kind of bottle you can throw in the beach bag, or take to a party and easily mix up gins with juice or other mixers. The pineapple notes obscure much of the juniper on the nose, but it yields on the palate allowing for some juniper and spice as well.

Seattle Gin *40% ABV*

SEATTLE DISTILLING COMPANY
VASHON, WASHINGTON

Contemporary, Recommended

Seattle Gin takes some of the best from the Pacific Northwest, combines it with a local red winter base spirit and a common (but uncommon in gin) botanical: hazelnuts. The nose is a spicy/floral melange, with minty juniper on the fringe. The spirit is smooth, with roasted nuts, rosemary and cinnamon at first. Juniper comes on the mid palate, coloured with a menthol-laden spearmint note. A long, warm finish has grain and lavender notes Lovely stuff for your next Negroni.

Solveig Gin *43.5% ABV*

FAR NORTH SPIRITS
HALLOCK, MINNESOTA

Contemporary

Rye gins are something of a lost art. Once much more common around the turn of the century, Solveig resuscitates the lost art by lending a herbal, citrussy brightness to it. Resinous pine, lemon zest and grapefruit oil on the nose, the palate bursts with fresh grapefruit, pine branches and ends with bright, freshly picked garden-grown thyme. A long, bright finish with a hint of rye coming through. Superb in a Gin and Tonic.

South River (Red) Gin 40% ABV

PAINTED STAVE DISTILLING
SMYRNA, DELAWARE

Aged

The counterpoint to its white Avant Garde gin, South River (Red) is rested for five months in a former red wine barrel, and therefore it's an unusual (for a gin) melon colour. The nose has hints of tea oil and soothing balm. The palate has a succinct juniper profile, with added notes of lemon, orange, herbal teas and a slight hint of Zinfandel wine. Interesting merging of gin, ageing and red wine notes. Complements other fortified wines (such as vermouths) in cocktails.

South River (White) Gin
40% ABV

Aged

Part of Painted Stave's Avant Garde Collection, it's designed to be a resuscitation of the pre-London Dry style of gin. South River is Navajo white in colour due to five months resting in a former white wine barrel. The nose is one part herbal and the other part resiny juniper. Gentle hints of sage and bay laurel set the stage for a triumphant, rich juniper display. Moderate in length with a warm juniper-led finish.

Spirit Hound Gin 42% ABV

SPIRIT HOUND DISTILLERS
LYONS, COLORADO

Contemporary

With locally picked botanicals, handcrafted stills and the foothills of the Rocky Mountains, Spirit Hound Distillers have both a beautiful location and a great gin. Fennel seeds on the nose, with lower notes of spice and citrus. The palate is rife with juniper and fennel. Spice notes lead to a finish reminiscent of chai spice. The finish is warming with fennel and anise cookies. Adds some zing to a Last Word cocktail, or makes a summery Gin and Tonic.

Spruce Gin 45% ABV

ROGUE DISTILLERY
PORTLAND, OREGON

Contemporary

The venerable company best known for its craft beers also has a line of spirits. Its Spruce Gin uses spruce to amp up the piny side of juniper. The nose is heavy with cucumber and wet leaves. The palate has a bit of piny crispness at the front, but it quickly devolves into a meditation on fresh cucumber with a dash of orange and ginger. The finish is short, but heavy on the heat.

Spy Hop Distilled Gin 42% ABV

SAN JUAN ISLAND DISTILLERY
FRIDAY HARBOR, WASHINGTON

Contemporary

Imparted with local, hand-foraged San Juan Island botanicals that include blackberry, rose and lavender, Spy Hop Gin goes for a regionally infused take on gin. The nose practically sings cardamom, the palate is spice forward and a bit edgy: coriander and cardamom again, with a dash of resiny juniper. A medium-short finish features fresh anise. Warm and earthy, a stark tonic water like Q makes a perfect companion for this gin.

Sunset Hills Virginia Gin
40% ABV

A. SMITH BOWMAN DISTILLERY
FREDERICKSBURG, VIRGINIA

Classic

Gentle quiet whispers on the nose, juniper is most clear, but there are intimations of citrus peel and fennel on the edges as well. Thick mouthfeel, but the flavour is rather restrained: the oily aspect of juniper, with the slightest peak of citrus early on. A rather tight finish with a faint pine note. Tends to get overpowered in drinks. Makes a fine tonic, but you might need to double the gin to get heard against louder ingredients.

Topo Piedmont Gin 46% ABV

TOP OF THE HILL DISTILLERY
CHAPEL HILL, NORTH CAROLINA

Contemporary, Recommended

Organic and distilled on a base spirit of North Carolina wheat, Topo Piedmont Gin has a robust balanced palate and works beautifully in a range of cocktails. At first aroma, there's ripe berry, creamy vanilla, lemon curd and pine. Sipping, there are notes of flaky, buttery pastry crust, velvety grass, cardamom and bright mint with juniper. A smooth, warming finish. This gin is as good with tonic water as it is in a Martini.

Wheeler's Western Dry Gin 40% ABV

SANTA FE SPIRITS
SANTA FE, NEW MEXICO

Contemporary

When I've driven through the deserts of western North America after a rain, the lasting image I have in my mind is the fresh aroma of sage on the air. Wheeler's Gin is more than just sage, the vibrant aroma is apparent upon first pour. The palate counters with celery and carrot notes, crisp dry juniper and quiet lemon zest. Long and smooth sage-led finish. Satisfying for a non-traditional take on a Martini, or paired with tonic syrup.

Wigle's Ginever 42% ABV

WIGLE WHISKEY
PITTSBURGH, PENNSYLVANIA

Holland Style, Recommended

Based on a 19th-century recipe, Wigle's Ginever is a regional reinterpretation of the Dutch traditional spirit, inspired by the melange of cultures that made up 19th-century Pittsburgh. The base spirit is rye, wheat and malted barley, and the attention to the base spirit is present even on the nose. Juniper on the tip of the tongue, while cardamom, vanilla and incredibly fresh lavender shine on the mid palate. Finish is a touch peppery, with a grassy/grainy back note.

Waterloo Antique Barrel Reserve Gin 47% ABV

TREATY OAK DISTILLING COMPANY
AUSTIN, TEXAS

Aged, Recommended

Waterloo Antique is the darkest barrel-aged gin we've seen. In the bottle, the colour almost looks like cola. The nose is caramelised with brown sugar and pecan pie notes. The palate reverts to form with a quiet expression of rosemary, grapefruit and even honeysuckle just before it transforms into loud allspice, clove and cedar. The finish is dry wood with nutty hints of pecan and molasses. This daring aged gin is perfect in an Alexandria cocktail.

Wheel House American Dry Gin 45% ABV

GOLD RIVER DISTILLERY
RANCHO CORDOVA, CALIFORNIA

Contemporary

Grain-to-glass, the base consists of white wheat and red winter wheat. The nose is warm with songs of grain, as well as liquorice, lavender and some vegetal brothy low notes, including ripened strawberry. The palate is spice forward, with plenty of juniper early on, setting things up for a finish with ginger, nutmeg and a dollop of chewy liquorice. Rich and warming, with a medium-short finish, it's smooth and well balanced. Good with tonic.

Wigle's Barrel-Rested Ginever 47% ABV

Aged, Recommended

If Wigle's Ginever is perfect for whisky lovers, then its barrel aged variation is something else altogether. A creamy nose with hints of applewood, vanilla and pine, the palate bursts with surprising complexities. Spruce, pine cones, freshly shed pine needles, juniper and then a finish with vanilla, cinnamon, custard and fresh grain. Medium-long warming finish. Beautiful spirit, a wonderful expression of tradition meets modern ingenuity: I recommend a Negroni or drink it on its own.

Wire Works American Gin
45% ABV

GRANDTEN DISTILLING
BOSTON, MASSACHUSETTS

Classic

....

If you were to look for a citrus that epitomised New England, it might be the hardy cold-resistant kumquat. Rare as it may be in gin, Wire Works puts it to work here with good effect. The nose is bright and junipery, as is the taste. Lemon zest and angelica back up a really perky, evergreen juniper note. Sweeter citrus crops up behind it, but the finish is long and juniper led. At 90 proof, it works well in Negroni and Vesper cocktails.

RIGHT The Solveig Gin bottle may be subtle but the gin within has a deep flavour.

Wigle Whiskey

Like all good ideas, the conception of Wigle's began over a few drinks. 'It seemed like a good idea at the time,' says Meredith Grelli, co-founder and new product development lead. 'After touring wineries, and with the latent history of Pittsburgh's pre-Prohibition whiskey on our minds, we suggested a family distillery back home in Pittsburgh.' Inspired by the wineries of Niagara-on-the-lake, Ontario, Meredith and co-founder Alex Grelli were ready to bring Whiskey back to Pittsburgh.

Wigle Whiskey
2401 Smallman Street
Pittsburgh, PA 15222
USA

www.wiglewhiskey.com

Notable Gins

Wigle's Ginever
42% ABV
Wigle's Barrel-Rested Ginever
47% ABV

The Wigle Whiskey distillery (never-mind the name, don't worry, we're talking about gin here) is located in Pittsburgh, Pennsylvania and has been doing grain-to-glass distilling with an emphasis on the organic and local since it opened its doors. But that precise expression of the grain in its gin was a result of Pittsburgh's historical past.

Pittsburgh was a diverse region even before the steel boom. Lauren Brock, new product developer at Wigle tells the story of how three traditions met in Pittsburgh, and how they inspired its gin: 'Scots were experts at turning grain into spirits, Germans could grow rye better than anyone else, and the Dutch were running distilleries making spirits from their homeland, including genevers from rye, wheat and barley.' It's not a coincidence that's the grains Wigle uses for its whiskeys are also behind its 'Holland-via-Pittsburgh' Holland-style Wigle's Ginever. 'Genever-style gins were the way of the world in Pennsylvania for most of its history and have all but disappeared,' Meredith says. A little bit spirit archaeology, a little bit something uniquely Pittsburgh, the folks at Wigle are doing something that won't be mistaken for just another contemporary gin.

It's not just the high-quality grains that make Wigle's Ginever, but also the botanicals, which add depth to the warm grain character. 'The year Alex and I developed our gin, I was consumed with botanicals,' Meredith says, talking of the jars and innumerable tinctures they went through while figuring out which would work best. 'We fell in love with the flavour of black cardamom paired with the juniper and whiskey.' Lavender was chosen for its surprising aroma, and cubeb because of how it supported the other botanicals and the flavour of the rye.

The process happens from start to finish on site. Organic grains are milled at the distillery, then distilled in a custom-built copper pot. The base for the gin is triple-distilled in order to provide a 'softer palette for the botanicals to display themselves'. The botanicals are added via botanical basket. Wigle ages some of its gin in used whiskey barrels to create a spirit that has the best of both worlds.

The future of gin is at an exciting crossroads. Lauren says, 'I see the future of gin as being one in which the customer is increasingly interested in the distillate, and not just solely in the botanical blend.' Meredith says she sees a future that leads to a 'regionalisation of gin expressions... we've got lots of interesting iterations, but what remains missing from the gin market is a sense of place.'

The team over at Wigle is currently looking at other expressions of gin as well, but they also produce organic whiskeys, bitters, honey spirits and rums.

OPPOSITE ABOVE At the Wigle Whiskey distillery in Pittsburgh, Pennsylvania, gin also gets a look in.
OPPOSITE BELOW The distillery hosts many events, from dinners and tastings to bottle-labelling parties.

Canada

Canada might not be first on your list when you think of places where gin is big. But it will be soon. Small-batch gins are everywhere, from the west coast to the Maritimes of the east. Distillers from places as disparate as Prince Edward Island and the Yukon Territory use potatoes to give their gin's base spirit a local touch, whereas British Columbia has exploded with gins featuring local, foraged, organic botanicals. Canadian gin has blossomed and come into its own since Victoria Gin's launch in 2008. There are now at least 30 gins in Canada, with more on their way. This guide cannot be exhaustive, because of how many new gins are hitting the market, but hopefully it helps demonstrate the range that Canadian gin has: from Prince Edward Island to BC, Canadian gin is truly in.

BELOW Long Table knows the value of small-scale production and labels its gins to endorse that stance.

Ampersand Distilling Co. Gin
43.8% ABV
AMPERSAND DISTILLING CO.
DUNCAN, BRITISH COLUMBIA
Contemporary

Just a short ferry ride from Vancouver across the Salish Sea, Ampersand Distilling Co is based on an organic farm, distilling a gin using an organic local wheat base and organic botanicals. Juniper, grapefruit zest and coriander on the nose, straddling the line between classic and contemporary. Spice and citrus on the palate, herbaceous juniper and a floral nuance with rose and violet colours. A dry, sweet finish. Use it for an Aviation.

AuraGin *40% ABV*
YUKON SHINE DISTILLERY
WHITEHORSE, YUKON TERRITORY
Contemporary

Straight from the Yukon, the distillers at Yukon Shine take a kind of potato native to the cold Canadian north, then combine it with barley and rye to create a rich base spirit. The nose is bright with non-Yukon fruits like lime and grapefruit, but the palate is richly coloured with traditional botanicals like cardamom, pepper, grains of paradise and cassia. All backed with a resinous juniper note. Smooth and robust and good in a Negroni.

Doctor's Orders Gin *40% ABV*
LEGEND DISTILLING
NARAMATA, BRITISH COLUMBIA
Contemporary

Legend Distilling forages its juniper berries in the wild, to capture a certain terroir that only locally grown British Columbian products can afford. The nose is filled with fruity and floral tones, with a gentle but distant traditional gin character underneath. The palate is initially classic with coriander and juniper, but it finishes with lavender, eucalyptus and blackberry. The finish is rich, dry and peppered with fading aromatic spice. Try it with tonic or citrus for a decent Tom Collins.

Endeavour Gin *45% ABV*
THE LIBERTY DISTILLERY
VANCOUVER, BRITISH COLUMBIA
Contemporary

The Liberty Distillery uses locally grown triple-distilled wheat spirit as the base for its gin. Twelve Botanicals and a copper pot still later, you have the Liberty Distillery's flagship gin. Upon pouring, floral aromas emerge: juniper, liquorice and a hint of honeysuckle is present. The taste is rich with black pepper, bright red grapefruits and a vivacious mid palate burst of juniper and citrus. A long, dry finish with a touch of coriander and liquorice-enhanced sweetness.

Gambit Gin 40% ABV
LUCKY BASTARD DISTILLERS
SASKATOON, SASKATCHEWAN

Contemporary

When in Saskatoon, use the saskatoons, right? The eponymous city seems a fitting place for a distillery to push the boundaries of contemporary gin with some local specialities. The nose is complex with lemon, camomile tea and anise. Once sipped, it's nicely bright with notes of lemon and coriander. A bright finish with peppery hints of celery. Robust and contemporary, it makes a nice Gin Fizz, or combine it with floral liqueurs.

Long Table London Dry Gin 45% ABV
LONG TABLE DISTILLERY
VANCOUVER, BRITISH COLUMBIA

Classic, Recommended

Handcrafted on a 300-litre (79-gallon) copper still, Long Table Distillery's gins embody the values of 'local' and 'sustainable'. Many of the botanicals are hand-picked or even foraged. The nose is fresh and classic, rife with pine and citrus. The palate is luxurious, with bright pine-note-forward juniper, lemon zest and just a touch of fennel. Long, dry finish with pepper and juniper notes. Especially good for classic dry Martinis.

Long Table Cucumber Gin 45% ABV
Flavoured

Takes the same botanical bill as its London Dry classic style gin and adds local British Columbian-grown cucumbers. The nose is literal with crisp, fresh cucumber, playing alongside glimmers of juniper and lemon. The palate begins with fresh cucumber as expected, but the spirit evolves, showcasing crisp juniper, citrus and baking spices. The finish is dry with a gentle peppery lift. Quite nice, especially with tonic water.

Iceberg Gin 40% ABV
ROCK SPIRITS
ST JOHN'S, NEWFOUNDLAND

Classic

Iceberg Gin is steeped in the romance of a lone man, sailing Arctic waterways in search of the perfect icebergs to melt down for use in his gin. The nose is clear with hints of rose water and juniper; however, overall it's rather subtle. The taste is classic and expected with juniper front and centre, then notes of citrus, coriander and angelica leading towards a finish that defines those notes a bit more clearly with grapefruit and orange.

Long Table Bourbon-Barreled Gin 45% ABV
Aged

The nose is surprisingly zesty, laden with bright grapefruit and citrus. Wood notes emerge in the lower notes as well, with vivid intimations of caramel, butter and cinnamon sugar. The palate is heavy, but surprisingly bright. Lemon zest early on, but later oak, buttery pastry, vanilla cream. The finish is rife with suggestions of mint, buoyed by a peppery heat. Delicious in a Negroni, or by itself on the rocks.

Oaken Gin 45% ABV
VICTORIA SPIRITS
VICTORIA, BRITISH COLUMBIA

Aged, Recommended

Oaken Gin is a rich shade of goldenrod. The nose is nicely aromatic, with subtle shades of orris, coriander and a floral/earthy bottom. When it hits the palate, lemon zest builds into a crescendo of juniper. It lasts only briefly, before succumbing to a sweet baking spice medley, with cinnamon, anise and a light floral lift. The ageing component of the spirit is evident, but never too in your face. Use it for an Alexandria or an Old Fashioned.

Okanagan Gin 40% ABV
OKANAGAN SPIRITS
KELOWNA, BRITISH COLUMBIA

Contemporary

Okanagan Spirits is a veteran of the craft distilling movement, having nearly a decade on many of the other local start-ups in Western Canada. From a fruit base, Okanagan draw on its extensive experience with liqueurs and eau de vies. The nose is slightly floral, with hints of rose, coriander and pine-shifted juniper. The palate is smooth with coriander and rose again, then hints of fennel and a long, dry finish. Good in Gin and Tonic, quite contemporary.

Prince Edward Artisan Distilled Gin 40% ABV
PRICE EDWARD DISTILLERY
HERMANVILE, PRINCE EDWARD ISLAND

Contemporary

Upon first pour, the spirit has an aromatic nose with menthol notes of spearmint and peppermint. Hints of lemon balm and a slight spice exist a little bit lower. The palate is rife with evergreen juniper at first. Mint comes through as intense with eucalyptus and mentholated tones. The finish is a little more of the same with shades of lemon and coriander. Provides a nice lift in a South-side Cocktail or with a citrus-heavy tonic.

Touch Wood Oaked Gambit Gin 40% ABV
LUCKY BASTARD DISTILLERS
SASKATOON, SASKATCHEWAN

Aged

Lucky Basted Distillers took its Gambit Dry Gin and rested the spirit in American oak barrels. The resulting gin is an amber-wheat colour. On the nose, oak and freshly cut wood, with dusty peach in the mid notes. Bright lemon hits the palate at first, with camomile, followed in quick succession by anise and fennel seed. Hints of nutmeg and clove make way for a crisp, slightly dry finish. Touch Wood Oaked Gambit Gin is smooth and great as it is, neat.

Piger Henricus Gin 43% ABV
THE SUBVERSIVES DISTILLERS
MICRODISTILLERY
KAMOURASKA, QUEBEC

Contemporary

I might not have guessed it at first if I hadn't read the label, but by Jove — there's parsnip on that nose. Parsnip is indeed one of the botanicals in this otherwise traditional gin. The palate begins with a crisp vegetal note, then herbaceous juniper, then a soft glow of coriander and cardamom on the finish. Subtle and subversive in a Corpse Reviver #2 or Last Word.

Schramm Organic Gin (Batch 14) 44% ABV
PEMBERTON DISTILLERY
PEMBERTON, BRITISH COLUMBIA

Contemporary

Eight organic herbs (clearly labelled on the bottle) plus locally distilled potato spirit, Schramm Organic Gin might be one of the most divisive gins out there. Exquisite in its bright aroma with rosemary up top, with spice and citrus as well. The rosemary segues into a bright mix of cinnamon, angelica and juniper. Hops loudly usher in a long astringent finish. May not be everyone's cup of tea.

Ungava Gin 43.1% ABV
DOMAINE PINNACLE MICRODISTILLERY
COWANSVILLE, QUEBEC

Contemporary

The neon-yellow colour might be the first thing you notice, but Ungava sets itself apart with six botanicals chosen to invoke a sense of the Canadian Arctic. The nose is lightly floral with hints of tea and juniper. The taste is smooth, but not entirely exotic. Coriander, with a spicy citrussy colour, is present early on. Seemingly traditional hints of lemon mid palate with a refreshing, but only gentle floral finish. Cloudberries perhaps? Great with tonic or in a Gin Alexander.

Victoria Gin (Batch 119)
45% ABV
VICTORIA SPIRITS
VICTORIA, BRITISH COLUMBIA

Contemporary, Recommended

Launched in 2008, Victoria Gin is the flagbearer for craft Canadian gin. Distilled in small batches on a German-made copper pot still, Victoria Spirits' gin is made with foraged and organic botanicals. The nose is orange, citrus, coriander and a wet piny note of fresh evergreen forest doused with rain. The palate is soft and slow, with rose and berry culminating in muted juniper and a citrus-led finish with hints of anise and baking spice.

Wallflower Gin 44% ABV
ODD SOCIETY SPIRITS
VANCOUVER, BRITISH COLUMBIA

Contemporary

Odd Society's spirits are designed in what may well be called the 'British Columbia style', with 100% local ingredients, all distilled grain-to-glass on site. The is abundantly floral, with notes of rose and elderflower. The taste is richly floral, too, with daisy, gardenia and bitter orange peel. A tart spice note segues into a dry finish with late hints of rose blossom. The gin's namesake, the coastal wallflower, is a member of the mustard family.

Wallflower Oaken Gin 44% ABV
Aged

As with Odd Society Spirits' Wallflower Gin, the nose is a summery assortment of floral aromatics. What sets it apart is the way that bitter orange and lemon zest notes emerge from the lows to give it a balanced, but surprisingly light nose for an aged gin. The palate has notes of oak, with bright candied orange and an efflorescent burst of rose. The finish continues to evolve with notes of mint, lavender and violet sweets.

RIGHT Victoria Spirits is not shy about the origin of the name of its home state, proudly displaying a portrait of the young British queen on its labels.

Yukon Shine Distillery

The romance of Canada (to me at least) lies in the vast expanse of the great north. It's the Northern Lights, the long winters, the cold and snow, the endless summer days where the sun shines for all but a couple of brief hours, and the vast wildness of the Taiga. This is the inspiration behind Karlo Krauzig's self-described 'one-man show' Yukon Shine Distillery. Set in his hometown of Whitehorse, Yukon Territory, his distillery makes both Yukon Winter Vodka and AuraGin.

Yukon Shine Distillery
Whitehorse, Yukon Territory
Canada

www.yukonshine.com

Notable Gin

AuraGin
40% ABV

OPPOSITE AuraGin goes through a total of five distillations at Yukon Shine Distillery.

Recent changes in the laws made opening a distillery possible. 'I saw this great opportunity to get in at the early stages of something destined to be huge.' Starting with personal preference, Krauzig opted for vodka and gin.

The 60th parallel is not the first place you usually think of when you think of a local food tradition, but despite the short growing season, Yukon Shine unabashedly embraces it. The grains and potatoes for the base spirit and the botanicals are sourced locally where possible.

If you talk potato and Yukon, you have to think of the Yukon Gold. Bred in Canada, it is one of the most widely grown potato cultivars in the country. It is fitting that Yukon potato spirit is part of the formula for AuraGin. It isn't the only thing though. It's blended with a distillate from Canadian rye seed mixed with malted barley to create a 'smooth velvety spirit'.

'Most gins play on juniper...in producing AuraGin I wanted juniper to add to the flavour and not dominate it.' Three kinds of citrus are added directly to the spirit, while another 12 botanicals including juniper are added to the gin via vapour infusion. 'The result is a citrus-forward gin where juniper is present but not overpowering,' Karlo says. Whittling it down to just those botanicals wasn't easy: 'I agonised for two weeks.' He tried all of the different traditional botanicals used in making gin, and tasted, then retasted until he found the ones that worked. During one experiment, 'at the last second I decided to throw the fruit directly into the spirit. The resulting spirit that began to pour out of the condensing column gave me goosebumps.'

AuraGin is part of a growing movement in which people are becoming more aware of what they're drinking and how it's being made. 'People are demanding more out of their experience.' Karlo also sees the trend towards contemporary gin as a positive thing for drinking in general. Some of the less traditional botanicals might help cultivate a more sophisticated palate and even 'hopefully replace some of the absurd flavoured vodkas'.

Designed to be complex and interesting enough to sip neat, Karlo recommends drinking AuraGin neat or on the rocks, but adds 'of course, I can't leave out the AGT (AuraGin and Tonic).

Thanks to changes in distilling laws, Yukon tradition finally has a chance to show its mettle to the gin world. The resulting spirit, I'd say, captures a different romance of the north, that feeling you get after coming in from the cold and huddling up with something warming. AuraGin is the light in the darkness.

Caribbean, Central & South America

Outside of the relative hotbeds of gin distilling in the United States and Canada, gin distilling is alive, but often with a local flavour.

Many regions of the Caribbean, Central and South America have some of the world's largest sugar cane or agave growing regions. It should come as no surprise then that many gins here use local ingredients. Gin is such a flexible canvas that the range within this one region could shatter any preconceived notions one might have of what gin can be.

Mexico

9 Botanicals Mezcal *45% ABV*

PIERDE ALMAS
OAXACA, MEXICO

Contemporary, Recommended

It's both a mezcal (the base spirit is distilled from maguey) and a gin (juniper is among the nine botanicals). The nose is smoky with charred wood, citrus and a touch of seared pine needles. The palate begins with mezcal notes, but you can detect the juniper building in the background. The finish smacks of charred corn husks and ruby red grapefruit. A bit unlikely but this really is a gin, with an agave base. Best served neat.

Argentina

Principe De Los Apostoles Mate Gin *40% ABV*

SOL DE LOS ANDES
MENDOZA, ARGENTINA

Classic

In the shadow of the Andes mountains, this gin features local botanicals and several touches specific to Argentina, such as the inclusion of yerba mate. The nose is half sweet grapefruit peel and the other half peppermint. The palate is quiet at first, with lemon peel rolling into a herbal mint and chive. Juniper comes on late, but boldly. A long, hot finish, leaning on peppermint. An assertive gin, good in a Negroni.

BELOW At Pierde Almas, every bottle in any one vintage is signed and numbered by the distiller.

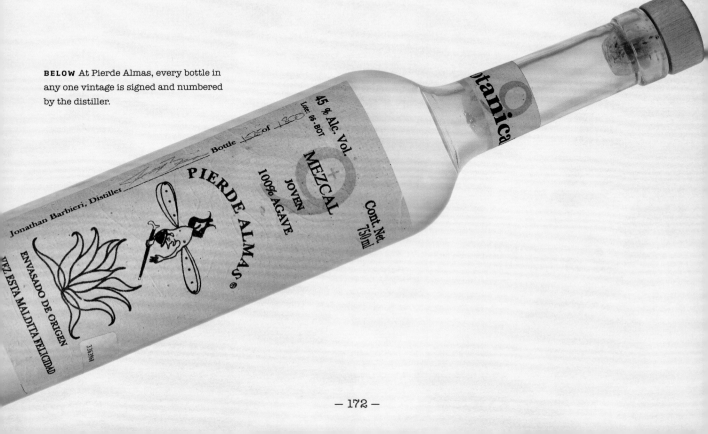

Colombia

Dictador Premium Colombian Aged Gin Treasure *43% ABV*

DESTILERIA COLOMBIANA
CARTAGENA, COLOMBIA

Aged

Drawing on Dictador's experience of ageing rum, Treasure is a gentle shade of Arylide yellow owing to time resting in barrels that previously held its namesake rum. There's a delightful aroma of lemon verbena and mint on the nose; the palate is intensely citrus forward with fresh lemon oil. Best drunk neat.

Dictador Premium Colombian Aged Gin Ortodoxy *43% ABV*

Aged

What happens when a well-known rum distillery takes a stab at gin? It shares two important things in common with rum. The base spirit is cane. And it's aged. Ortodoxy is Dictador's classic-style attempt at gin. The nose is juniper, orris and coriander, with a low touch of angelica. The palate is quite sweet with creamy lemon, blueberry pie and subtle juniper. Clean finish, with a hint of oak and mint.

Jamaica

Old Tom Gin *40% ABV*

J WRAY AND NEPHEW LTD
KINGSTON, JAMAICA

Classic

It is not an Old Tom by style. It's just a name. Jamaica's most popular gin is primarily aimed to be a mixing spirit to go with tonic or cola. Hints of hay and citrus on the nose. The palate has cane spirit/rum-like notes with sweet lemon. A tight, pungent finish with acidic notes. It can be a little rough on its own – probably best suited to mixing in cocktails.

RIGHT Yerba mate, an important part of Argentinian and other South American food cultures, is a significant ingredient in Principe De Los Postoles Mate Gin.

Tasting Notes

Rest of World

A DISCERNING
TASTING SURVEY

Australia

If the US craft gin explosion happened first, then the UK was not far behind and now Australia is the new frontier: gin distilleries are cropping up all over the continent, with many bringing something of their native land to the gin. It's not unusual to see botanicals included that are completely unheard of outside of their homeland. Bush tomato? Try West Winds Gin. Finger lime? How about Stone Pine Gin. Lilly Pilly? That's in Botanic Australis. Tasmanian Pepperberry? Wattleseed? Eucalyptus? Meen? There's an incredible food tradition spanning a diverse range of endemic flora that Australian gin distillers are starting to use for creating gins that are both delicious and truly Australian.

BELOW At Mt. Uncle Distilery, the symbols on its neck labels leave no doubt as to the country of origin.

Four Pillars Barrel Aged Gin 43.8% ABV
FOUR PILLARS DISTILLERY WARRANDYTE SOUTH, AUSTRALIA

Aged

This light gold gin is aged by taking the Four Pillars standard gin and ageing it in a solera of nine French oak barrels. Sweet citrus on the nose, with coriander, lemon verbena and lemon balm. Citrus notes dominate the palate, highlighting the woody, resinous juniper, and hints of oak. Cinnamon, cassia and other notes appear later, giving an impression of vermouth aromatics.

Four Pillars Gunpowder Proof Gin
58.8% ABV
Contemporary

Contemporary floral and spice-forward notes on the nose, with an intriguing paprika note just beneath the surface. Sweet aromatic spice gives the nose an intriguing balance. Not as intense as the strength might suggest, Gunpowder is sippable on its own, with the botanicals betraying the full power of the spirit: bright citrus, coriander, vanilla, gingerbread spice and sappy pine notes end in green leaf and menthol.

Four Pillars Rare Dry Gin
41.8% ABV
Contemporary

The four pillars that underpin this gin are: the still, the water, the botanicals and love. The love and attention to detail is evident in the first sip. Malty, creamy vanilla along with some fennel. Coriander and eucalyptus imparting a slight menthol touch as well. The palate showcases cocoa up front, coriander anise and fennel in the middle. The profile is quite contemporary, but booming with sunny spice. The finish brings a pleasant burst of heat to close things out.

Botanic Australis Gin 40% ABV
MT. UNCLE DISTILLERY WALKAMIN, AUSTRALIA

Contemporary

The side of the bottle reads like a field guide to Australian flora. Three kinds of eucalyptus, bunya nut, river mint and finger lime — we're far from finished too. The nose is peppermint and eucalyptus, as if a mint cordial. The palate adds some spruce and juniper up front, some peanut butter and sweet spice on the back. A long mentholated finish, which is completely unlike anything I've ever tasted in a gin, at least in the northern hemisphere.

Great Southern Dry Gin
40% ABV

GREAT SOUTHERN DISTILLING CO.
ROBINSON, AUSTRALIA

Classic

Like many Australian gins, the Great Southern Distilling Company uses some endemic botanicals (such as bloodroot), along with a grape spirit and a few traditional gin botanicals to create its gin. The nose is lemony, cardamom and slightly piny. Mixed spices at first, with subtle green juniper in the middle and a finish rife with hints of cubeb. Try it in a Monkey Gland for a spicy, Australian take on the classic.

The Retiring Gin 40% ABV
WILMOT, TASMANIA
Contemporary

The Retiring Gin is Bert Shugg's retirement passion, designed to be an artisanal small-batch Tasmanian spirit. Distilled from dextrose, the botanicals are added via four separate vapour infusions before being blended. Equal parts hibiscus and candied lemon on the nose; the palate is floral, with still lots of candied citrus, raspberry-lemon cakes, juniper and some peppery baking spice on the finish.

New Zealand

Lighthouse Gin 42% ABV
GREYTOWN FINE DISTILLATES LTD
GREYTOWN, NEW ZEALAND

Contemporary

Inspired by the southernmost point of New Zealand's northernmost island, it includes several New Zealand-specific botanicals: local oranges, kawakawa, and the yen ben lemon. The nose is one part gentle citrus, two parts fresh brothy kitchen herbs. The taste has a touch of the herbal note up front, but it's quickly pushed to the background by spruce and juniper. A hint of orris and bread segues into a clean, medium-long finish.

Ginnifer Golden Gin 49% ABV
GREAT SOUTHERN DISTILLING CO
ROBINSON, AUSTRALIA

Aged, Recommended

Aged in a French oak barrel, Ginnifer Golden Gin is shimmering and golden. A gentle, slightly orange/lemon aroma emerges from the spirit when poured, with cinnamon coming forth as it warms. The palate is sublime, a rich, thick, custardy vanilla comes forth, with anise and pepper. Finish is buttery and medium with just the right amount of warm, slow-moving spice notes. Sip in an Alexandria or Halja Cocktail.

West Winds Cutlass 50% ABV
GIDGIE DISTILLERIES
GIDGEGANNUP, AUSTRALIA

Contemporary

Featuring the native bush tomato, The Cutlass is the higher proof sister to the 40% ABV Sabre. The nose is bold and invigorating, with zesty lime peel, spicy coriander and dark chocolate. The palate veers more towards the classic at the start, with juniper, citrus and lightly warming spice. The citrus takes a turn towards sherbet near the finish, just as a milk chocolate note resurfaces. Dry, warming finish with resinous juniper on full display.

Vaiŏne Pacific Gin 40.2% ABV
VAIŎNE
AUCKLAND, NEW ZEALAND

Contemporary

Vibrant nose with orange and lemon. Juniper and some cassia/angelica notes hover on the fringe. The taste begins as classic, with hints of lemon, vanilla, almond and resiny juniper, then it's the citrus that takes the show mid palate. Orange and particularly lime, which leads into a long, bright, citrus-forward finish. Try it in a Tom Collins, Gimlet or Gin Fizz: anywhere you have a cocktail that is crying out for a citrus lift.

Four Pillars

Four Pillars Distillery is located in the Yarra River Valley, just outside of Melbourne in Australia. The region has a cool climate, particularly well suited to growing grapes, and has a bustling wine industry, with vintners bottling the high-quality Chardonnays that the region is renowned for. So it's no surprise that co-founders Stu Gregor and Cameron MacKenzie came from the wine industry. Lifelong gin drinkers, it was while working their day jobs that they formulated a plan to begin distilling gin.

Four Pillars Distillery
21–23 Delaneys Road
Warrandyte South, Yarra Valley
Victoria 3134, Australia

www.fourpillarsgin.com.au

Notable Gins

Four Pillars
Barrel Aged Gin
43.8% ABV
Four Pillars
Gunpowder Proof Gin
58.8% ABV
Four Pillars Rare Dry Gin
41.8% ABV

'Gin was a logical step for us wine folks. It's aromatic and textural and it requires a good degree of sensory training and an understanding of balance.'

It took a few years of working on the side to get Four Pillars Distillery up and running. Cameron talked about what it was like creating a modern Australian gin. It's more than 'wombats and kangaroos', 'Modern Australia is a blend of cultures.' He tinkered with nearly 80 different botanicals until he identified the classics he wanted to use, and the local botanicals that worked well alongside them.

Among the classics, Four Pillars Gin includes cardamom, coriander, lavender, cinnamon, star anise, angelica and oranges. Drawing from Australian tradition, lemon myrtle also makes the mix. Lemon myrtle is an evergreen, native to the Australian rainforest. Its lemon-scented leaves were part of the Indigenous Australian food and medical tradition. Tasmanian pepper isn't part of the pepper family, but the berries do have what Cameron describes as 'a soft white-pepper spice character'.

Partner Matt Jones soon joined the team and by December 2013, the distillery was open and their gin was on the market. The distillery had upgraded from the glass lab stills of the experimental phase to a 450-litre (118-gallon) CARL pot still named Wilma (after Cameron's mum). In 2015 it upgraded its facility to add two new stills: Judith (named after Stu's mum) and Ilene (named after Matt's mum).

They see the future as bright for gin and distilling in Australia as a whole. An oft-cited statistic is that the nation imports 95% of its gin. Clearly there's room for growth. 'We have some of the most unique botanicals in the world, incredible clean water and so on. The future for gin in general is wonderful,' Cameron says, adding that the gin renaissance has inspired many and 'we are seeing some amazing new styles of gins and loads of brilliant craft producers'.

Australia seems to be one of the most exciting nations to watch for gins, with a vast culinary tradition that gin distillers are just starting to tap into. Four Pillars makes Rare Dry Gin, a barrel-aged variation and the navy strength Gunpowder Proof, which bottles at a stunning 58.8% ABV. But gin drinkers might appreciate some of the other interesting things it is putting out. After distilling a batch of gin, it takes the organic oranges (now having been steamed in gin), and uses them to make a product called Breakfast Negroni marmalade. So you can now spread an aperitif on your toast. Brave new Australia indeed.

RIGHT & OPPOSITE Four Pillars follows other distilleries in naming its stills, but goes one step further by indicating on each bottle which still has been used to make the gin inside.

Vaiŏne

New Zealand is a pretty good place to live if you have an interest in learning how to distil spirits. It's the only place where it's legal to distil for personal consumption. The tradition of moonshining certainly exists in many other countries, though. Some turn a blind eye; others take their chances, being far from the watch of the government.

Vaiŏne
PO Box 11562
Ellerslie 1542
Auckland
New Zealand

www.vaione.com

Notable Gin

Vaiŏne Pacific Gin
40.2% ABV

New Zealand is different though. In the early 2000s, John Sexton spent his leisure hours tinkering in his garage, building a miniature distillery. As a man who loved gin, he went on to develop a gin to his personal specifications.

'I spent many hours as my dad's sidekick learning the ins and outs of distilling,' says John's son, Anthony Sexton. A rum drinker by choice, he was his dad's taste tester as well and quickly learned his way around gin.

Anthony says that 2008 was the tipping point, when he and his dad won the National Stillmaster Champion award for his gin and vodka, as well as being named champion distiller. 'From this point the idea took hold and we began to put together a business plan.' In 2012, they put up their own money and brought Vaiŏne out of the garage and to gin lovers in New Zealand and beyond.

Dairy farming is among the country's largest industries, and Vaiŏne uses these resources as the foundation for its gin: it's distilled on equipment built by hand from recycled dairy farm equipment, and the base spirit is distilled from whey. Anthony points out, though, that whey wasn't chosen simply out of convenience: 'This is by far the most pure-tasting spirit base on the market and this is exactly what we wanted, to really let the botanicals stand out as stars in our gin.'

Citrus is clearly the star when you sip Vaiŏne, but it's actually a blend of 12 different botanicals that combine to create the gin: juniper, coriander, cardamom, cassia, cubeb, liquorice, bitter almond, angelica, orris and then two kinds of citrus (lime and orange). 'There was a lot of experimentation as our tastes evolved as we went through the process', and the final taste is a result of more than four years of trial and error. The result is a 'Pacific theme' with a 'sense of tradition'. Something that is South Pacific in character but has inspiration from the British tradition.

Founding distiller John Sexton passed away in 2014, and Anthony now is leading the effort to make his dad's dream a reality, but he sees a bright future for gin: 'It is just in its infancy in New Zealand, but I'm already starting to see an increase of interest and quality with craft products... gin is currently under-represented in the New Zealand market and will continue to grow its share over the next decade.' He adds a cautionary note: 'Distillers need to be more descriptive of the style of gin they are producing, if gin is to reach the heights it is surely capable of.'

Anthony is hard at work on some new gins to expand the Vaiŏne gin line in the near future. But for now, he recommends a 'two parts Schweppes tonic to one part Vaiŏne gin, in a stemless wine glass'.

LEFT Anthony Sexton proudly displays his award-winning gin.

Asia & Africa

This short list includes some of the world's biggest gin-drinking regions. But many of their local gins aren't as of high a quality or widely available outside their local markets. With the gin renaissance making its way around the world, a couple of the nations here might well be the next regions to watch.

BELOW It is no surprise to find that a country visited so frequently by the British Navy has a gin distillery, in this case Mandalay, dating back more than a century.

Myanmar

Finest Dry Gin 41% ABV
MANDALAY DISTILLERY
YANGON, MYANMAR

Classic

The nose is slightly rum-like, with notes of sweet grass and just a smidge of orange. The palate is somewhat watery and thin, with notes of hay and spice setting the stage for a finish redolent of lemon and orange sweets. Medium-length finish with ethanol overtones throws the whole thing a little bit off. Best as an inexpensive mixing gin.

Myanmar Dry Gin 40% ABV
PEACE MYANMAR GROUP
YANGON, MYANMAR

Contemporary

Very sweet, almost sweet-like nose with strong lime sweet tones. The palate is heavy on the fake citrus up front, with orange and lemon, before a very mild and sedate pine note comes through. It has none of the usual sharpness of gin, however. The finish is long and dull with little depth. The sweet artificial citrus notes might be off-putting to some. Use this as a mixing gin for cocktails.

Philippines

Ginebra San Miguel 40% ABV
GINEBRA SAN MIGUEL INC.
PHILIPPINES

Classic

Ginebra San Miguel is the top-selling gin in the world, and the only gin brand to have an eponymous basketball team as well. According to the International Wine and Spirit Research group, each Filipino consumes nearly a litre and half (3 pints) of gin per year. The base spirit is distilled from cane. A harsh juniper nose with a hint of salt and acetone. The palate is sweet straw and juniper focused. A lightning fast finish, with a chemical aftertaste.

Uganda

Waragi Gin 40% ABV
UGANDA BREWERIES LTD
KAMPALA, UGANDA

Classic

Waragi translated means 'war gin', and although the term is often used to describe a variety of local moonshine products, this is in fact a legally distilled gin (and you can occasionally buy it outside of Uganda as well, as it is exported). Waragi is distilled from cane, like many other gins from Asia and Africa. Vaguely herbal, subtle aroma on the nose. The spirit is flat and thin, albeit quite smooth with a faint pine-needle taste. Underwhelming and it's a mostly harmless curiosity outside of Uganda.

The
Drinking
of Gin

A brief history of the gin and tonic

The refreshing summer tipple that we know as the Gin and Tonic hasn't always been the drink we are familiar with today. The origin of the concoction lies in places as far apart as the UK, India and Peru.

The indigenous cultures of the Andes were long aware of the healing properties of trees in the cinchona family and this plant species is widespread in the rainforests of Western South America. Europeans learned of the plant through their encounters with the Quechua peoples. At least five different species of cinchona have been used historically for their quinine-containing bark.

The Quechuas used the bark to stop the shivers and relax muscles. The bark on its own is incredibly bitter, so it was mixed with sweetening agents to make it more palatable. This tradition would follow the Europeans when they brought its bark back to Europe in the 17th century. It was quickly discovered that the drug was effective in treating another disease that caused shivers in its sufferers. Europeans now had in their grasp a powerful cure for malaria, a deadly disease once endemic to warm, swampy regions around the world where mosquitoes could flourish. As Europeans began their expansion around the world, this medicine would play an important role in enabling them to do so.

French scientists in the early 19th century were able to isolate quinine from the bark of the tree, enabling more doses of the powerful anti-malarial to be carried by navies or explorers as they ventured into places around the world where the disease was prevalent. Throughout the 1820s–50s, British naval and army doctors had a great deal of success using quinine as a proactive treatment. In other words, everyone took their daily dose and it greatly reduced, and in some cases completely eliminated, casualties from malarial fever.

Britain's colonial presence in India had a major effect on the drink as we know it today. In 1858, when the British government took rule over India, there were over 125,000 Britons living in India, with nearly a third of that number living as civilians.

This large population was required to take a daily dose of quinine, just as the soldiers were. However, when dealing with everyday people, perhaps a little bit more carrot than stick is required. In short order, entrepreneurs such as Erasmus Bond and Schweppes took to commercialising the now centuries-old technique of adulterating quinine with sweetener and another liquid. These commercially available tonic waters known as 'Indian tonics' were soon widespread in India. So it doesn't seem so much of a stretch to imagine how one person, fatefully, decided to add some gin to their tonic water. It was through British colonialism that the Gin and Tonic evolved and made it back across the world. By the 1880s, mentions of 'Gin and Tonic' appeared in British newspapers, meaning that the combination had made it back to the UK.

The drink has endured, and even prospered, around the world, remaining a summer staple to many, even those who don't need the daily medicinal dose of quinine.

Tonic water has since evolved greatly and now contains much less quinine than its forebears. Some supermarket brands contain no more than a token quantity as tribute to its Indian origins. Many modern brands are now sweetened with high-fructose corn syrup rather than sugar.

Fortunately, as with gin on the whole, tonic water has undergone a renaissance in the last decade. New brands such as Fever-Tree and Q Tonic are returning less sweet, slightly more bitter styles of tonic water into vogue. There's been a rapid proliferation of craft tonic syrups, which have more in common with the remedies of old. These syrups are often dark brown in colour, and contain pulverised cinchona bark and other herbs. They are combined with seltzer or soda water to create a more historical take on the popular summer cocktail.

OPPOSITE The G&T: a classic cocktail the world over.

Gin and Tonic

The Gin and Tonic

GLASS: ROCKS

1 part gin

2 parts tonic water

GARNISH: LIME WEDGE

Build in a highball glass. Fill glass with ice. Gently squeeze lime over ice. Add gin; add tonic. Stir. Garnish with a lime wedge and serve.

The Evans Gin and Tonic

GLASS: COLLINS

1 part gin

2 parts tonic water

GARNISH: LIME AND LEMON WEDGES

Build in a Collins glass. Fill glass with ice. Gently squeeze lime and lemon over ice. Add gin; add tonic. Stir. Garnish with both wedges and serve.

The Gin and Tonic (w/syrup)

GLASS: HIGHBALL

1 part tonic syrup

2 parts gin

3 parts soda water

GARNISH: LIME WEDGE

Pour tonic syrup and gin into a highball glass. Stir until well combined. Add ice and soda water. Stir again until well combined. Gently squeeze lime wedge over drink, garnish with a lime wedge and serve.

The Cure-All

GLASS: HIGHBALL

1 part gin

2 parts tonic water

3 dashes Angostura bitters

¼ lime

GARNISH: LIME WEDGE

Squeeze lime over ice in a highball glass. Add gin, tonic water and bitters. Gently stir with ice until well combined. Serve.

RIGHT Gin Tonica, Gin & Elderflower Tonic (see page 189) and the classic G&T.

One Possible Gin Tonica

GLASS: LARGE RED WINE GLASS

5 parts gin

2 parts tonic water

2 black cardamom pods

Peel of 1 lemon, spiralled by peeling all the way around the fruit in one long stroke.

GARNISH: LEMON PEEL, JUNIPER BERRIES

Chill a large red wine glass. Gently open cardamom pods so that you can smell the aroma. Place lemon peel in wine glass so that it hugs the edges. Pour gin over the cardamom and lemon. Let it sit for one minute. Add tonic. Serve.

Gin Tonica (short for Gin and Tonic) is something of a phenomenon in Spain. Take a gin, add a tonic, serve it in a large red wine glass, often called a balloon or copa glass, then throw out all you know about Gin and Tonic garnish. Twist the peel of an entire lemon. Add some cardamom pods. Maybe a juniper berry or ten. The garnish has been pushed from mere formality into an entire art. What aroma will it impart? How will it look? What flavours does that gin require to hit the next level? The large glass gives the gin and aromas more space to do their work. Then there's the ice. The science of the ice in a classic Gin Tonica is a big deal as well. Twice frozen ice? Cracked in a certain way to maximise chilling and reduce dilution? Yep, it's all there.

Entire bars devoted to the concept have opened all over Spain, including Bobby Gin in Madrid, and Elephanta and Xixbar in Barcelona.

The style is making its way around the world. The London Gin Club, for example, is one of many bars outside of Spain that serve Gin and Tonics in this style. Many bars in New York City serve their Gin and Tonics in oversized balloon glasses. So the next time your G&T arrives in a red wine glass, you know where it all started.

Top places for a G&T

The London Gin Club (at The Star)
22 Great Chapel Street
London, UK
www.thelondonginclub.com

Great selection of gins, with an extensive menu dedicated to Gin and Tonics, served in copa glasses with specially paired botanicals. Even has a house-designed gin, 7 dials.

Oceana
120 West 49th Street
New York, USA
www.oceanarestaurant.com

Its gin collection is among the best in the city, but it sets itself apart with its line of house-made tonic syrups, each defined only by a flavour profile like 'citrus' or 'bitter'.

Le Pourvoyeur
184 Jean Talon E
Montreal, Quebec, Canada
www.lepourvoyeur.com

Self-fashioned 'gin pub' with well-made cocktails and gin-tasting flights. Distinguishes itself with egalitarian gin selection, giving equal weight to local (in particular Québécois), French, Spanish and Scottish gins.

The G&T Bar
Friedrichstraße 113
Berlin, Germany
www.gintonic@amanogroup.com

Single-minded dedication to the art of Gin and Tonic that comes with a dash of the unusual. Worth trying are the line of Tanqueray + tonic + tea (yes!) + a dash of bitters cocktails.

Elephanta
37 Torrent d'en Vidalet
Barcelona, Spain
www.elephanta.cat

Friendly staff and and an expansive selection of gins and tonics including local specialities and well-known favourites, all garnished and dolled up in true Gin Tonica style.

Some perfect gin and tonic combinations

How do you pick the perfect gin to go with your tonic?

It's easy when there's a companion gin and tonic already on the market. Take for example the case of Six O'Clock Gin. The gin itself has notes of elderflower, coriander and juniper, with orange rind on the finish. The companion tonic rounds things out with a bit more citrus up top and a long, dry finish. Combine the two and something wonderful happens. Mix in a rocks glass, with ice of course.

Pinckney Bend Distillery in Missouri, USA, produces a gin that is bright, citrussy and warming. Its tonic syrup is complex with warm, woody and musky floral overtones. Put them together with a bit of soda water, and create magic in your glass.

But not every gin distiller is so prescriptive as to have designed a companion tonic that considers the flavours of both so fully as to bring out the best in both. And Pinckney Bend's gin is equally delicious when combined with plenty of other tonics, and its tonic syrup complements many others gins, too.

There's a lot of considerations to bear in mind. If you're working with a classic, clean tonic water like Fever-Tree, nearly anything goes. If you're working with one of the bolder-flavoured tonic waters or tonic syrups, though, a little bit of gin-sense can make a big difference between an okay drink and a great one.

Strong-grain gin with tonic

There is a growing trend for gins with a pronounced base spirit that has a strong grain flavour. Some of these work well with regular tonics, some of them not so well. This is why Bradley's Bourbon Barrel Aged Kina Tonic syrup is such an interesting option for the home bartender. It adds some woody, caramelised depth to whatever you mix it with. Given how well grain and wood notes work together, the two can create some magic with gins you might not normally consider as Gin and Tonic material. Vor Gin from Iceland works well with tonic; however, when paired with this syrup, it takes both to a whole new level.

1 part Vor Gin
2 parts Bradley's Bourbon Barrel-Aged Kina Tonic
5 parts soda water
NO GARNISH

Gin and Hansen's tonic

When working with a really citrussy gin or citrus tonic, you can pair like with like, or look for an interesting or intriguing contrast. I think this combination of Jack Rabbit Gin from Utah and Hansen's Tonic with California citrus, creates something a little unexpected that brings out the best in both.

1 part Jack Rabbit Gin
2 parts Hansen's Tonic
GARNISH WITH ORANGE TWIST

Gin and bitter tonic

Imagine this: you're on a camping trip. A beautiful summer night. You've brought a top-notch gin, but the only tonic water that's left are cans that are in the ice box. It might not be your cup of tea. You might wish you'd brought your craft syrup from home; however, you have to make do. You know the tonic will provide some requisite bitterness, but for that next level? Try packing some of The Bitter Truth's Gin and Tonic Bitters. Guaranteed to elevate your next Gin and Tonic.

3 parts Lord Astor London Dry Gin
4 parts Canada Dry tonic water
3 dashes The Bitter Truth Gin and Tonic Bitters
GARNISH WITH LIME WEDGE (OPTIONAL)

Flavoured gins with tonic

When mixing tonic with flavoured gins, you can always play it safe and come out with a gin that leads with the intended flavour. However, the right tonic can really change the impression a gin leaves. Back River Cranberry Gin from Sweetgrass Farm Winery is a good gin that delivers what you expect. When paired with Fever-Tree's Mediterranean Tonic Water, the herbal notes combine to create a Gin and Tonic that might be the perfect accompaniment at a Thanksgiving dinner or harvest celebration.

1 part Back River Cranberry Gin
3 parts Fever-Tree Mediterranean Tonic Water
1 dash Angostura bitters
GARNISH WITH LIME WEDGE

On the other side of the coin, Williams Chase Seville Orange Gin has a bright citrussy orange-led palate with a dry finish. I suggest pairing it with a less citrus-forward tonic water to allow the Seville Orange notes to shine. Q Tonic does this nicely, and then we add a lemon twist for a little bit of aromatic complement, which also adds some contrast to highlight the orange notes.

1 part Williams Chase
   Seville Orange Gin
2 parts Q Tonic
GARNISH WITH LEMON TWIST

Gin with elderflower tonics

There are a few elderflower-heavy tonics on the market right now. It would be a mistake to take the bright elderflower aromatics of Warner Edwards Elderflower Gin or Knockeen Hills Elderflower Gin and pair it with such a literal tonic. In fact, I think some of the most classic-style gins not only add the most to an elderflower tonic, but also benefit the most from that high, bright floral note. I left out a garnish in this case because the elderflower aroma from the tonic is bold enough for this G&T.

2 parts Sunset Hills Virginia Gin
3 parts Fever-Tree Elderflower Tonic
NO GARNISH

A variation on elderflower tonic is available from Jack Rudy's Cocktail Co. who makes an elderflower tonic syrup of its own that adds a bold floral richness to any gin. For contrast, I chose a gin with some pronounced menthol notes. Ripe with hints of mint and eucalyptus, Mt. Uncle Distillery's Botanic Australis Gin has 14 native Australian botanicals. Nope, elderflower is not among them. The combination of the two is a little bit of east meets west, north meets south, with the two combining to create something unique.

2 parts Botanic Australis Gin
1 parts Jack Rudy Cocktail Co.'s
   Elderflower Tonic
3 parts soda water
NO GARNISH

Gin with Fentiman's tonic

Fentiman's Tonic can be a bright complementary addition to a gin and tonic that truly elevates the drink to new heights. Or it can absolutely overpower a gin. Fortunately there are many more opportunities of the former variety to use it in. I tried it with Schramm Organic Gin from Pemberton Distillery. Schramm gin is uniquely and powerfully herbal with a complex melange of citrus, rosemary and hops. Pairing it with a bold tonic creats a loud harmony of lemongrass, citrus and fresh herbs.

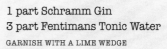

1 part Schramm Gin
3 part Fentimans Tonic Water
GARNISH WITH A LIME WEDGE

Tonic water

What is Tonic Water?

Tonic water is usually bottled and carbonated. Most commercially produced types are sweetened, ranging from the only slightly sweet taste of Q Tonic or Fever Tree to the overwhelming cloying notes of sweetened supermarket brands. The amount of quinine in supermarket brands is miniscule, with only a slight hint of bitterness. Premium brands vary, some use other flavours such as elderflower or lemongrass to create a different flavour profile; others still play with sweetening or quinine content to produce a more bitter or more sweet drink.

But generally when we talk about tonic water we're talking about something that is ready to drink directly from the bottle.

Tonic Water Tasting Notes

Canada Dry Tonic Water

INGREDIENTS: CARBONATED WATER, HIGH FRUCTOSE CORN SYRUP, CITRIC ACID, SODIUM BENZOATE (PRESERVATIVE), QUININE, NATURAL FLAVOURS

Crisp and effervescent, with a good deal of fizz towing the line of sweetness and saccharine. Finish is still sweet, with a bitter note that marks a sudden coda. Though it might be lacking in complexity, there's appeal in the simplicity. Utterly devoid of pretentiousness, it's going to let your gin be your gin. It might be too sweet for some.

Fentimans Tonic Water

INGREDIENTS: CARBONATED WATER, CANE SUGAR, CITRIC ACID, TONIC FLAVOUR (WATER, LEMON OIL, ETHANOL, LEMON GRASS OIL), QUININE (10MG)

'Botanically brewed' seems an odd descriptor for a tonic water, but the reasoning is clear from first taste: lemon zest dominates early, but it takes on a greener slightly vegetal character as a protracted bitter astringency comes on. Lemongrass and a faint tartness endure on their own. It's a loud tonic water that complements classic-style gins nicely, but its notes can clash with contemporary gins or obscure, subtle gins.

Fever-Tree Tonic Water

INGREDIENTS: SPRING WATER, CANE SUGAR, CITRIC ACID, NATURAL FLAVOURS, NATURAL QUININE

A bright and clean tonic, it has a perceptible lemon and orange overtone on the nose. Very smooth tasting, with a subtle, restrained effervescence that allows for the flavours of the tonic and gin to take centre stage. Finish has a clean quinine-led bitterness that has a faint tartness of lime and bitter orange in the background. Nicely balanced and highly recommended, as it allows the gin to dominate but hits all the expected marks for sweetness and bitterness.

Fever-Tree Elderflower Tonic Water

INGREDIENTS: SPRING WATER, CANE SUGAR, FRESH ELDERFLOWER EXTRACT, CITRIC ACID, NATURAL FLAVOURS, NATURAL QUININE

Vibrant elderflower notes abound, both on the nose and on the palate. A concise effervescence carries the floral notes which, as they fade, leave notes of fresh spring leaves and a touch of citrus, with a very subtle bitterness to finish. It's an elderflower tonic that delivers on its promise. Although it's largely one note, it does its job well in a G&T.

Fever-Tree Mediterranean Tonic Water

INGREDIENTS: SPRING WATER, CANE SUGAR, CITRIC ACID, NATURAL FLAVOURS, NATURAL QUININE

Herbal and botanically complex on the nose, this has hints of thyme and lemon. The fizz is gentle, and the palate is quite smooth, allowing the flavours to come through nicely. Herbal notes whisper above the bubbles, fading into a mild, only slight bitter finish. A unique tonic that adds notes to pair nicely with juniper, but are only found rarely in gin.

Fever-Tree Naturally Light Tonic Water

INGREDIENTS: SPRING WATER, PURE FRUCTOSE (FRUIT SUGAR), CITRIC ACID, NATURAL FLAVOURS, NATURAL QUININE

Along with Q Tonic, Fever-Tree Naturally Light is low in calories and noticeably less sweet than other tonics. Subtle hints of bitter orange with only a touch of sweetness. Crisp, clean and smooth, it's refreshing and gives the gin beneath space to shine, highlighted with only a slight citrus lift and a crisp astringent finish. Similar to Fever-Tree's full calorie option, it has only a slightly noticeable dip in sugariness.

Hansen's Cane Soda

INGREDIENTS: TRIPLE-FILTERED CARBONATED WATER, CANE SUGAR, CITRIC ACID, NATURAL FLAVOURS WITH EXTRACTS OF CALIFORNIA CITRUS, QUININE

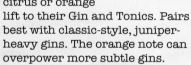

Moderately sweet and effervescent with a strong citrus note right from the can. Strong orange flavour with only a mild astringency. Best for those who really like a strong citrus or orange lift to their Gin and Tonics. Pairs best with classic-style, juniper-heavy gins. The orange note can overpower more subtle gins.

Q Tonic

INGREDIENTS: CARBONATED WATER, ORGANIC AGAVE, NATURAL BITTERS, HANDPICKED QUININE, CITRIC ACID

Crisp and bubbly, with only a slight sweetness, astringent and slightly tart on the finish. The focus is on the quinine and bitterness, largely due to the mild sweetness. Allow all the notes of a gin to shine through most clearly, but those used to a sweeter Gin and Tonic might find it too astringent. Recommended.

Schweppes Indian Tonic Water

INGREDIENTS: CARBONATED WATER, SUGAR, CITRIC ACID, FLAVOURINGS INCLUDING QUININE, SWEETENER (SODIUM SACCHARIN)

Slightly sweet with a syrupy undertone that's cut cleanly with a brisk dose of quinine. It is slightly more intense than other mainstream brands. The restrained sweetness lends itself nicely to mixing, allowing the natural sweetness of citrus to shine through better (if you are choosing to add citrus to your G&T that is).

Tonic syrups

What are Tonic Syrups?

Tonic syrups are concentrated combinations of cinchona, herbs and spices, with added sweetening, bottled and designed to be combined with soda water on mixing. They differ from tonic waters in that they exclusively use cinchona bark in combination with other raw botanicals, and are often very dark in colour. Ranging from burnt sienna all the way to burnt umber, a Gin and Tonic made with a syrup will be readily identifiable by its golden/red coloration.

Tonic syrups have gained traction among gin drinkers because they afford flexibility in one's drink. If you want a more bitter drink, or less bitter, gin sippers can vary the amount of syrup they add. The disassociation of the carbonation and flavouring also allows drinkers to adjust the taste.

If you are curious about how tonic syrups are made, see page 194 for a recipe.

Tonic Syrup Tasting Notes RATIOS ARE GIN:TONIC:SODA WATER

El Guapo Bitters British Colonial Style Tonic Syrup

SUGGESTED RATIO: 4:1:6

The nose is rich with forest, wood and soil. It's summery and fresh with a strong earthy note. The palate is actually quite woody, with a very strong citrussy lift mid palate. Tart and somewhat sweet, and sweetened with cane sugar, it ends with a crisp bitter note and just a touch of ginger. It's also cloudier than many other commercial tonic syrups, with an appearance similar to that of a homemade syrup.

Jack Rudy Cocktail Co. Small Batch Tonic

SUGGESTED RATIO: 2:¾:5

Lemon chiffon in colour, distinctly lighter than most other tonic syrups. The nose has lemon, orange and cinchona, with low notes of ripe berry and camomile. On the palate, lemon, lemongrass and a hefty dose of bitter orange and quinine. The finish is relatively concise, leaving the palate clean and whet for the next sip.

Jack Rudy Cocktail Co. Elderflower Tonic

SUGGESTED RATIO: 2:¾:5

The nose is heavy and thick with perfumed notes. Yes, elderflower, but also pungent tones of jasmine and orange blossom. The palate is floral as you might expect, but robust with all the intensity of a bouquet. Dense with elderflower, rose, among other floral tones, it settles into a long bitter, earthy finish.

Bradley's Kina Tonic

SUGGESTED RATIO: 3:2:6

Subtle on the nose with a delicate mix of rich, earthy spices such as cinnamon and orange oil, with just a faint intimation of ginger in the low notes. The palate is pleasingly sweet, with a tart mid note and a long finish pleasantly heavy on wood and cinchona. Very nice. Recommended.

Bradley's Bourbon Barrel-Aged Kina Tonic

SUGGESTED RATIO: 3:2:'TO TASTE'

Warm nose with hints of ginger, cinnamon and orange oil. The palate is crisp and clean with hints of bark, bitter orange and rind and a long astringent finish with cedar, lemon and good bitterness.

Pinckney Bend Classic Tonic Syrup

SUGGESTED RATIO: 1:1:4

Created specifically for pairing with Pinckney Bend Gin, this is an awesome drink. The nose is woody and floral with hints of rose, birch and hibiscus. The palate is sweet with woody undertones, warm spice and a little bit of citrus. Crisp and not too bitter, it's a good complement to citrus-forward gins. Sweetened with both cane and agave.

GARNISH WITH LIME

Liber & Co. Spiced Tonic Syrup

SUGGESTED RATIO: 2:¾: 'TOP WITH'

Powerful and pleasant with a couple of Asian notes standing out early on, with ginger, lemongrass up top and a pleasant spice backing of clove, cardamom and even a touch of pepper. On the palate, it begins with a slight sweetness, before the spice notes rise quickly. There's a slight tinge of lemon rind and a crisp bitterness, with notes of black pepper on the finish. Beautiful, loud tonic syrup at its best. Recommended.

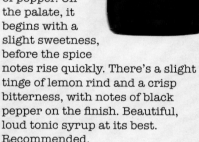

Homemade tonic syrups

Craft tonic syrups might be one of the most exciting innovations to have taken the gin world by storm in the last decade. Kevin Ludwig and Jeffrey Morganthaler are largely credited with helping bring the idea of homemade tonic syrups into the home with their recipes from 2007 and 2008, to which the recipe below owes a debt of gratitude.

Locating cinchona bark (the ingredient which brings the quinine to the party) is probably the biggest challenge home tonic makers will encounter; however, owing to its increasing popularity, it's now widely available on Amazon or in speciality supermarkets, such as Kalustyan's in New York City (you can order online).

As with the homemade cold-compounded gin recipe, once you master the basics, you can really take this in any direction you want. The recipe is a template to get you started. Like something less bitter? Replace the gentian with more citrus. Looking for something a bit more spiced? Try adding ginger or nutmeg.

This goes really well with your homemade gin as well.

INGREDIENTS

475ml/16fl oz water
350g/12oz sugar
5g/⅕oz of cinchona bark, chunks or chips, not powder
10g/⅓oz juniper berries
5g /⅕oz gentian root
2 cardamom pods, broken
1 allspice berry
½ stick of cassia
Peel of 1 lemon, using a vegetable peeler
Juice of ½ lemon
2 tsp citric acid
Pinch of salt
2 tsp vodka

Combine the bark, juniper, gentian, cardamom, allspice, cassia and lemon peel in a saucepan on the hob. Bring to the boil, then reduce the heat and allow to simmer for 15 minutes. With about 5 minutes left to go, add the lemon juice, citric acid and salt.

Remove from the heat, and remove the large solids from liquid using a cafetière (French press) or coffee filter. Then do one more round of filtration. If you're using a coffee filter, this may take up to half an hour. Gravity filtration is a slow process. If your filter becomes clogged up with small solids, pour any liquid left in the filter back into your saucepan. Grab a new filter and start again with any of the remaining unfiltered liquid.

Once completely filtered, return to the hob in a clean saucepan, add the sugar and stir. Bring to boiling (100°C/212°F), remove from heat and leave to cool. Once your syrup is cool, add the vodka and stir well to evenly distribute. Pour into a sterilised bottle or jar and seal. The syrup will keep in the fridge for about three months.

We suggest a ratio of two parts gin to one part tonic syrup, topped with soda water to taste. Cheers!

Red or yellow cinchona?

There are two major types of cinchona available. By far the most common is red cinchona, which has the maple, wooden and tea-like notes usually found in commercial tonic syrups. Yellow cinchona, also known as calisaya, while much harder to find, has a higher quinine content and less quantities of the other alkaloids found in cinchona.

When you find cinchona bark commercially available, unless specifically specified, it's probably the red variety. And unless you're concerned about your tonic syrup's anti-malarial properties compared to other brands, you can safely stick to the red and get good results from your homemade syrup.

More cinchona

The medical name for having too much quinine is cinchonism. Many bartenders and home tonic makers have made perfectly safe tonic syrups. But it's worth keeping an eye on. If you want more bitter in your tonic syrup, add something like gentian, but don't add more cinchona.

Tips for making a tonic syrup that doesn't overdo it on the quinine:

• Use whole bark rather than powdered.
• Use red cinchona rather than yellow cinchona.
• Use filtration to extract solids from your syrup. Use a combination of a coffee filter/ water filter to produce a non-cloudy syrup.
• Sample your syrups and taste in moderation.

Making homemade infused gin

Unless you live in New Zealand, the only kind of gin you can make at home is an infused, bathtub/cold-compounded gin. This gin doesn't need to be distilled. It will still have a bright juniper-focused character, and can technically still be described as a gin. However, unlike most gins it will have a cloudy, dark appearance.

Fear not, as many widely available gins have used this method to make good, even excellent gins. Tru2's Organic Gin has a cloudy golden hue; Master of Malt makes a series of popular Bathtub Gins; Bendistillery adds juniper via infusion to make its Crater Lake Gin – the infusion method is is far from forbidden in the gin world.

The best part about infusing gin at home is that you can customise the mix to your liking. Want a strong juniper-only infused gin? How about lots of exotic spices? Maybe fresh herbs? There are no limits once you've mastered the basic foundation.

But first a word on kits

Given the resurgent interest in gin, a large number of kits have appeared on the market. If you live in a place where you have access to a high-quality spice grocer, you can usually find all of the ingredients you want at a better price. Even Amazon has most of the ingredients you might want for sale. The kits make a nice gift, but for those looking to be a bit more creative, I think that going the DIY route is cheaper and more rewarding.

What do you need?
250ml/8fl oz 100 proof or higher vodka
250ml/8fl oz 80 proof vodka (*Pick something you would drink in both cases. Anything you taste in the vodka, you will taste in the gin.*)
A bell jar, big enough to hold about 600ml (1 pint) of liquid/solids. (*This is where the infusion will take place. You're going to need to filter the solids out at the end, so my advice is don't do it in the vodka bottle.*)
Muslin cloth or cafetière (French press) or a water filter
Botanicals (*Pick your own or use my recipe below as a starting point. A little bit of some things goes a long way!*)

Aaron's Clawfoot Bathtub Gin
10g/⅓oz of juniper berries. (*Before adding to vodka, pulse 1 or 2 times in a food processor to break up the berries.*)
Grated zest of 1 lemon
3-4 small pieces of lime zest
A few coriander seeds
A small piece of dried liquorice root
5 white peppercorn berries
5 cubeb berries
5 grains of paradise
Pinch of fennel seeds
Pinch of caraway seeds

Pour the 100 proof vodka into a bell jar. Add botanicals. Seal and give a good shake. Place the jar in a dark, room-temperature place that won't be subject to large temperature fluctuations. Shake once daily. Your gin will be ready for filtering in as few as two days if you prefer a lighter style, though you can let it go as long as a week if you want. The resultant gin will have a much bolder flavour.

To decant the liquid, strain through a muslin cloth to extract the large solids. There may be some fine sediment present. The liquid may take some time to drip through. If you have a cafetière (French press) available, it requires a little less patience to use. For those looking to spend a little bit more money, a two-step process of muslin cloth, then using a store-bought reusable water filter will result in the clearest gin with the least amount of sediment in it.

Add the 80 proof vodka and shake well.

I think the best cocktail to make with homemade gin is the Negroni (page 200). The bold herbal/spice notes come through so much more vividly, and complement the bitter notes of the Campari in a really lovely way.

Gin cocktails

Martini

No cocktail has inspired so much discussion about its name and origins as the Martini. Writers have made their careers discussing the cocktail and its origins. The name has inspired a new suffix, so much so that any family-friendly restaurant can serve a 350ml/12 fl oz brightly coloured drink in an oversized glass, add '-tini' to the end of it and have a new drink on its menu. Even our superheroes and iconic characters drink Martinis. But enough of the cultural significance.

Leaving the origin stories to the experts, the Martini is perhaps the most quintessential gin cocktail, and one that leaves an incredible amount of leeway for one's individual tastes. Though many older recipes favour a ratio of one part gin to one part dry vermouth, more modern recipes have taken that ratio from 5:1 to 10:1 to even ∞:1 (though one might legitimately argue in the latter case that the Churchill Martini, in which one simply looks at the vermouth bottle while drinking, is just chilled gin and therefore not even a cocktail, but we digress).

Early recipes often included bitters, or a small dash of some other ingredient as well. Recipes in the late 19th century used Old Tom gin rather than dry gin. Modern recipes use both contemporary and classic-style gins. The garnish: Lemon Twist? Olive? Onion? There's a surprising amount of flexibility here, just don't think about swapping out the gin for vodka. Yes, we're looking at you Mr Bond. Call it whatever you want, just don't call that a Martini.

The Gibson

GLASS: COCKTAIL OR MARTINI

6 parts gin
1 part dry vermouth

GARNISH: ONION

Same method as the Official IBA Martini (opposite), but garnish instead with a single pickled silverskin onion.

The Official IBA Martini

GLASS: COCKTAIL OR MARTINI

6 parts gin

1 part dry vermouth

GARNISH: LEMON PEEL OR PIMENTO-STUFFED OLIVE

Stir in a mixing glass with ice. Strain into a chilled cocktail or Martini glass. Squeeze oil from lemon peel into drink and garnish with lemon peel or a pimento-stuffed green olive.

The Pascal Martini

GLASS: COUPE

7 parts gin

2 parts dry vermouth

2 dashes Fee Brothers Black Walnut Bitters

2 dashes maraschino liquid

GARNISH: MARASCHINO CHERRY

Stir all ingredients in a mixing glass with ice and strain into a chilled coupe glass. Garnish with a maraschino cherry and serve.

Top places for a Martini

The Connaught and Coburg Bars

The Connaught Hotel
Carlos Place, Mayfair, London, UK
www.the-connaught.co.uk

There is perhaps no more a luxurious and relaxing atmosphere than the intimate Coburg Bar and David Collins-designed Connaught Bar for a tip-top gin cocktail in London. Overseen by the legendary mixologist Ago Perrone, known as the 'Martini magician'.

Dukes Hotel

St James's Place
London, UK
www.dukeshotel.com

Renowned, and with good reason, Dukes Hotel is one of the best places in the world to grab a Martini. Revel in the history, as this is where Ian Fleming, creator of James Bond, drank. It's easy to see why he was so inspired. The Martinis themselves featuring Sacred Gin and Vermouths stand on their own.

Bathtub Gin

132 9th Avenue
New York, USA
www.bathtubginnyc.com

Hidden as per the speakeasy tradition, well known on the strengths of its cocktails. Though they'll also pour some Nolet's Reserve tableside, for our money the best drink is the house Martini: Fords Gin and Dolin Vermouth served up with olive and lemon.

Gin Palace

10 Russell Place
Melbourne, Australia
www.ginpalace.com.au

This venerable, intimate Melbourne institution serves up top-notch Martinis buoyed by a fantastic gin selection rife with local favourites. For those interested in learning more, it offers a Martini masterclass and holds local gin tastings.

Negroni

It's rare that any cocktail has an origin story that is so cut and dried as the Negroni. While others are normally steeped in myth, akin to playing a 150-year game of telephone, the story of the Negroni goes something like this.

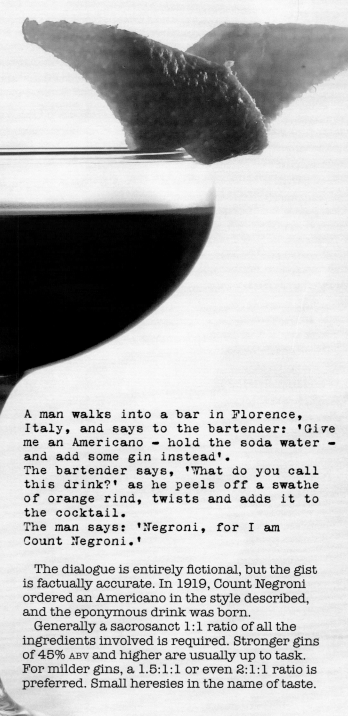

Negroni (modern variation)

GLASS: COUPE
2 parts gin
1 part sweet vermouth
1 part Campari
GARNISH: ORANGE TWIST

Shake ingredients with ice and then strain into a chilled coupe glass. Garnish with orange twist.

A man walks into a bar in Florence, Italy, and says to the bartender: 'Give me an Americano – hold the soda water – and add some gin instead'.
The bartender says, 'What do you call this drink?' as he peels off a swathe of orange rind, twists and adds it to the cocktail.
The man says: 'Negroni, for I am Count Negroni.'

The dialogue is entirely fictional, but the gist is factually accurate. In 1919, Count Negroni ordered an Americano in the style described, and the eponymous drink was born.

Generally a sacrosanct 1:1 ratio of all the ingredients involved is required. Stronger gins of 45% ABV and higher are usually up to task. For milder gins, a 1.5:1:1 or even 2:1:1 ratio is preferred. Small heresies in the name of taste.

The Official IBA Negroni

GLASS: ROCKS

1 part gin
1 part sweet vermouth
1 part Campari

GARNISH: ORANGE TWIST (OPTIONAL)

Stir ingredients in a mixing glass with ice.
Strain and serve over ice in a rocks glass.
Optionally garnish with a twist of orange peel.

Unusual Negroni

GLASS: ROCKS

1 part gin
1 part Aperol
1 part Lillet Blanc

GARNISH: NONE

Stir ingredients in a mixing glass with ice.
Strain and serve over ice in a rocks glass.

Top places for a Negroni

Bar Termini
7 Old Compton Street, London, UK
www.bar-termini.com

Bar Termini fashions itself as an authentic Italian
coffee and aperitif bar. From a classic Negroni to
the boundary-pushing, pink peppercorn Negroni,
any of these options are winners. It was opened by
Tony Conigliaro, he of esteemed 69 Colebrooke Row,
which is also a fantastic place for a cocktail.

Amor y Amargo
443 East 6th Street, New York, USA
www.amoryamargony.com

To be sure, the gin is good. Amor y Amargo elevates
the other two components of the drink to new
heights. House-crafted vermouth comes directly
from the tap, and for the adventurous, swap out
Campari for any of its numerous amaros.

Clyde Common
1014 SW Stark Street, Portland, Oregon, USA
www.clydecommon.com

Jeffrey Morganthaler's experiments with barrel-
ageing cocktails spawned a movement. He's now
bar manager at Clyde Common, where he's kept the
tradition alive with a Negroni on the menu that's
rested for two months inside a bourbon barrel.

The Drawing Room
1222 Barrington Street, 3rd Floor
Halifax, Nova Scotia, Canada
www.henryhouse.ca

A cosy, intimate cocktail bar tucked away on the
third floor of a pub and restaurant. The speciality
among its selection of pre-Prohibition era cocktails
is a smoked Negroni that is half cocktail theatre,
half unique and delicious.

Caffe Rivoire
Piazza della Signoria, 4R, Florence, Italy
www.rivoire.it

For those in the Count Negroni fan club, Caffe
Rivoire, via ownership lineage, is the current title
holder of the Negroni legacy. Though other bars in
Florence claim to be the birthplace of the Negroni,
this is one place where you can appreciate the
legacy while enjoying a good cocktail.

Gimlet

The Gimlet is a simple, refreshing cocktail whose origins lie in gin and lime's medicinal past. Sailors in the British Navy got their daily dose of vitamin C to prevent scurvy in the form of lime juice. By the second half of the 19th century, Lauchlan Rose's method of preserving lime juice without alcohol was standard issue on ships.

Officers were drinking gin at this time, and it's likely that the Gimlet's origins are here, though the name itself is less likely to be a reference to a rear admiral (Thomas Gimlette) and more probably a metaphorical reference to a boring tool for piercing small holes in wood and barrels, common on naval vessels. The Gimlet was appearing in print and cocktail books by the 1920s.

Rose's Lime Juice is a key ingredient in the Gimlet, but it's undergone some significant changes in the century and a half since Lauchlan invented it. The sweetening methods vary around the world, and it's certain that the original wasn't artificially coloured. However, the particular 'stewed lime' note of Rose's Lime Juice is vital to the classic cocktail, and therefore it has remained the standard. For those who prefer something a little truer to the original methods, a recipe for homemade lime cordial is opposite.

The Gimlet

GLASS: COCKTAIL OR ROCKS

4 parts gin

1 part lime cordial/
   sweetened lime juice

GARNISH: LIME TWIST

Stir in a cocktail or rocks glass with ice and serve. Optionally, garnish with a lime twist.

Fresh Gimlet

GLASS: ROCKS

4 parts gin
1 part lime juice, freshly squeezed
1 part simple syrup
2 lemon verbena leaves

GARNISH: MINT LEAF AND LEMON VERBENA LEAF

Gently muddle lemon verbena leaves and gin in a shaker glass. Add simple syrup, lime juice and ice. Shake vigorously. Strain into a rocks glass over ice. Garnish with a mint and lemon verbena leaf on top.

Lime Cordial

8 limes
240ml/8fl oz lime juice, freshly squeezed
100g/3¼oz sugar

First wash 8 limes thoroughly. Peel each of them, preferably with a vegetable peeler to create wide swathes. Heat the lime juice in a pan over a high heat and bring to the boil, allowing it to reduce in volume by half. Remove from he heat and leave the lime juice to cool for about 10 minutes.

Return to the burner and heat again, adding the sugar. Bring back to the boil. When the mixture boils, add the lime peel, then immediately remove from heat and leave to cool. Once cool, strain out the solids and bottle. The mixture should be kept in the fridge.

Top places for a good gin cocktail

69 Colebrooke Row
69 Colebrooke Row, London, UK
www.69colebrookerow.com

It doesn't specialise in gin exclusively, but the drinks it creates and pairs with some of the inspired inventions from Tony Conigliaro's lab are among the best in the business. The Woodland Martini stands out, but is not the only great option.

Dutch Kills
27-24 Jackson Avenue, Long Island City, NY, USA
www.dutchkillsbar.com

Simple, classic, well-prepared drinks in a railroad-style bar, a short subway trip outside of Manhattan. It's the cocktail bar of choice in my neighbourhood. Nice gin selection and good bartenders – only the best parts of the NYC cocktail bar experience.

Liberty
517 5th Avenue, Seattle, Washington, USA
www.libertybars.com

A well-curated gin selection behind the bar, and a fantastic drink selection in general. Several in-house barrel-aged cocktails (including a Negroni) are available, but the winner for my money is the Hollywould. If something less bitter is your thing, try the tea-infused gin.

Penrose
3311 Grand Avenue, Oakland, California, USA
www.penroseoakland.com

It's love at first sight when the first line on a cocktail menu calls out a local gin by name. Terroir gin, mezcal and absinthe? Sign me up. The playful combinations of base spirits and the house-made tonic make it worth a visit.

Pouring Ribbons
225 Avenue B, New York, USA
www.pouringribbons.com

It begins with creating a graph of its cocktails to allow patrons to discover new drinks or old favourites by how similar they are to other drinks they know. But its seasonal, rotating menu can always be counted on for a few fantastic gin quaffs.

Classic gin cocktails

A purist will say that all gin cocktails were designed to work well with classic-style dry gin. While that may be technically true, there are some drinks that work best when paired with a bold juniper-forward gin, so some of these drinks can also work with contemporary-style gins.

That said, these drinks are some of the best starting points for highlighting the character of classic gin that has made it an enduring favourite behind bars for mastering the cocktail craft.

Pegu Club

GLASS: COUPE

45ml/1½fl oz classic gin

15ml/½fl oz lime juice, freshly squeezed

15ml/½fl oz orange curaçao

2 dashes orange bitters

2 dashes Angostura bitters

GARNISH: NONE

Add all ingredients to shaker with ice.
Shake well and strain into a chilled coupe glass.

20th Century Cocktail

GLASS: COCKTAIL OR COUPE

45ml/1½fl oz classic gin
20ml/¾fl oz lemon juice,
   freshly squeezed
20ml/¾fl oz Lillet Blanc
15ml/½fl oz crème de cacão

GARNISH: LEMON TWIST

Shake ingredients with ice and
strain into a chilled cocktail glass.
Garnish with a twist of lemon and
serve.

Bronx Cocktail

GLASS: COCKTAIL OR COUPE

60ml/2fl oz classic gin
20ml/¾ fl oz orange juice,
   freshly squeezed
15ml/½fl oz dry vermouth
15ml/½fl oz sweet vermouth

GARNISH: ORANGE TWIST

Shake ingredients with ice and
strain into a chilled cocktail or
coupe glass.
Garnish with a twist of orange and
serve.

Clover Club

GLASS: COUPE OR STEMMED WINE GLASS

45ml/1½fl oz classic gin
20ml/¾fl oz lemon juice,
   freshly squeezed
7.5ml/¼fl oz raspberry syrup
1 egg white

GARNISH: NONE

Add all ingredients to a shaker
and shake without ice for 10–15
seconds. Then add ice and shake
vigorously again until well chilled.
Strain into a chilled coupe or
stemmed wine glass. Serve.

Vesper

GLASS: COCKTAIL GLASS

90ml/3fl oz classic gin

30ml/1fl oz vodka

20ml/¾ fl oz Cocchi Americano

GARNISH: LEMON TWIST

Shake ingredients with ice until well chilled. Strain into a cocktail glass. Garnish with a twist of lemon and serve.

Gin and Jam

GLASS: ROCKS

90ml/3fl oz classic gin

30ml/1fl oz dry vermouth

1 dash lemon juice, freshly squeezed

1 tbsp jam of your choice (orange marmalade or blueberry jam recommended)

GARNISH: ½ TBSP JAM

In a cocktail shaker with ice, combine gin, vermouth, lemon juice and 1 tbsp jam. Shake for about 15 seconds to ensure that the jam is well mixed with other ingredients. Strain using a hawthorne strainer (the jams will clog the pores on a cobbler shaker) into a rocks glass over three or four ice cubes. Spoon half a tablespoon of jam over the ice cubes in the glass. Serve.

TOP PLACES WITH

Amazing

GIN COLLECTIONS

The Feathers Hotel

24 Market Street,
Woodstock,
Oxfordshire, UK
www.feathers.co.uk

The bar that began the arms race for having the most gins available might look unassuming at first glance, perhaps even cosy. They set the bar high with 161 gins in 2012. Though they don't hold the record today, the list remains impressive and the cocktails are definitely worth seeking out.

Premium Gin Emporium at The Old Bell Inn

Huddersfield Road,
Delph, Saddleworth,
Greater Manchester, UK
www.theoldbellinn.co.uk

This inn is also a former world record holder, with over 400 different gins in stock. The Old Bell Inn offers cocktail classes in addition to having an incredibly impressive array of gins from around the world.

The Gin Palace

42 Middle Abbey Street,
Dublin, Ireland

The Gin Palace features over 150 gins from around the world and boasts the largest gin collection in Dublin. Check out their gin club or try a gin sampler and find a new favourite.

Contemporary cocktails

Contemporary gin takes on a lot of different flavour profiles due to the range that the style embraces. So without trying to narrowly specify a cocktail to one gin, we try to give a general characteristic that when paired with the cocktail recipe below, really amps it up to the next level. See page 67 for details of suitable contemporary gins. These are only recommendations as a starting point. As you get to know more contemporary gins, feel free to substitute gins that better align with your palate and preferences.

Alaska Cocktail

GLASS: COUPE

60ml/2fl oz spice-forward
  contemporary gin
20ml/¾fl oz Yellow Chartreuse
2 dashes orange bitters

GARNISH: LEMON TWIST

Stir ingredients together with ice and strain into a coupe glass. Add a twist of lemon and serve.

Corpse Reviver #2

GLASS: COUPE

⅛tsp Absinthe Verte

30ml/1fl oz spice-forward
    contemporary gin

30 ml/1fl oz Cocchi Americano

30ml/1fl oz Cointreau

30ml/1fl oz lemon juice,
    freshly squeezed

GARNISH: LEMON TWIST

Place absinthe in the coupe glass.
Rinse around edges, then pour our
whatever remains. Put ingredients
into a shaker with ice. Shake and
strain into a coupe glass. Garnish
with a lemon twist, then serve.

Aviation

GLASS: COUPE

60ml/2 oz floral contemporary gin

15ml/½fl oz lemon juice,
    freshly squeezed

7.5ml/¼fl oz maraschino liquid

7.5ml/¼fl oz crème de violette

GARNISH: MARASCHINO CHERRY

Shake ingredients with ice, strain
into a coupe glass. Garnish with a
cherry and serve.

French 75

GLASS: CHAMPAGNE FLUTE

60ml/2fl oz floral contemporary gin

20ml/¾fl oz simple syrup

15ml/½fl oz lemon juice,
    freshly squeezed

150ml/5fl oz Champagne

GARNISH: NONE

Add gin, simple syrup and lemon
juice to a shaker with ice. Shake
well and strain into a flute glass.
Top with Champagne. Serve.

Singapore Sling

GLASS: HIGHBALL

30ml/1fl oz citrus-forward
    contemporary gin
30ml/1fl oz pineapple juice
15ml/½fl oz lime juice,
    freshly squeezed
15ml/½fl oz Cherry Heering
15ml/½fl oz Cointreau
7.5ml/¼fl oz Bénédictine
1 dash Angostura bitters

GARNISH: MARASCHINO CHERRY
AND PINEAPPLE SLICE

Shake all ingredients in a shaker
with ice. Strain into a highball glass
over ice. Garnish with a cherry and
piece of pineapple and serve.

Last Word

GLASS: COUPE

20ml/¾fl oz spice- or herb-forward
    contemporary gin
20ml/¾fl oz Green Chartreuse
20ml/¾fl oz lime juice,
    freshly squeezed
20ml/¾fl oz maraschino liquid

GARNISH: NONE

Shake ingredients together with ice
and carefully strain into a chilled
coupe glass. Serve.

TOP PLACES WITH
Amazing
GIN COLLECTIONS

Hop Sing Laundromat
1029 Race Street, Philadelphia,
Pennsylvania, USA
www.hopsinglaundromat.com

A speakeasy of traditional
style, it's located behind a
nondescript, unmarked door
in the Chinatown district
of Philadelphia. Fantastic
cocktails (gin and otherwise)
made by top-notch bartenders,
with a veritable library of 100+
gins behind them.

Dutch Courage Officers' Mess
51 Alfred Street, Brisbane,
Australia
www.dutchcourage.com.au

With over 100 gins from
around the world, each neatly
categorised for the novice
gin drinker as well as the gin
connoisseur who knows what
they like, this is a veritable
gin-lover's paradise. Have your
gin of choice any one of three
ways, or expand your horizon
with a flight.

Doce Gin Club
Carrer de l'Almirall Cadarso,
12, Valencia, Spain
www.doceginclub.com

Among the participants in
a *Guinness Book of World
Records* arms race, the leader
at the start of 2015 is Doce Gin
Club with over 500 different
commercially available gins.

Aged gin cocktails

Aged gin in the modern sense of the term is quite new. Because of the wide range in flavour profiles of aged gins, the brands used to design these drinks are specified here, as it is a bit harder to swap out one barrel-aged gin for another. As there is no rich history of barrel-aged gin from which to draw historical recipes, many of the drinks here are originals. Once you become acquainted with barrel-aged gin in general, experiment using these recipes as templates.

Halja Cocktail

GLASS: COUPE

30ml/1fl oz Corsair Barrel-Aged Gin
60ml/2fl oz whipped-cream-
   flavoured-vodka
15ml/½fl oz crème de violette
15ml/½fl oz lime juice,
   freshly squeezed

GARNISH: HUNDREDS AND THOUSANDS (CANDY
SPRINKLES)

Shake ingredients together with ice and strain into a chilled coupe glass. Garnish with some hundreds and thousands, then serve.

Old Fashioned

GLASS: ROCKS

6.75ml/2¼fl oz Few Barrel Gin

3 dashes Angostura bitters

¾ tsp caster/superfine sugar
   (or 1 sugar cube)

GARNISH: ORANGE TWIST (OPTIONAL)

Add the sugar and bitters first with
a small splash of gin. Gently muddle
the three ingredients together
until the sugar is well integrated,
or, if using a cube, at least until it
is broken up. Add the rest of the
gin and stir. Add ice and optionally
garnish with an orange twist, if
desired. Serve.

Justin Kneitel's Hot Toddy

GLASS: MUG

45ml/1½fl oz Few Barrel Gin

20ml/¾fl oz lemon juice,
   freshly squeezed

1 tsp sugar

60ml/2fl oz near boiling water
   (93°C/200°F)

GARNISH: CINNAMON STICK

Stir together gin, lemon juice
and sugar in the cup you plan on
drinking it out of. Stir in hot water
slowly, stirring constantly until the
sugar is dissolved. Add a cinnamon
stick and serve immediately, while
still piping hot.

Justin Kneitel's Debonaire

GLASS: ROCKS

60ml/2fl oz Few Barrel Gin

20ml/¾fl oz Amaro Ramazzotti

15ml/½fl oz Clément Créole Shrubb

¾ tsp Tempus Fugit Dark
   Crème de Cacao

GARNISH: ORANGE TWIST

This is a room-temperature
cocktail, no ice is needed. Place
ingredients in a rocks glass. Stir
with a bar spoon, add a twist of
orange and serve.

Alexandria

GLASS: COUPE

45ml/1½fl oz Waterloo Antique Barrel Reserve Gin

30ml/1fl oz crème de cacao

30ml/1fl oz double cream

GARNISH: FRESHLY GRATED CINNAMON AND NUTMEG (A PINCH OF EACH)

Shake the liquid ingredients well in a shaker with ice cubes. Shake for 15 seconds. Strain into a chilled coupe glass. Garnish with a fine dusting of fresh (if possible) nutmeg and cinnamon over the top. Serve.

Varuna

GLASS: COUPE

60ml/2fl oz Roundhouse Imperial Barrel-Aged Gin/ Ginskey

20ml/¾fl oz lime juice, freshly squeezed

15ml/½fl oz 1:1 simple syrup

7.5ml/¼fl oz coconut rum

1 egg white

GARNISH: GRATED NUTMEG

Add egg white, gin, lime juice, simple syrup and rum to a shaker without ice. Shake for 10–15 seconds. Then add ice and shake vigorously for another 15 seconds. Strain and serve into a chilled coupe glass. Grate a small amount of nutmeg on top of drink and serve. Cocktail by Justin Kneitel.

Old Tom cocktails

Many cocktails that originated in the late 19th century were designed to be mixed with Old Tom gins. Many have since been adapted or updated to work with the dry gins that came into vogue in the 20th century; however, these drinks are more than historical curiosities or windows into the past. Many of them, true to the cocktail creator's intentions, are superb cocktails in their own right. You can update them, but until you've had a Tom Collins or Martinez with Old Tom gin, I'm not sure you can truly say you've tasted them.

Tom Collins

GLASS: COLLINS/HIGHBALL

60ml/2fl oz Old Tom gin

30ml/1fl oz lemon juice,
    freshly squeezed

7.5ml/¼fl oz simple syrup,
    or to taste*

Soda water, to top

GARNISH: LEMON CIRCLE
AND MARASCHINO CHERRY

Fill glass halfway with cracked ice. Add gin, lemon juice, simple syrup and water. Stir to combine and top with soda water. Garnish with lemon and cherry. Serve.

* To taste might be a better recommendation. As some Old Tom gins are actually sweetened with sugar, you might find the cocktail needs less sweetening. For Old Toms that are botanically sweetened, you may find that the drink is too sour, in which case double or triple the simple syrup.

Martinez

GLASS: COCKTAIL OR COUPE

90ml/3fl oz Old Tom gin
15ml/½fl oz sweet vermouth
7.5ml/¼fl oz maraschino liquid
2 dashes Angostura bitters

GARNISH: ORANGE TWIST

Add all ingredients to a shaker with ice. Shake and strain into a chilled cocktail or coupe glass. Garnish with an orange twist and serve.

Casino Cocktail

GLASS: COUPE

60ml/2fl oz Old Tom gin
4ml/⅛fl oz maraschino liquid
4ml/⅛fl oz lemon juice, freshly squeezed
3 dashes orange bitters

GARNISH: NONE

Shake all ingredients together with ice. Strain into a chilled coupe glass. Serve.

Tuxedo Cocktail 1

GLASS: COUPE

30ml/1fl oz Old Tom gin
30ml/1fl oz dry vermouth
4ml/⅛ fl oz maraschino liquid
½tsp absinthe verte
2 dashes orange bitters

GARNISH: LEMON TWIST AND MARASCHINO CHERRY

Stir all the ingredients in a mixing glass with ice. Strain into a chilled coupe glass. Garnish with a lemon twist and a maraschino cherry. Serve.

Ford Cocktail

GLASS: COCKTAIL OR COUPE

30ml/1fl oz Old Tom gin

30ml/1fl oz dry vermouth

7.5ml/¼fl oz Bénédictine

2 dashes orange bitters

GARNISH: ORANGE TWIST

Add all ingredients into a mixing glass of ice. Stir and strain into a cocktail glass or coupe. Garnish with an orange twist and serve.

Pink Gin

GLASS: COUPE

60ml/2fl oz botanically sweetened Old Tom gin

4 dashes Angostura bitters

GARNISH: LEMON TWIST (OPTIONAL)

Add bitters to the inside of a chilled coupe glass. In a separate mixing glass, stir gin with ice until well chilled. Strain into a coupe glass and optionally garnish with a twist of lemon. Serve.

Holland-style gin cocktails

Holland gin was often a synonymous term for genever. These gins had a rich, grainy character that was complemented rather than dominated by botanical additions. Many of the new gins coming out of the United States today are drawing heavily from the Holland gin tradition and therefore do their best work in cocktails originally designed for this other style of gin. A few good examples include Corsair Genever (page 148), Merrylegs Genever-Style Gin (page 158) and Wigle's Ginever (page 164).

Improved Holland Gin Cocktail

GLASS: COUPE

60ml/2fl oz Holland gin
7.5ml/¼fl oz simple syrup
7.5ml/¼fl oz maraschino liquid
⅛ tsp absinthe
2 dashes Angostura bitters

GARNISH: LEMON TWIST

Add all ingredients to a mixing glass with ice. Stir and strain into a coupe glass. Garnish with twist of lemon and serve.

Holland Fizz

GLASS: COLLINS

60ml/2fl oz Holland gin
15ml/½fl oz lemon juice, freshly squeezed
7.5ml/¼fl oz simple syrup
1 dash Angostura bitters
1 egg white
Soda water, to top

GARNISH: LEMON TWIST

Add all ingredients except soda water to shaker and shake without ice for 10 seconds. Then add ice and shake vigorously. Strain into a Collins glass and top with soda water. Garnish with lemon twist and serve.

Death in the Gulfstream

GLASS: COUPE

60ml/2fl oz Holland gin
15ml/½fl oz lime juice, freshly squeezed
7.5ml/¼fl oz simple syrup
5 dashes Angostura bitters

GARNISH: LIME TWIST

Add all ingredients to a shaker with ice. Shake and strain into a chilled coupe glass. Garnish with a twist of lime and serve.

Sloe gin & cordial cocktails

Sloe gins and other cordial gins are often enjoyed on their own; however, in the tradition of cocktails like the Sloe Gin Fizz, it's sometimes just a matter of knowing what else to do with it. In many of these drinks, sloe or damson gin can often be used interchangeably owing to similar profiles. Some of the more exotic cordials like raspberry or cranberry might be a bit more difficult. Raspberry or strawberry cordials work well opposite Calvados in the Savoy Tango, whereas cranberry makes a good fizz.

Savoy Tango Cocktail

GLASS: COUPE

45ml/1½fl oz sloe gin
45ml/1½fl oz Calvados

GARNISH: NONE

Put ingredients in a shaker with ice. Shake well, strain into a coupe glass and serve.

Sloe Gin Fizz

GLASS: COLLINS

60ml/2fl oz sloe gin
20ml/¾fl oz lemon juice, freshly squeezed
15ml/½fl oz simple syrup
Soda water, to top

GARNISH: LEMON TWIST

Put ingredients in a shaker with ice. Shake and strain into glass over ice. Top with soda water to taste. Optionally, garnish with a lemon twist and serve.

Blackthorne Cocktail

GLASS: COUPE

30ml/1fl oz sloe or damson gin
30ml/1fl oz sweet vermouth
1tsp simple syrup
1 dash Angostura bitters
2 dashes orange bitters

GARNISH: LEMON TWIST

Stir ingredients in a mixing glass with ice. Strain into a coupe glass. Garnish with a lemon twist. Serve.

Use these as starting templates to get to know the drink, and branch out as you become better versed in the flavour profiles of different cordial gins.

Flavoured gin cocktails

Some flavoured gins are created by skewing the botanical mix in one direction or another in order to call it flavoured gin. This may be done to either capitalise on the strength of an existing product's name, or else to better convey the flavour itself. Flavoured gin is generally less sweetened than its cordial counterparts and may still be described as dry.

I wouldn't recommend swapping out flavoured gins for cordials necessarily. Cordial gins might be too sweet in these drinks, and flavoured gins may require additional sweetening to work well.

You can often treat flavoured gins in a similar way to contemporary gins of the same type. Try swapping out a cucumber-flavoured gin for Martin Miller's Gin (page 99), or William Chase Seville Orange Gin (page 109) for Bluecoat Gin (page 144) for instance.

Flavoured Gins are singular beasts, but I've never met one that didn't work in a gin and tonic.

Spring Orchard

GLASS: HIGHBALL

60ml/2fl oz Seagram's
    Apple Twisted Gin
45ml/1½fl oz St. Germain
    Elderflower Liqueur
90ml/3fl oz soda water

GARNISH: NONE

Shake gin and elderflower liqueur together with ice. Strain into a highball glass over ice and top with soda water. Serve.

Southside Cocktail

GLASS: ROCKS

60ml/2fl oz Gordon's
    Elderflower Gin
30ml/1fl oz lime juice,
    freshly squeezed
20ml/¾fl oz simple syrup
1 sprig fresh mint

GARNISH: MINT LEAF

Remove a single mint leaf from the sprig. Set aside. Shake all other ingredients in a shaker with ice. Shake hard so that the mint leaves release their oils. Strain into a rocks glass over a few ice cubes. Garnish with the single mint leaf.

Hesperus

GLASS: COUPE

90ml/3fl oz Williams Chase
    Seville Orange Gin
30ml/1fl oz vodka
15ml/½fl oz Lillet Blanc

GARNISH: LEMON TWIST

Stir liquid ingredients together with ice until well chilled. Strain into a coupe glass. Twist lemon zest over drink, then use as a garnish. Serve.

Aaron's top 10 gins

Barr Hill Gin
45% ABV (USA) see page 141

Citadelle Réserve Gin (2013)
44% ABV (France) see page 119

Dorothy Parker
44% ABV (USA) see page 152

Halcyon Gin
46% ABV (USA) see page 154

Hernö Juniper Cask Gin (Batch 5)
47% ABV (Sweden) see page 128

Pink Pepper Gin
44% ABV (France) see page 120

Plymouth Gin
41.2% ABV (UK) see page 102

St. George Terroir Gin
45% ABV (USA) see page 159

Sipsmith VJOP
57.7% ABV (UK) see page 103

Vor Gin
47% ABV (Iceland) see page 125

The Top 100 places to drink gin: Europe

UK

69 Colebrooke Row
69 Colebrooke Row
London
www.69colebrookrow.com

214 Bermondsey
214 Bermondsey Street
London
www.214-bermondsey.co.uk

**Claridge's Bar
at Claridge's Hotel**
49 Brook Street
London
www.claridges.co.uk

**The Connaught Bar
& Coburg Bar**
Carlos Place,
London
www.the-connaught.co.uk

Duke's Hotel
St. James's Place
London
www.dukeshotel.com

The Feathers Hotel
24 Market Street
Woodstock, Oxfordshire
www.feathers.co.uk

Graphic Bar
4 Golden Square
London
www.graphicbar.com

**The London Gin Club
(at the Star)**
22 Great Chapel Street
London
www.helondonginclub.com

Merchant House
13 Well Court
London
www.merchanthouselondon.
com

Mr. Fogg's
15 Bruton Lane
London
www.mr-foggs.com

Nightjar
129 City Road
London
www.barnightjar.com

The Portobello Star
171 Portobello Road
London
www.portobellostarbar.co.uk

**Premium Gin Emporium
at The Old Bell Inn**
Huddersfield Road
Delph, Saddleworth
Yorkshire
www.theoldbellinn.co.uk

Purl
50-54 Blandford Street
London
www.purl-london.com

White Lyan
153 Hoxton Street
London
www.whitelyan.com

**The Worship Street
Whistling Shop**
63 Worship Street
London
www.whistlingshop.com

SCOTLAND

Bramble Bar
16A Queen Street
Edinburgh
www.bramblebar.co.uk

Bruach Bar
326 Brook Street
Dundee
www.bruach-bar.com

Gin71
71 Renfield Street
Glasgow
www.gin71.com

DENMARK

The Bird and the Churchkey
Gammel Strand 444
Copenhagen

Ruby
Nybrogade 10
Copenhagen
www.thebird.dk

Gilt
Rantzausgade 39
Copenhagen
www.gilt.dk

Helmuth
Boulevarden 28
Aalborg
www.helmuthaalborg.dk

FINLAND

A21 Cocktail Lounge
Annankatu 21
Helsinki
www.a21.fi

FRANCE

Le Coq
12 rue du Chateau d'Eau
Paris
www.facebook.com/pages/
BAR-LE-COQ-PARIS

Prescription Cocktail Club
23 rue Mazarine
Paris
www.facebook.com/pages/
Prescription-Cocktail-Club

GERMANY

Becketts Kopf
Pappelallee 64
Berlin
www.becketts-kopf.de

Couch Club
Klenzestr. 89
Munich
www.couch-club.org

The G&T Bar
Friedrichstraße 113
Berlin
www.amanogroup.de

Lebensstern
Kurfürstenstraße 58
Berlin
www.lebensstern-berlin.de

Victoria Bar
Potsdamer Str 102
Berlin
www.victoriabar.de

ICELAND

Hverfisgata 12
Hverfisgata 12
Reykjavik
www.kexland.is/kexland/
hverfisgata

ITALY

Caffe Rivoire
Piazza della Signoria, 4R
Florence
www.rivoire.it/

Nottingham Forest
Viale Piave, 1
Milan
www.nottingham-forest.com

NETHERLANDS

Door 74
Reguliersdwarsstraat 74I
Amsterdam
www.door-74.com

Henry's Bar
Oosterpark 11
Amsterdam
Www.henrysbar.nl

Snappers
Reguliersdwarsstraat 21
Amsterdam
www.snappers-amsterdam.nl

NORWAY

Chair Oslo
Thorvald Meyers Gate 45
Oslo
www.chairoslo.no

RUSSIA

Chainaya Tea and Cocktails
1-ya Tverskaya-Yamskaya
Ulitsa, 29, Moscow
www.facebook.com/
chainayabar

SPAIN

Bobby Gin
Carrer de Francisco Giner, 47
Barcelona
www.bobbygin.com

Bristol Bar
Calle del Almirante, 20
Madrid
www.bristolbar.es

Doce Gin Club
Carrer de l'Almirall Cadarso,
12, Valencia
www.ocaginclub.com

Elephanta
37 Torrent d'en Vidalet
Barcelona
www.elephanta.cat

Dry Martini
Calle Santalo, 46
Barcelona
www.drymartiniorg.com

Old Fashioned
Carrer de Santa Teresa, 1
Barcelona
www.oldfashionedcocktailbar.
com

SWITZERLAND

Old Crow
Schwanengasse 4
Zürich
www.oldcrow.ch

SWEDEN

Corner Club
Lilla Nygatan 16
Stockholm
www.cornerclub.se

Hush Hush
Linnegatan 11
Gothenburg
facebook.com/pages/
Hush-Hush

The Top 100 places to drink gin: The Americas & Rest of World

USA

Acacia
2108 E Carson Street
Pittsburgh, Pennsylvania
www.acaciacocktails.com

Amor Y Amargo
443 East 6th Street
New York City
www.amoryamargony.com

Apotheke
9 Doyers St.
New York City
www.apothekenyc.com

Bar Congress
200 Congress Avenue
Austin, Texas
www.congressaustin.com/bar-congress

Bar Tonique
820 N Rampart Street
New Orleans, Louisiana
www.bartonique.com

Bathtub Gin
132 9th Ave
New York City
www.bathtubginnyc.com

The Berry and Rye
1105 Howard Street
Omaha, Nebraska
www.theberryandrye.com

Billy Sunday
3143 W Logan Blvd
Chicago, Illinois
www.billy-sunday.com

Bourbon and Butter
391 Washington Street
Buffalo, New York
www.bourbonbutter.bar

Crudo
3603 E Indian School Road
Phoenix, Arizona
www.crudoaz.com

Clyde Common
1014 SW Stark Street
Portland, Oregon
www.acehotel.com/portland

Downtown Cocktail Room
111 Las Vegas Blvd South
Las Vegas, Nevada
www.downtowncocktailroom.com

Dutch Kills
27-24 Jackson Avenue
Long Island City, New York
www.facebook.com/dutchkillsbar

Gin Palace
95 Avenue A.
New York City
wwginpalaceny.com

The Hawthorne at the Hotel Commonwealth
500A Commonwealth Avenue
Boston, Massachusetts
www.thehawthornebar.com

Hop Sing Laundromat
1029 Race Street
Philadelphia, Pennsylvania
www.hopsinglaundromat.com

Liberty
517 5th Avenue
Seattle, Washington
www.libertybars.com

Madam Geneva
4 Bleeker St
New York City
www.madamgeneva-nyc.com

Middle Branch
154 E 33rd St
New York City
www.facebook.com/MiddleBranch

Oceana
120 West 49th Street
New York City
www.oceanarestaurant.com

Oyster House
1516 Sansom Street
Philadelphia, Pennsylvania
www.oysterhousephilly.com

PX
728 King St.
Alexandria, Virginia
www.barpx.com

Penrose
3311 Grand Avenue
Oakland, California
www.penroseoakland.com

Polite Provisions
4696 30th Street
San Diego, California
hwww.politeprovisions.com

Pouring Ribbons
225 Avenue B
New York City
www.pouringribbons.com

Scofflaw
3201 W Armitage Avenue
Chicago, Illinois
www.scofflawchicago.com

Traymore Bar
2445 Collins Avenue
Miami, Florida
www.comohotels.com/metropolitanmiamibeach

Whitehall
19 Greenwich Avenue
New York City
www.whitehall-nyc.com

Wisdom
1432 Pennsylvania Avenue, SE
Washington DC
www.dcwisdom.com

CANADA

Clive's Classic Lounge
740 Burdett Avenue
Victoria, British Columbia
www.clivesclassiclounge.com

The Drawing Room
1222 Barrington Street, 3rd Floor
Halifax, Nova Scotia
www.henryhouse.ca

Le LAB
1351 rue Rachel Est.
Montréal, Québec
www.barlelab.com

Milk Tiger Lounge
1410 4 St SW
Calgary, Alberta
www.milktigerlounge.ca

Nota Bene
180 Queen St W
Toronto, Ontario
www.notabenerestaurant.com

Le Pourvoyeur
184 Jean Talon E
Montreal, Quebec
www.lepourvoyeur.com

Spirithouse
487 Adelaide St W
Toronto, Ontario
www.spirithousetoronto.com

Toronto Temperance Society
577A College Street
Toronto, Ontario
www.torontotemperancesociety.com

CENTRAL & SOUTH AMERICA

Salinger
Alfonso Reyes 238
Mexico City, Mexico
www.facebook.com/pages/Salinger

878
Thames 878
Buenos Aires, Argentina
www.878bar.com.ar

Astor São Paulo
Rua Delfina 163
São Paulo, Brazil
www.barastor.com.br

Frank's Bar
Arévalo 1445
Buenos Aires, Argentina
www.franks-bar.com

AUSTRALIA

Bulletin Place
1, 10-14 Bulletin Place
Sydney
www.bulletinplace.com

Dutch Courage Officers' Mess
51 Alfred Street
Brisbane
www.facebook.com/dutchcourageofficersmess

Gin Palace
10 Russell Place
Melbourne
www.ginpalace.com.au

NEW ZEALAND

Scarlett Slimms & Lucky
476 Mount Eden Road
Auckland
www.slimms.co.nz

REST OF WORLD

28 Hong Kong Street
28 Hong Kong Street
Singapore
www.28hks.com

Arola at the JW Marriott
Juhu Tara Road
Mumbai, India
www.marriott.com/hotels/travel/bomjw-jw-marriott

Ginter at the Intercontinental Dubai Marina
Bay Central Dubai Marina
Dubai, United Arab Emirates
www.ihg.com/intercontinental/hotels/gb/en/dubai

Harry's Bar
Off Paul Kagame Road
Lilongwe, Malawi

Imperial Cocktail Bar
Ha-Yarkon St 66
Tel Aviv, Israel
www.imperialtlv.com

Mother's Ruin
219 Bree Street
Cape Town, South Africa
www.facebook.com/mothersruincpt

Index

Figures in *italics* indicate captions.

PUBLISHER'S ACKNOWLEDGEMENTS

The publisher would like to thank the many gin distillers from around the world who kindly provided images of their gins and distilleries reproduced here.

Thanks also to the following people who helped in the production of this book:

The Merchant House, London: Nate Brown and Lewis Hayes

Graphic Bar, London: Gio Cascone and Urban Leisure Group

Thanks also to Sasha Gitin for special photography of gin bottles and to Simon Murrell for special photography of gin bottles and the cocktails on pages 182-218.

PICTURE CREDITS

5 dieKleinert/Alamy; 6 FALKENSTEINFOTO/Alamy; 7 centre INTERFOTO/Alamy; 7 Meridian Images/Alamy; 8 INTERFOTO/Sammlung Rauch/Mary Evans Picture Library; 10 Photo Researchers/Mary Evans Picture Library; 11 top Photo Researchers/Mary Evans Picture Library; 11 bottom Tracy Hebden/Alamy; 12 Mary Evans Picture Library/Alamy; 17 bilwissedition Ltd. & Co. KG/Alamy; 18 Peter Jordan_F/Alamy; 19 North Wind Picture Archives/Alamy; 21 North Wind Picture Archives/Alamy; 23 Classic Image/Alamy; 25 INTERFOTO/Alamy; 26 Niday Picture Library/Alamy; 27 Everett Collection Historical/Alamy; 32 Anson Smart; 36 Photology1971/Alamy; 37 Anthony Cullen; 39 Anthony Cullen; 41 Alastair Wiper; 44 Botanical art/Bildagentur-online/Alamy; 48 Quagga Media/Alamy; 49 Florilegius/Mary Evans Picture Library; 50 Quagga Media/Alamy; 51 Mary Evans Picture Library; 52 Photo Researchers/Mary Evans Picture Library; 53 Patrick Guenette/Alamy; 54 Mary Evans Picture Library; 55 Mary Evans Picture Library; 57 bottom right Design Pics Inc/Alamy; 58 left Quagga Media/Alamy; 58 right Patrick Guenette/Alamy; 59 bilwissedition Ltd. & Co. KG/Alamy; 60 left Photo Researchers/Mary Evans Picture Library; 60 right INTERFOTO/Alamy; 61 left Patrick Guenette/Alamy; 62 World History Archive/Alamy; 62 author photographs Eileen Proto; 63 author's photograph Eileen Proto; 70 Mary Evans Picture Library; 72-3 Peter Horree/Alamy; 79 Anson Smart; 109 Levon Biss; 152-153 both Paola Thomas; 173 www.gbpcreative.ca; 181 Anson Smart

AUTHOR'S ACKNOWLEDGEMENTS

It's nearly impossible to write a book of this scale without the generosity of so many distillers, bartenders, craftsmen and women who shared their stories, invited me to their space, and poured their gins with me. This book is an ode to them, for the story of gin is being writ with every new gin and cocktail. Thanks to each and every one of you.

Thanks to my wonderful loving wife, Kate Garrigan, who let me fill two rooms of our New York City apartment with gin. She greeted every box and bottle with a smile and her support. Thanks for helping me make this happen, and I promise – I'll give you back your bookshelf. Once we finish the gin!

Special thanks to David T Smith, I'm not sure I could have a better friend and thought partner-in-gin throughout this whole writing experience. Thanks, Buddy.

Thanks to Justin Kneitel for your cocktail advice and sageful wisdom throughout the years. How many gins have we shared since that last call G&T at the very genesis of all of this?

And of course sincere thanks to the many others who have supported or helped me along the way. Thank you Matt Carland, Dawn Antoline-Wang, Henry Wang, Thomas Christensen, James Lester, Gene Shook, Ellen Noonan, Leah Potter, Leah Nahmias, Katie Almirall, Sara Smith, John Sgammato, Eileen Proto, Chris Nyberg, Laura Grow-Nyberg, Abby Bathrick, Jon Karp, Lesia Lozowy and Patrick Gilmartin (I still haven't forgotten that first G&T you served me all those years ago). Thank you for sharing your stories Ian Hart & Hilary Whitney, John Lundin, Dr Anne Brock & Hannah Lanfear, Ben Capdeville & Holly Robinson, Sam Galsworthy, Meredith Grelli, Lauren Brock, Emily Vikre, Jon Hillgren, Jason Barrett, Cameron MacKenzie, Anthony Sexton, Karlo Krauzig, Anders Bilgram, and Jonas Naessens.

And Finally, last but not least, thanks to my wonderful family: Mom, Dad, Alicia & Jeff Jurek, Andy & Jen Garrigan and John & Patty Garrigan. Thanks for your support and help – the next gin and tonic is on me.